D0220096

The Internet Research Handbook

The Internet Research Handbook

A Practical Guide for Students and Researchers in the Social Sciences

Niall Ó Dochartaigh

SAGE Publications
London • Thousand Oaks • New Delhi

SAGE Publications Ltd
6 Bonhill Street
London EC2A 4PU

SAGE Publications Inc.
2455 Teller Road
Thousand Oaks, California 91320

SAGE Publications India Pvt Ltd
32, M-Block Market
Greater Kailash - I
New Delhi 110 048

British Library Cataloguing in Publication data

A catalogue record for this book is available from the British Library

ISBN 0 7619 6439 8
ISBN 0 7619 6440 1 (pbk)

Library of Congress Catalog Card Number available

Typeset by SIVA Math Setters, Chennai, India
Printed in Great Britain by The Cromwell Press Ltd,
Trowbridge, Wiltshire

Contents

Boxes and diagrams

Chapter 7

Chapter 8

Chapter 10

Abbreviations

FPE	Front Page Express
IE4	Internet Explorer 4
IE5	Internet Explorer 5
ISP	Internet Service Provider
NN	Netscape Navigator
NSC	Netscape Composer
TCP/IP	Transmission Control Protocol/Internet Protocol
URL	Uniform Resource Locator

Acknowledgements

Gabhaim buíochas le mo thuismitheoirí, Niamh agus Eoin, le mo sheanmháthair, Frances agus le mo sheanathair, Labhrás. Gabhaim buíochas faoi leith le Frances as mé a ghríosadh chun oibre. 'Nach bhfuil an leabhar sin críochnaithe agat fós?' a deireadh sí liom go rialta.

Thanks to Patricia Sleeman who wrote chapter 9 on archives and statistics and who helped me with a host of queries from her base at the National Digital Archive of Datasets in London. Colleagues in the Department of Political Science and Sociology in Galway provided useful advice and support while I was writing the book, in particular Anne Byrne who read some of the draft and whose comments were extremely useful. Thanks to Professor Chris Curtin for helping to create a work environment in which it was possible to spend time on research and to Kay Donohue for her help with a million and one things. Ann Kelly in the Library at NUI, Galway, was generous with her time and advice. A lot of other people at NUI, Galway, contributed to the book, often without realising it. The students who took the Internet Research Methods classes and the Politics and the Internet course made an essential contribution to this book through their questions and their discoveries.

Jenny Pournelle set up meetings and both her and Yvonne Ivory acted as the best hosts I could possibly have when I carried out research in California. Several people generously gave me their time at UCSD and UCLA including Phil Agre, Anne Gilliland-Swetland, Karl Lo and Bob Trippi.

James and Lisa and Niamh Quinn-Tierney put me up in Boston yet again, let me use their house as an office and entertained me like royalty. James even allowed me to drive back from the airport. Danny and Andy Sokatch gave me great help as always. Jeffrey Beale at Harvard patiently answered all of my questions about cataloguing.

This book couldn't have been completed without regular breaks to go swimming, walking and drinking. Providing company on some of these important breaks as well as informal advice and encouragement ('have you not finished that book yet?') were Mick and Oonagh and Eoghan, Colin and Lisa, Mike and Tanya, Aogán and Alice, Philip and Bushy, Paul and Lawrence, Moira and Andy, Eoghan and Susan, Tony, Pádraig, and Ger and Roger and Louis. Thanks especially to Patrick King for being almost always willing to come out to Tí Neachtain when I asked.

Mike Fitzpatrick gave me an introduction to real-world surfing in Co. Sligo. It's about a million times better than the Internet version.

This book has its genesis in the three years I spent working as a webmaster at INCORE in Derry setting up a web service on ethnic conflict. I was lucky to have great, friendly, easygoing people to work with. Gillian Robinson and John Darby couldn't have been more supportive and encouraging. It was a pleasure to work with Gráinne Kelly.

Pat Curran generously taught me a lot of what I know about computers in general. Guus Meijer, Martin Melaugh, Lyn Moffett, and Catherine Sharkey, Roger McGinty and Mike McCool all contributed to the genesis of the book in different ways.

Patricia Sleeman, who wrote chapter 9, thanks Frances Blomeley, Richard Davis, Sally Hughes and Philip Monaghan for all their help. Jonathan Newman and Stu Weibel clarified points relating to copyright and to the Dublin CORE respectively.

Thanks to the readers who initially read the proposal for this book and made useful suggestions and to the series editors who made some good points and provided some useful advice on an earlier draft of the book. Thanks to Beth Crockett at Sage who never got too upset when I missed a deadline.

Special thanks and a hug to Aogán Mulcahy who put me in touch with Sage in the first place and who has always been a great person to talk to about work and lots of other things.

I try to spend as little time as I possibly can staring at computer screens and listening to them hum. For this reason this Internet book was written using a series of blue and black and red pens. Martha Shaughnessy did a good job of deciphering the resulting scrawls and typing them up.

Thanks most of all to Carol-Ann and Caoimhe. Carol-Ann made sure I never took myself too seriously while I was writing this book. She listened to me rant on whenever I had a problem and helped me solve lots of them by being cool and calm and always right about everything (almost). This book was meant to be finished before Caoimhe was born. By the time it was actually finished she could stand up on her own, clap her hands, wave goodbye and grind her teeth together, but not all at the same time.

About the *Internet Research Handbook*

Why bother with this book?

If you have just started using the Internet you may be wondering why on earth you would possibly need a book about it. Nothing could be simpler. Point, click and off you go, travelling effortlessly to distant Websites on far-off continents. To many new users it can seem just about as easy as falling off a bike. If on the other hand you have been using the Internet for a while and find that it still takes half an hour to find a simple piece of information, you won't need to be convinced of the need for a handbook. The Internet is easy to use if you are just looking for 'anything' on a particular topic or if you have a specific task in mind like buying a car or booking a holiday. To do this requires very few skills. Research, on the other hand, is a 'systematic way of asking questions' (Drew, 1980: 8, cited in Bell, 1993: 2). For those carrying out serious research on the Internet a very different set of skills is required. Using the Internet for research involves learning how to mine sites and databases rigorously so that you extract all of the relevant information in the shortest possible time. It involves maximizing the possibilities opened up by email contact with other researchers around the world. It involves learning about the major databases which are devoted to the social sciences and learning how to do the detective work necessary to evaluate and to cite documents whose authorship and origins are often unclear. This book provides clear but detailed advice in all of these areas.

Understanding

The importance of understanding how things work on the Internet is stressed throughout this book. Understanding in this case means knowing just enough about the technical side of the Internet to be able to make effective use of it in your research. This is not a technical book. Time spent learning the technology should be kept to the essential minimum. Otherwise it is time stolen from research into the subject you are really interested in. For those who are interested in knowing a little more about the technology there are short items throughout the book, safely isolated from the main text in inset boxes.

Who it's aimed at

This book is intended for use as a textbook for courses on Internet research both at undergraduate and graduate level, courses which introduce students to efficient and critical use of the Internet as a research resource. It is also aimed at postgraduate students who are about to start research for a dissertation, and at experienced academic researchers who are trying to incorporate the Internet into their research practice. It will also be of use to researchers in a wide range of areas, from media to government, to the voluntary sector, who are concerned with issues of current debate and controversy. It can be used by such researchers as a handbook to be consulted at different stages of the research process, each chapter generally dealing with different, if overlapping, stages of that process. It assumes two types of reader, the first being those who have been typing on a computer for a while but are just starting to use the Internet. For these users chapter 2 on research tools is essential reading, providing the basic information needed to begin making optimum use of the various Internet tools. It acts as a reference chapter to refer back to throughout the research process. The second type of reader will have been using the Internet, fitfully and sometimes productively, for quite a while. Some of them may skip chapter 2 but even those who have been using the Net for quite a while may find some useful basic tips in that chapter. The experienced Net user will find some familiar material in most chapters but much of it should be new even to them.

This book assumes that the reader already has access to the Internet through their college or university or through an Internet service provider (ISP). It does not spend any time telling you how to get connected to the Internet. In part it is the purpose of this book to promote the use of the Internet as a mainstream research resource by setting out, in clear and simple terms, best practice in its use in research. To this end it introduces the reader to the high academic standards which must be applied if the Internet is to be accepted as a valid resource for quality academic research.

The book deals with the Internet as a thread which runs through the entire research process, from formulating a research question to publishing the results of your research. It is organized according to broad stages of the research process. It describes how the Internet can best be integrated into existing research practice while also being used to develop new forms of research practice and new possibilities. It should be used in conjunction with a more general text on social science research methods. It outlines a wide range of possibilities but don't panic – few people will need to use all of the resources described in this book.

Technical details and conventions used in the book

Most of the time this book avoids giving detail which is specific to one computer system or piece of software. Where there are differences between Mac and PC users it outlines the options for both. When dealing with Web browsers it gives examples from the two most commonly used browsers, Netscape Navigator (version 4 for the Mac) and Internet Explorer (versions 4 and 5 for the PC). Appendix 4 gives commands for Netscape 6, the most recent version of the Netscape Web browser. Internet addresses (URLs) appear in bold text throughout the book. Virtually all Internet addresses begin with http:// so I have left out this part of the addresses, except in the bibliography. When I'm illustrating general points about the Internet, I generally use a Web and email address for imaginary universities called 'Any College' and 'My College'. I've done my best in this book to focus on resources which are likely to last. Nonetheless, as with all books about the Internet, some of the detail in this book will be out of date by the time it is published.

Terminology

When I use the term 'Internet' I mean everything on other computers that you can access from your computer. That includes not just Web pages but library catalogues, email and databases of all kinds. Some of this material is not classified as part of the Internet by certain technical definitions. However, where no distinction between these materials is obvious to the user, where they are all just sources of information available through Internet technology, there is little point in forcing a distinction between them. By 'online' I just mean on the Internet, unless I say otherwise.

A term used a lot in this book is 'the real world'. Clifford Stoll, who is sceptical of the grand claims made for the Internet, uses it to describe the offline world, anything that is not on the Internet or not on a computer (Stoll, 1995a). The phrase embodies a certain scepticism about the Internet which I would like to echo in this book. The Internet is an incredibly valuable research resource. It will unavoidably run through any serious research project in the future. That said, it is a resource which brings with it certain temptations for the researcher: the temptation to increased isolation from the people who are around them in the real world, the temptation to a dependence on email networks which can provide a shallow and even misleading sense of community. There is the possibility that specialist researchers in particular will feel increasingly detached from the physical community they live in. This book stresses the importance throughout the research process of staying in touch with that real world, of drawing on its rich resources of human contact and printed materials which, in the end, are a far more important resource to the researcher than anything to be found online.

Chapter summary

Chapter 1, 'Research and the Internet', discusses the impact which the Internet is having on the ways in which we conduct research. It outlines how the Internet can best be integrated into the traditional research process. The Internet is a good source for very specific types of research materials and the chapter describes these materials. It includes a section on understanding the Internet which provides just enough technical detail to help the researcher make sense of the Internet as a whole.

Chapter 2 on research tools introduces the principal Internet tools, from Web browsers to email. Experienced Internet users will be able to skip most of this chapter but even they should find a few snippets of interest. It is really directed at those who are just beginning to use the Internet tools. It is a preparatory chapter, designed to help you kit yourself out before you begin your research. It is also intended to act as a short reference manual on the tools to which you can return at different stages of your research.

One of the first stages in the traditional research process is the literature search – finding out what has been written on your topic. Chapter 3, 'Searching for books and articles', is about using the Internet to search for published materials. It teases apart the differences between the myriad journal article databases which are available and describes the new means of finding printed material which the Internet has opened up, from allowing direct contact with publishers to allowing easy access to dissertations and theses.

Many of the most experienced Internet researchers insist that the greatest benefit the Internet has brought is easy contact with other people interested in the same subject. This is the subject of chapter 4, 'Making contact'. Such contact was always useful to researchers but the Internet makes it much easier and allows, via mailing lists, the sort of one-to-many contact which was previously only possible through publication or at conferences.

Chapter 5, 'The Web', is the first of four chapters which deal with searching the 'open Web', that realm of information chaos which can induce despair in even the most experienced of Internet researchers. It aims to develop an understanding of how information is organized on the Internet. The Internet may be chaotic but it is chaotic in very specific ways. Understanding the nature of the chaos is a vital first step in learning to navigate through it. The chapter deals with advanced skills for using Web browsers which will be of interest even to experienced Web users. It also looks at the way in which debates and struggles over the issues of privacy and censorship impact directly on the social science researcher.

Chapter 6, 'Searching by subject', provides advice on using the services which are devoted to cataloguing or classifying Web resources according to the subject area they deal with. This is the method by which libraries have traditionally catalogued books and displayed them on the shelves. For the researcher conducting a systematic enquiry to find all of the relevant information on their research topic, it's important to start searching of the open Web with these services, rather than with the keyword search engines which are much more popular and which are dealt with in the next chapter. Searching by subject allows you to find all of the material in your area which has already been classified and described by other people. It will save you vast amounts of time and you can use the keyword search engines for 'mop-up' purposes, to find materials which have not yet been classified or included in subject guides.

The keyword search engines, the famous names like AltaVista, Google, and all the rest, are the most popular way of searching the Internet. Chapter 7, on searching by keyword, provides detailed advice on how best to use these search engines. The aim is to help the researcher to find all of the information directly relevant to their research in the shortest possible time. It profiles individual search engines, describes how best to use the different search options and provides 'Eleven steps to effective searching'.

Chapter 8, 'Classification, evaluation and citation' is about how to deal with those documents which you've retrieved from the open Web. Internet documents are notoriously difficult to judge in terms of credibility and quality. It can even be difficult to find basic citation information for these documents. This chapter provides detailed advice on classifying, evaluating and citing Web documents.

Chapter 9 deals with archives and statistics. Archives have in the past been relatively inaccessible to researchers. Archives store original materials and often hold the only copies of those materials available anywhere. As archives have gone online they have become much more accessible. It is easier to find out what is stored in the various archives. In some cases you can view the actual documents online. Many more researchers can now realistically consider including archives in their searches. Making archives more widely available is potentially one of the greatest benefits which the Internet will offer to researchers.

Data archives are archives of statistical data, a research source which has always been important to social scientists. The Internet not only allows easier access to datasets produced and stored all over the world. In many cases you can also manipulate data online, creating tables customized to your needs.

Publication is the ultimate goal for many researchers, to spread their findings to a wider audience and hopefully to have some influence on other people. You can use the Internet to publish your research results but you need to be very careful how you go about it. Chapter 10, on Internet publishing, discusses the need to plan carefully what you put on the Internet, where you put it and how you ensure that people know it's out there. It also provides short straightforward advice on writing simple Web documents.

1

Research and the Internet

Why bother with the Internet?

It is easy to find reasons not to use the Internet as a research resource. It plays host to 'hate' politics, to child pornography and to the obscenities and ravings of lonely individuals with nothing better to do than vent their frustration online. The fanatical and the demented flood the Net with worthless Web pages and meandering rants. All that, and it's endlessly frustrating to use. Even if there is useful information out there you will waste huge amounts of time clearing a path to it through the ocean of garbage. It is hard to tell whether the documents you retrieve are credible or not, whether they were written by a thoughtful and wise expert who is patient, diligent and kind or by someone who knows far less than you do about the subject.

That said, it would be a mistake to allow the Internet to be defined or characterized by the proportion of nonsense it plays host to. It may be useful to think of the Internet not as a chaotic and therefore useless library but as a category like 'printed matter'. Printed matter includes not only books and newspapers but milk cartons, junk mail, stickers in phone booths and chocolate bar wrappers. The fact that mounds of printed matter exist which are of no real value to a researcher does not mean that we abandon all printed matter as being irrelevant. At the same time, there are important differences between the two categories. It is easy enough to distinguish one type of printed material from another, to tell a newspaper from a cigarette packet. The Internet equivalent of a cigarette packet or a soggy beer mat covered in drunken scrawls can be a bit more difficult to isolate and exclude from your research, but it can be done.

Rather than writing off the Internet as a serious research resource, it is necessary to develop a new set of research skills which address the challenges which the Internet presents. It is necessary to revive and reinforce certain traditional research values like scepticism, flexibility and rigour, while at the same time developing new approaches to the research process which allow you to make optimum use of this new resource. An increasing proportion of the information produced by and about human society is now being channelled through the Internet. As Phil Agre has written, 'The Internet is not a separate cyberspace reality. It is a new nervous system for the physical world' (Agre, 1996a). Social scientists, above all those concerned with understanding different aspects of collective human behaviour, cannot consider ignoring the Internet as a research resource.

Transforming academic research

Information overload

Information overload is a term particularly beloved in the world of business. The increased volume of information is causing very immediate problems for businesses which seek to make major decisions based on the fullest possible information. Being comprehensive on a topic is now far more difficult than it was before the advent of the Internet. This has major implications for the researcher. It is much less realistic now than it was a few years ago to aim for a 'comprehensive' approach to your research, looking at everything which is relevant. It is even more important to establish clear boundaries to your research and to be ruthless about ignoring materials beyond those boundaries. This narrowing of focus, however, has its own dangers and it would be wrong to react to information overload by narrowing your focus excessively.

Microspecialization

The nightmare scenario is that the researcher will be inclined to solve the problem of information overload by narrowing their area of enquiry so much, with the aim of being as comprehensive, as expert, in one field as they possibly can, that it is relevant only to a small cluster of specialists.

This has of course always been a trend in academic research, summed up in the old quip about an expert being someone who knew more and more about less and less until finally they knew everything about nothing. It is a trend which the Internet could accelerate dramatically. In a 1997 article, 'Electronic Communities: Global Village or Cyberbalkans?', Van Alstyne and Brynjolfsson outlined the increased potential for the splintering or 'balkanization' of research which the Internet provided. For one thing it allows increased ongoing contact between specialists around the world. By allowing academics to pull away from the people who are physically around them and are involved in other subjects, it allows them to indulge their specialization more. It thus reduces the extent to which they engage with the subjects and areas of speciality of those around them. University departments are enabled by the Internet to build stronger links to departments in their field based at other universities. It is far easier now for departments to participate in joint research projects based at several different institutions than it was. The consequent weakening of ties with other subjects in their own university could have major consequences for the future of universities as coherent institutions (Agre, 2000b). The university has always been important not only as an institution concerned with thought but also as a physical location where people from a wide range of disciplines were routinely in contact with each other. It's a space in which people can get ideas from other disciplines which enrich their own subject area. This is an aspect of the university which may suffer if campuses become increasingly 'virtual'.

There is the danger in the long term, as specialist international networks develop and strengthen via the Internet, of a quite dramatic narrowing of focus and of research interests.

Ending marginalization

On the flip side the Internet is transforming for the better the research of people who were geographically marginal, physically isolated from others working in the same area and from important sources of information on their subject. It is now reasonable, for example, for a researcher outside the USA to conduct research related to US government activity because they now have access via the Internet to a huge proportion of the printed documents produced by that government. Researchers who are studying a subject which no one else in their own college or university is interested in can now remain much more easily in contact with the current debates in their field if they find the right list or Website. Through searching databases of books and articles or visiting the Websites of publishers they can remain as up to date about the literature in their field as anyone in a large well-resourced university. For many researchers who are geographically isolated this is a genuine transformation.

Internationalization of research

Allied to the reduced importance of location is the internationalization of knowledge. For the first time researchers have instant and easy access to information about other universities and research centres across the globe. It is far easier now to find out about courses and reading lists at other universities, to see how departments and disciplines are organized, to see how researchers thousands of miles from you slot your particular speciality into their categorization of knowledge. It can be quite a shock to find out that categories you may regard as fixed such as 'law' or 'government' or 'politics' can have very different meanings and very different boundaries depending on the country you are in. The Internet starkly reveals just how 'nationally specific' different academic systems are. Not only does the Internet give the researcher much easier access to the research on their subject which is carried out in other countries, but it also clearly reveals the lack of a common international understanding of what different subjects consist of.

It will be interesting to see if it contributes to a true 'internationalization' of social science research, if researchers across the world settle on an agreed vocabulary which they can use to discuss their subjects with those beyond their own country's borders.

Mentoring/supervision

The role of mentor or supervisor, an individual or committee who can advise a researcher on where to begin their research, and who can comment on their work, has always been an important part of research. The Internet is contributing to a number of long-term shifts in the relationship between supervisor and researcher, particularly in the university setting where email has become so ubiquitous. Email contact has made it easier to maintain contact over long distances, to pass draft chapters and comments back and forth, to ask quick questions and receive quick replies and to discuss the progress of the research.

This ease of contact has both positive and negative aspects. On the positive side it is arguable that it is no longer as important to be located in the same place as your mentor unless you are involved in lab-based work where you'll work alongside your supervisor. You can, theoretically, work with your 'ideal' supervisor no matter where they are, or maintain regular contact while doing research fieldwork, no matter how far away you are. Contact can be maintained so inexpensively and frequently that effective supervision can be provided without much personal contact. It is also arguable that this is an extremely negative development, that such long-distance relationships, with meetings at long irregular intervals, are much weaker than face-to-face relationships. It raises questions about whether important aspects of the mentor–student relationship can be maintained without regular face-to-face contact. Can the degree of mutual understanding, interdependency and mutual commitment which are ideally part of this relationship develop without such contact?

If a researcher is also drawing much of their support and sustenance by email from a network of specialists in their field, does an email relationship with a mentor provide any greater quality of contact? That is, if the relationship weakens does it continue to be of any great value?

It may be that the Internet will actually make face-to-face contact more highly valued. In an environment where casual email contact with people all over the world in your area of specialization is possible, what may mark out the student–mentor relationship from relationships conducted through email is the extra quality which comes from face-to-face contact in the 'real world'. The email supervisor could well come to be seen as a poor second best.

The research process

The research process rarely progresses from one clearly defined stage to the next. Much more often it's a messy circular process. It usually includes periods of total despair as you hit one dead-end after another as well as periods when you plough forward relentlessly and everything seems to come together beautifully.

For the sake of clarity I'll talk here about different aspects of the research process as though they were a series of clearly defined stages.

The research question

The first step in the research process is to decide what it is you are trying to find out, to devise a question or questions which sum that up as precisely as possible.

This demands a lot of preliminary reading and a lot of thought about how your work will relate to existing work in this area. What exactly is it that you will contribute that has not been done already? The result should be a clearly phrased question or questions. The question may have changed dramatically by the time you finish your research but it is important to have some solid question to organize your research around in the early stages. The Internet rewards, above all, those who know what they want to know, and who can frame their questions precisely. In particular, it rewards the researcher who can describe their research in terms of keywords. Clearly no subject can be boiled down into a few keywords or phrases. It is a crude method of searching for material but it is a method which the technology forces the researcher into.

Given how important keyword searches will be in your research it is important to identify useful keywords at the same time as you develop your research question. You should develop lists of keywords at two levels. Firstly, there are broad general terms for searching library catalogues and article databases. This will include the broad subject headings your topic comes under. You can find these by checking the subject classifications of a few key books in the area and picking those which seem most relevant to your research. They will also include terms which are commonly found in the titles of articles and books on the topic and which are likely to be used as keywords by writers on this topic.

Secondly, there are precise, unique terms which you can use on the big Internet search engines, keywords which ensure that you only bring back documents which are directly related to your topic. (See chapter 7 for detailed advice on developing keyword searches for the Internet search engines.) This list of keywords and key phrases will develop and grow as your research progresses. From the very beginning of your research you should develop a keyword chart, recording the keywords used and the sources they have been used to search. Then, if you come up with a keyword or phrase two years into your research which turns out to yield particularly rich returns you can go back and run it against the sources you have already searched using other keywords. When you come across a new database or search engine you can run all of the relevant keywords through it in one sitting, ensuring that you have scoured it for information as comprehensively as possible.

The literature search

The literature search, which involves finding out what has already been published on your subject, is a core research task which has been transformed beyond recognition by the development of the Internet. Access to online library catalogues across the world, to databases of articles and of theses and dissertations, has made it possible to do swift and wide-ranging searches of the literature. It also makes more urgent the question of how widely you should search. This is particularly the case when you extend your literature search onto the open Web. There you are faced with the question of what type of material to include in your search. Do you draw the line at policy papers or think-tank briefs, do you exclude or include conference papers, reports from non-governmental organizations or political parties? The Internet forces you to think a lot more about this question, not only because of the sheer volume of material available, but also because of the range of material you now have access to.

Collecting citation details

Research books have always warned the researcher to take down citation details the first time they look at a particular book or article. It saves a lot of time chasing down references when you finish your research. This is especially important when it comes to Internet materials. Chapter 8 deals in detail with citation but from the very beginning you should be collecting the following details for each Web document you plan to use: author, title, site (the Website it belongs to), date (date produced, last updated or viewed depending on what information is available), section title (where relevant) and URL. For detailed information on each of these elements see chapter 8.

Contact

Contact and conversation with real people have always been integral to research. At the very least this involves the formalized contact a researcher has with their supervisor. But much more than this, contact by letter or interview with experts in the field, and social and academic contact with people around you who share the same interests, play an important role in directing you to obscure sources, keeping you on track, encouraging you, sparking off ideas and insights. The Internet massively expands the possibilities for contact with other people. There is the potential there for a rapid increase in the quality of research through the sharing of information between specialists.

Collecting data

Many primary sources, ranging from newspapers through documents produced by organizations to documents in online archives, are now accessible through the Internet. Along with survey results and interviews, written primary sources are the raw material of social science research. In the long run it is conceivable that improved access to such primary materials will be the greatest contribution of the Internet to research. Archives and other specialized collections of primary sources are generally confined to one location or to several locations. If you wanted to see the archives of a certain newspaper, there were a limited number of places where collections of the newspaper were held. If you lived outside the USA, for example, and wanted to do research on a small provincial US newspaper, it was entirely likely you would have to travel to the USA to consult it. Through the Internet the researcher now has access to the (albeit limited) archives of thousands of newspapers. Many archives and special collections only granted access to postgraduate students and academics. It was difficult for undergraduates to do research on primary sources. The wealth of primary sources on the Internet opens up new possibilities for original research at undergraduate level.

Issues around collecting original data through surveys, interviews or questionnaires on the Internet and around doing ethnographic research are dealt with in books and articles such as Bertot and McClure (1996), Kaye and Johnson (1999), Kollock and Smith (1999), Mann and Stewart (2000), Hine (2000) and Jones (1998). People gathering such data are just beginning to develop tools and models of good practice for this type of work. It is an extensive topic in its own right and is not covered in this book.

Evaluation and citation

Research has always required that the researcher take a sensibly sceptical approach to everything they read, being careful not to place too much trust in the claims of any one person.

The fact that the Internet allows access to a far wider range of material of much more variable quality than that found in a university library makes that attitude of scepticism more important than ever before. The skills required to evaluate documents in terms of credibility and authority need to be much more developed when it comes to dealing with documents out on the open Internet. Equally, the traditional academic practice of citation, of ensuring that all of your sources can be located again if necessary, becomes that much more important in a medium where documents can simply disappear if a Webmaster deletes a file. Not since the days of single-copy handwritten manuscripts has it been so easy for a document to disappear from the face of the earth for ever.

Publication

The last stage of the research process, ideally, is publication. The Internet has made it possible for very specialized documents, which it will never be economical for a publisher to produce, to be widely distributed. It opens possibilities for researchers to distribute their work more widely than would ever have been possible before.

The Internet impacts differently on the various stages of the research process. For some stages the impact is more dramatic than for others, but taken as a whole these changes suggest that the Internet is at the heart of a fundamental transformation in the way academic research is carried out.

Understanding the Internet

The Internet is a fact

The Internet is not an organized system or an archive, it is not primarily a network or even a network of networks, it is a fact. It is the fact that millions of computers across the world can communicate with each other. When you click a blue-underlined hyperlink on your computer screen, your computer sends a message to another computer asking it to send you the file the hyperlink refers to. The Internet is the fact that this other computer will understand the request and will send the file. When it comes right down to it the Internet is just files on other people's computers which they allow the outside world to look at.

The 'networks' and lines which carry your request include phone lines, satellite dishes, and myriad varieties of cables. Such lines of communication have existed for a long time. Most of them were not built specifically to carry Internet traffic and they are not the essence of the Internet. The Internet ultimately is the simple fact that millions of people and companies and institutions across the world have linked their computers up to this communications network and allowed the outside world to browse through certain sections of their computers.

Understanding this makes it simple to answer one of the most frequently asked questions about the Internet: 'Why is there nothing about my favourite topic on the Internet?' There is nothing there because nobody has decided to put it up. When someone does put up something on your favourite topic, whether they do it from a bedroom in South Africa or a university computer lab in Japan, it will be available to the world instantaneously, though it may take you a while to find it. To put this information 'on the Internet' they will just move a file to that part of their computer (or to another computer) which is open to the outside world.

Very few organizations or agencies are obliged to put all or even any of their information online. Often they will just put up those materials which they want to highlight, which show them in the best light. The researcher needs to bear in mind that the motives for putting information on the Internet are often far from lofty. Very few people will put up everything which they have available in printed form.

The Internet only took off in 1994

The Internet has existed since the 1960s. That is, computers have been able to communicate over long distances since then. For a brief history of the Internet see appendix 3. However, it was only in 1993 and 1994, when easy-to-use browsers such as Mosaic and Netscape became widely available and made such communication simple to use, that two important things happened.

1. A wider public began to use the Internet, particularly university students with free access.
2. Seeing that the public were using the Internet, everyone from universities to governments to businesses began to connect their computers to the Internet and to place information on them for people to look at.

This marked the beginning of the current phase of rapid growth in Internet use.

The World-Wide-Web

The World-Wide-Web appeared in 1993. It is based on http, the HyperText Transfer Protocol, and the major innovation it introduced was 'hypertext'. Hypertext is the blue-highlighted text you see in Web documents on Netscape or Internet Explorer. 'Hidden' in every piece of blue text is an Internet address which could point you to another document on the computer you are connected to or could point you to a document on a computer on the other side of the world. It allowed people for the first time to put information on the Internet to create very elaborate documents. People could include links to other documents in the body of a document. They could also include graphics, sound and even video to create full multi-media documents.

   It is important to bear in mind that the World-Wide-Web is just an easy-to-use framework for organizing files, whether documents or images. The 'Web' is not to be confused with the information people put up on their computers. Everybody puts up their own information. The Web 'protocol' just means that all the machines understand each other and display documents from other machines in a standard way. Equally, Web browsers such as Netscape and Internet Explorer are not to be confused with the Web itself. They are just ways of looking at Web documents. The Internet is still first and foremost the simple fact that the computer you are sitting at is connected to millions of computers around the world on many of which people have put up information. Netscape or Internet Explorer just provides an easy way to cruise around that information.

Online databases

In the years before the appearance of the World-Wide-Web a number of different initiatives had been taking advantage of the fact that computers could connect to each other over long distances. Online services which preceded the Web included large databases of academic articles which were accessible via telnet and which were used by university researchers (see chapter 2 and appendix 3 for more on telnet). They also included large commercial databases of newspaper and magazine articles aimed at those doing business research. The business services were so complicated and expensive to use that they were effectively limited to professional searchers who earned a living searching them. Some of the database companies even required you to buy a specialized computer terminal which could only be used to link to their database. The academic article databases were not particularly easy to use either and you could only get access to them if your university was subscribed to them.

In the past few years these types of online services have moved onto the Internet, allowing users to search them through simple Web pages. These large powerful databases, many of them charging fees for use, are now effectively part of the Internet. In addition new databases of articles have been set up which perform the same function as the online databases but which are based entirely on the Internet. To the user there is no visible difference between these services, and when I refer to the Internet in this book I include the online databases which became part of the Net in the late 1990s.

What the Internet is good for

For many types of information the Internet is worse than useless. It rarely has the full text of books and even if it does it is probably cheaper and simpler to get the printed copy. If it provides the full text of academic articles it is usually only to paying subscribers. The vast majority of published academic work is not freely available through the Internet. There is no point doing Internet searches for types of material which are just not there. This section describes the main types of material which the Internet is particularly good at providing.

The new (events which took place after 1993)

Any event which attracted public interest and occurred after about 1993, when the Web really took off, is well covered by a variety of sources on the Web. You will find newsgroup and email discussion archives, stories in newspaper archives, personal sites and statements by interested groups. Conversely, if it happened before then you will find only a fraction of the information. The shallowness of the Internet, in historical terms, is also a feature of the pay databases of academic articles and of newspapers. Newspaper archives on the Internet rarely go back beyond the 1980s. Article databases rarely go back beyond the 1970s and, in the case of many journals, go back no more than a few years. For many information providers on the Internet the only time that counts is 'now'.

The old

As well as being packed with current information the Net is a useful source for printed materials more than about seventy years old. This is because printed materials go out of copyright several decades after they are first published. The regulations vary between countries but the upshot is that most documents and books from the 1920s and before can be placed on the Net by anyone who wants. There are projects dedicated to doing this, Project Gutenburg (**promo.net/pg**) being the original example, a project which puts the full text of out-of-copyright books on the Net. The usefulness of this to you depends on whether or not people have dedicated themselves to putting up works in your particular area of interest. Moreover, the value of putting common books online, books which can be found in most libraries and book-shops, such as the works of Shakespeare, is perhaps questionable.

The academic (within limits)

Universities were at the forefront of the development of the Internet and were among the first large organizations to put up information about them-selves. If you want to know about a university's courses, its departments, its staff and its publications then the Net is probably the prime source for much of this information. The Internet is also a prime source for informa-tion <u>about</u> academic articles and books. That said, the databases of journal articles are far from comprehensive, leaving out large numbers of the smaller journals. Although they are incredibly useful the big services which allow you to download (for a fee) the full text of current articles only include a proportion of journals and then only relatively recent issues. The Internet has also sparked off the establishment of many electronic journals, journals which do not have a print counterpart and which usually allow free access to everyone.

The far-away

It used to be difficult for, say, a US-based specialist in German politics to keep up with day-to-day events in Germany in great detail. Now that local and national newspapers, governments and activists around the world put information on the Net it is a much easier task. It is possible to follow events in a far-away country in much greater detail than was ever possible through newspapers or television, particularly by direct access to the news wire stories and to the Websites of groups active on particular issues. There is evidence that many immigrant groups in the USA and elsewhere are keeping in touch more closely with events in their countries of origin as a result. Emigrant groups scattered around the world, whether Bosnians, Croats, Serbs, or Albanians, Sri Lankan Tamils, or Sinhalese, Turks or Kurds, can now stay current with events at home in a way which was not possible before. The political implications of this are just beginning to unfold but the research implications are clear. It is now much more viable to do research on current events in a country located far away from the researcher's base.

The activist

For centuries one particular type of organization and individual, the activist, has produced documents which they never even attempted to profit from, which they gave away or sold cheaply as part of their attempts to persuade people of the rightness of their cause – documents such as political pamphlets, religious tracts, idealistic manifestos. For many social scientists, those studying social movements or political parties, for example, such documents are valuable research resources. The Internet has provided activists who are not concerned with making a profit from their writings with an opportunity to spread their message more widely. As a result researchers have the sort of access to those types of materials which they could only have dreamed of up to a few years ago.

The not-for-profit

Closely related to the 'activist' category, the 'not-for-profit' sector includes charitable organizations and non-governmental organizations (NGOs). They share with activists a desire to get their message out while not necessarily seeking to make a profit from it. Some of these organizations, such as the Red Cross/Red Crescent Societies (**www.ifrc.org**) and Amnesty International (**www.amnesty.org**) put large volumes of their material on the Web.

Government and officialdom

Governments and official bodies have always produced massive volumes of printed material, often published only because they were legally obliged to do so. Many of these publications were of interest only to a small specialized audience and were particularly difficult to get hold of outside their country of origin. Many governments, the US government in particular, have gone online so enthusiastically that it is a source of worry to some that they are abandoning the printing of certain government publications (Stoll, 1995a: 34). Instead they are making them available via the Internet alone. It emphasizes just how important the Internet has become as a storing-house for such materials. For very practical reasons, including savings in printing and distribution costs, many government documents are now much more accessible than they were to those outside that government's country. The downside is that, for many inside the country without easy Net access or Net research skills, they are effectively less accessible.

The marginal

Whether it is lesser used languages, small religious groupings, minor political groupings or specialist subjects with a limited audience, it is one of the revolutions effected by the Internet that marginal groups in society which did not have the resources to print publications or the distribution network needed to spread them are now able to make materials available worldwide. For the researcher concerned with studying a marginal group it provides access to the sort of materials which used to be extremely difficult to track down and get hold of. For members of those groupings it provides the potential to strengthen group identity through regular contact even though members may be spread across the globe.

News and business

A large proportion of the world's newspapers, TV stations and magazines have gone online. Never before has it been possible to get access to so much up-to-date news from so many sources. Businesses large and small treat the Internet as an advertising medium and a means of distributing the information about themselves that they would like you to know. If your research involves work on companies and corporations the Internet makes information about them more accessible than ever.

Archives

Archives have always been among the most inaccessible of research resources. It was hard to find out what they contained and you had to visit the archive to view the material. Some archives have now put some of their collections online while many more allow you to search their catalogues online.

Statistics

Statistics are a form of social science research data which it has always made sense to computerize. Data archives, computerized collections of statistics, including many dealing with the social world, have been available online for several years. With the development of the Internet such data collections, from the US census (**www.census.gov**) to 'The Data Archive' based at Essex University in the UK (**www.essex.ac.uk**), have become much more accessible to the general public.

The lonely, the deluded, the obsessive

Individuals who fall into these categories seem to be heavily over-represented on the Net. Anyone who has browsed more than a few personal home pages will have realized this. If this forms part of your research interest the Net is a treasure-trove. This aspect of the Net may be of particular interest to psychologists, anthropologists, ethnographers and sociologists of various persuasions.

2

Research tools

Introduction

This chapter describes the basic functions of the core Internet tools. It is aimed at those who have just begun to use these tools but even experienced Internet users will find some items of use. Internet research involves using your computer in new and slightly different ways. For this reason the chapter includes a section on those basic computer skills which are particularly important in Internet research.

This is a preparatory chapter, designed to help you kit yourself out properly before you begin your research. It is also intended as a short reference manual on the tools which you can return to for basic information at different stages of your research.

Your local set-up

Computer and Internet facilities vary widely from one college or university to another. In some places the people in charge of these facilities will have made them incredibly user-friendly. Sections of this chapter will be irrelevant because your local set-up will be so easy to use. In other places the people in charge will be so far behind the times or under-resourced that it will seem impossible to figure out how to find any of these tools on your local system. In both cases it is important to note that your local set-up is very possibly unique, or customized in a unique way by your college or university. This book cannot provide a guide to that set-up and to its particular quirks and benefits. It is essential that you get to know your local set-up at the same time as you are reading this chapter. Everything outlined in this chapter should be available on all but the oldest and most under-resourced systems. If it is not, it is easy for your computer people to get hold of and install.

Memory

Using the Internet can be very demanding on a computer's memory. Newer computers should have no problems but in older computers you may have to add memory in order for things to work more quickly. One way you will know you do not have enough memory is because your computer will keep crashing when you have more than one or two other pieces of software open at the same time as the Web browser. Memory is not complicated. It is hardware that you can see and touch. To install extra memory will involve someone opening up your computer and physically slotting some memory chips into the innards of the machine. If you have a slow machine get this done before you even begin using the Internet for research.

Terminology

There are a few basic terms I will use quite a bit in this chapter. They are terms which are thrown around a lot by computer people but whose meaning non-computer people are not always clear about.

Hardware   Any bit of computer equipment you can touch. A keyboard, a monitor, all the circuit boards, memory chips and electronic bits and pieces you would see if you smashed your computer to bits with a hammer (as you will occasionally be tempted to do).

Software   Any computer program. When it comes right down to it a program is a huge collection of instructions to your computer. A word processing program will include hundreds of thousands of lines which basically say things like 'When the user selects "bold text" from the menu make the text bold'. Software programs or, as they are often called, packages, will usually have been installed on your computer before you get it. They include things like Microsoft Word, a word processing program, or Netscape Navigator, a Web browser program. In the first case Microsoft is just the name of the company which makes the package while 'Word' is the actual name of the package. Likewise, Netscape is the name of a company, Navigator is the name of the software package.

In the case of these popular packages new versions with extra features are produced regularly. Thus the first version of Microsoft Word was Word 1 while Word 6 and Word 7 are later versions. One of the biggest problems with software is that older versions of the software are often unable to read documents created in newer versions because there are so many extra features they do not understand. Newer versions should have no problems reading documents created in earlier versions.

If you open a file of any kind, your computer automatically opens the program which is used to create or alter that file. You can also open a program by clicking or double clicking an icon representing it or by choosing it from the start menu (on a PC).

Default   The 'default' is what the software is set up to do unless you specify otherwise. Default settings can be changed by you, usually through a menu command called 'options', 'preferences' or 'settings'. For example, the default setting for the Web page that comes up when you open Netscape

Navigator is the Netscape home page. You can change that setting so that a different page comes up automatically when you open Navigator.

Basic computer skills

Introduction

When you use a computer for Internet research you use it in a very different way than if you were just using it for word processing. You switch back and forth between programs regularly; you work simultaneously with text, images and communication software. This section deals with basic computer skills which are particularly important when doing Internet research. Because they are not so important for other uses of a computer a lot of people spend years using computers without learning these skills. The instructions for PCs below apply to PCs running Windows 95, Windows 98 and Windows 2000.

Switching between programs

It is a cardinal rule for efficient use of a computer that you do not keep starting up and shutting down computer programs. When you finish working on a document you should 'close' that document or window, not 'exit' the whole program. Instead of shutting down programs you need to learn how to switch between them. Many users switch between programs just by clicking on the windows to bring the window they want to the front of the screen. When you have a lot of windows open and you are doing a lot of switching, you have to keep moving the windows around. It can become very confusing. It also means that you never fully understand the difference between two different programs, like Word and Navigator, and two windows within one program – as when you have two or more Word documents open at the same time. If you get into the habit of switching between programs you will find it is not only less confusing but also the first step to understanding the distinction between different programs.

When you are carrying out Internet research you will usually have a minimum of two programs open: your Web browser and a word processing package. The word processing package needs to be open for you to take notes on your research. As well as your word processing package your computer will have a simple text editor. On the Mac this is called 'simple text'; on the PC, 'Notepad' (**Start→Programs→Accessories→Notepad**). It has no frills and is therefore much leaner than the word processing packages. If you use this for taking notes instead of a word processor your Web browser will work that little bit faster. You can then transfer those notes into a word processor later for further editing.

You may find you will also have your email package or perhaps a graphics package open at the same time. You should only shut one of these packages down if you are reasonably sure you have finished using it or that you will not be using it for a good hour or so.

Alt tab/Apple tab (**alt→/apple→**)   On both Macs and PCs there is a simple shortcut for switching between programs. On a PC, hold down the alt key, and hit the tab key. On a Mac, hold down the apple key, and hit the tab key. You will see icons for the computer programs which you have open. Continue holding down alt/apple and hitting tab to highlight the program you want to switch to. If you let go of the alt/apple and tab keys that program will come up on the screen. On newer Macs **apple tab** will switch between all of the open programs without showing icons. On newer PCs it allows you to switch between every window you have open.

As well as the alt tab/apple tab shortcut, both Macs and PCs provide other ways to switch between programs.

Mac   On the top right of your Mac screen is a little image. It shows you what program you are currently using. If you click on it and hold the mouse button down you will see a list. This is a list of all the programs you currently have open plus the 'Finder' which is your desktop display showing your hard disk and other items on the desktop. Drag the mouse down this list till you have selected the program you want to work on, then let the button go. The menu bar for that program will appear along the top of the screen and any windows you have open in that program will come to the front of the screen. If you want windows from other programs hidden, so the screen is not so cluttered, you can 'hide' the other programs. To switch back and forth between programs just go and repeat the operation or use apple tab to do the exact same thing.

PC   Things work quite differently on a PC. In the top right of every window are three buttons allowing you to minimize, maximize and close the window. To hide a window click on the minimize button at the top right of the window. Each of the windows you have minimized appears as a little block along the bottom of your screen and you can open them again just by clicking on the block.

File structure: understanding how your computer is organized

Many computer users can and do remain blissfully ignorant of how files are organized. They never need to know because of the way they use the computer, opening files by double-clicking on them, not paying any attention to where they save them because all their documents are usually there in front of them when they start up the machine. For the ordinary user this causes few problems unless they accidentally save a document in the wrong folder. For the Internet researcher it is not an option to remain in such blissful ignorance. When you are using a few programs simultaneously, when you are saving different types of files, when you are copying things from a Web document to a word processing document, you need to know where these items are being saved on your computer.

Whenever you save a file, whether on a Mac or a PC, you are given the option of where to save it. Most computers will save all Web documents in one place, all image files in another, all email attachments in yet another folder. But you do not have to accept this and in fact should not accept this. If you have images, attachments, Web documents and word processing documents which all relate to chapter 1 of your research project you will want to keep them all together in one folder. Instead of just saving files wherever your computer decides they should go you need to get used to saving them where you want them.

Macs and PCs follow the same basic system of organizing files. There are folders (they used to be called directories on PCs but not anymore) and in the folders there are files. Folders are just a handy way of organizing your files. If you have a dozen documents related to the first chapter of your research project it makes sense to put them all in a folder called 'chapter 1' and to put this in another folder called 'research'. It makes it easy to find them all again. The files are the hard content. Each file is a single item but files can be of vastly different sizes and types. If you type a line of gibberish on a word processor and save it, that is a file. If you type a 300 page book and save it as one very long document, that is also a file. If you save a photo from the Web, that is a file.

You need different programs to look at different types of files. You need image software to view an image file and word processing software to view a word processed file. Usually when you double click on the icon of a file your computer automatically opens the program needed to view that file.

However, a lot of material you download from the Web will automatically be opened up by your computer in programs you do not want them opened in. For example, your computer may automatically open all html documents in your Web browser. But, if you want to edit these documents you need to open them in a word processing package. There is nothing to stop you doing this. Just open up the word processing package, choose **file→open** (in the case of Microsoft Word) and select the html document you want to open. Many packages will show only files created in that package when you choose '**file→open**'. To see other types of files at this point just choose 'all files' under the option 'List files of type:'.

Sometimes you will save documents from the Web as plain text with a .txt extension. If you double-click on them to open them your computer may well try to open them in a simple text editor. Many of these editors cannot handle long documents and they will balk at this. In this case just open your word processor again and use '**file→open**' to open the documents.

File extensions   A file extension is the last part of a file's name. It tells you what kind of file it is – if, for example, it is a graphics file or a text document. Your computer uses file extensions to decide what software to open to view a particular file. It used to be that every file on a PC had to have a three-letter extension. This is no longer the case and the Macs never required extensions. Despite this it became very common to use them, simply to let people know at first glance what type of file they were dealing with. Below is a list of the most common file extensions.

.txt plain text file with none of the formatting like italics, headers and lists which you get in word processing documents.

.doc word processing document in Microsoft Word, full of elaborate formatting. Just to confuse things, people who put plain text documents on the Web sometimes give them a .doc extension, just to indicate that they are a document.

.wpd word processing document in Corel WordPerfect.

.htm/.html html documents, that is Web documents that you view through your Web browser. The .htm extension tells you that the document was probably created on an older PC which only allowed a three-letter extension.

.exe an executable, a computer program. If you have Netscape on your computer, somewhere in your file system will be a file called **netscape.exe** or something similar. If you double click on it Netscape will start up.

Drives and disks   Drives (on the PC) and disks (on the Mac) are really the highest level folders you can get. Unlike the lower level folders, drives and disks are real physical items. You can actually open your computer and take out your hard disk (on the Mac) or your C drive (on the PC) (but don't). They are really just the big folders that all the other folders and files are stored in.

PC drives   On a PC the C drive (C:\) is the computer's hard disk, the big folder in which everything is stored. Not only does it contain all the documents you have created but also it contains everything needed to run the machine. If you went rampaging through the C drive, deleting files at random, you could make your PC a wreck, impossible to use. Most of what is on the C drive you never need to know about. You just need to know where your documents are stored on it. You can explore the drive by opening 'My Computer', selecting C:\ and then choosing **file→explore** and having a look inside the various folders.

The A drive (A:\) is the 'floppy' disk, though they are no longer floppy. It is the disk you stick into the front of the computer. If you want to take files away from the computer you save them on the A drive.

The D drive (D:\) is usually the CD-ROM. If you are using a PC which is part of a network you will often find that the network has over a dozen drives, from A to Z. A will still be the floppy disk but as a user you and all other users could be on another drive like the F or the U drive. It does not make any difference which one. The computer people locally have just decided to give a certain drive over to student users. So, rather than having a whole C drive to yourself, you will have a bit of space on another drive. It makes no real difference. There is no need to explore the other drives. It is just important to know they are there when you are looking for your own files so you do not get too confused.

Finding files

One way to find files is to search down through the folders. Another is to use the Find facility on the Mac (switch to finder. choose **file→find** and enter part or all of the file name). On the PC choose 'Find' from the Start menu and enter all or part of the file name. Alternatively, open 'My Computer', select your main drive (C:\ in most cases) then choose **file→explore** and in Explorer choose **Tools→Go to**. In each case you will get back a list of the files containing the name you typed in. The list will show you what folders these files are in.

Understanding the Internet by understanding your own computer

There is one final reason why you should get to understand the file system on your own computer. I have mentioned already that the Internet is essentially just files on other people's computers that they allow the outside world to view. These files are organized just like the files on your own computer are. Understanding how files are organized on your own computer is an essential first step in understanding how Websites are organized.

Copy and paste (ctrl c, ctrl v/apple c, apple v)

Anyone who has used a computer for word processing will have used the copy and paste commands from a pull-down menu in Word or a similar package. When you 'copy' text it is copied to a clipboard. If you then copy something else it replaces the first item on the clipboard, though on newer computers the clipboard will store several items at the same time. When you use the paste command whatever is in the clipboard is pasted wherever you last clicked the cursor.

The joy of copy and paste is that these commands are available in pretty much every software package and that they use the same shortcut commands in every package: ctrl c for copy, ctrl v for paste (on the Mac, apple c and apple v). Before you copy select the text you wish to copy by clicking and dragging the mouse across to highlight it. Using these shortcuts and using alt tab (apple tab on the Mac) to switch between packages is the most efficient way to copy text from one package to another. Doing Internet research requires regular copying from one package to another, from your Web browser to your word processor to your email package. Using these shortcuts instead of drop-down menus saves a lot of time.

Moving within windows

All Mac and PC users will have experience of working with windows on the computer screen, moving and resizing, minimizing and maximizing them. One simple feature of windows which some new users are unfamiliar with is the scroll bar at the right hand side of the window. The small square within the vertical scroll bar shows you how far down a document you are. If it is half way down the bar you are at about the half way point in the document. By moving the box (click and drag) you can move very quickly through the document. Drag it to the bottom of the scroll bar, let go of the mouse button and you are at the end of the document. As you drag the box down the scroll bar you can see the page numbers on a word processed document change on the bottom of the window in some packages. This allows you to go quickly to whatever page you want in the document.

The scroll bar also allows you to travel through a document in several different ways. Most users will be used to using the arrows at the top and bottom of the bar to scroll through, a line at a time. If you click on the bar anywhere below the box you will go down by exactly one screen. If you click above the box you go up exactly one screen. The exact same function is performed by the page up and page down keys on your keyboard.

This is the best way of moving through a Web document which you are scanning quickly to see if it is of any use to you. Move through the document exactly one screen at a time, missing nothing. When you have downloaded a document, go down one screen. If the box in the scroll bar barely moves you know you are dealing with a very long document. If it moves way down you know you have a short document.

If you move down a Web document as it is still downloading you will see the little box in the scroll bar jumping like a jerky puppet. This is because it is constantly readjusting where it is in the document. If you went down a page when only two pages had downloaded, the box would have moved half way down the scroll bar. As more material downloads it jumps back up to show that it is now only a tenth or a twentieth way through the document.

Moving through files and folders

There are several different ways in which you will find yourself viewing lists of your files: in 'My Computer' (or your hard disk on the Mac); when you save a document; when you go to open a document. Because Internet research requires you regularly to move through files and folders it is worth knowing a few methods for quickly moving through lists of them. The arrow and paging (page up, page down) keys work with lists of files and folders in the same way as they work with documents. Page up and page down will bring you up or down by exactly one screen at a time. The arrow keys will move the list up or down one line at a time. Making sure that you have clicked on the list of files and folders, type the first letter of the file or folder you are looking for. The computer will jump down to the first file or folder beginning with that letter. When you have built up large collections of files you will find this a useful way of moving quickly to the file or folder you are looking for.

Dealing with 'OK'

Particularly on the Internet you are regularly asked to click on boxes which say 'ok', or 'continue' or 'I accept'. Using the mouse to click on them is unnecessary and wastes time. Just hit the return key (↵) on your keyboard to accept the option which is highlighted.

Working with images

For many experienced computer users their first encounter with image files takes place when they start using the Internet. This can be a bewildering encounter. The first thing to note is that all images on a Web page are separate individual files. They are graphics files, created not in a word processor but in a graphics package. Many of the images you see on the Internet were created in the following way: a picture was scanned into a computer using a scanner (a piece of hardware you can buy for a few hundred pounds or dollars); the picture was saved as a graphics file, maybe after being altered in a graphics package; it was saved as either a gif or jpeg file. You will recognize these files from their extensions, **.gif** and **.jpeg** (or **.jpg**) (see inset). These are the two graphics formats which are universally recognized on the Internet. There are dozens of other graphics formats, including formats specific to Macs or PCs, but all Web browsers will recognize gif and jpeg images. The person who saved the image then wrote a Web document and included a link to this image. That is, the image is not actually part of the Web document, it is a completely separate file. If you want to save it you have to click on the image using the right mouse button. This will give you the option to save. You can then work with it on your own computer using a graphics package. On PCs there is a simple graphics program called 'Paint' (**Start→Programs→Accessories→Paint**). Because images are such an important part of so many Web documents it is essential that you be able to store and view these images on your own computer.

Image formats

GIF (Graphics Interchange Format)
This is better for areas of solid color, as in graphic art.

JPEG (Joint Photographic Experts Group)
This handles more colors and is better suited to photographs.

To do any serious editing of the images, however, you will need to get hold of a more advanced graphics package. You may already have a graphics package on your computer. To check, save a gif or jpeg file to your computer then double click on the file. The image may open in your Web browser. Newer browsers will automatically open graphics within the browser rather than in a graphics package. This is bad for you because the Web browser does not allow you to play around with graphics files, to reduce or enlarge them, to add captions or save them in different formats – things you may need to do for legitimate research purposes. In this case you still need to get a graphics package. You can then open image files by opening that package and then choosing 'open file'. Do not bother with a big elaborate package like Photoshop unless you plan to become a graphic designer. These packages require too much learning for your purposes. Instead get a freeware or shareware package such as PaintShop Pro or Lview Pro (for PCs), GIF Converter, or JPEGView (for the Mac). (Freeware and shareware are explained below.) These packages each work differently and each deal with a slightly different set of formats. Virtually all can deal with gif and jpeg images but if you use images from a rare format make sure the package you use can recognize this format.

Copying the screen

You will often find that you want to copy something on your screen but you cannot figure out how because it is not a graphics file or a piece of text – an icon or a menu bar for example. On PCs the way to copy such an item is to tap the 'print screen' key usually located on the upper right of your keyboard. You will hear a little noise but there will be nothing else to tell you that you have just copied the screen to the clipboard. Switch to the simple graphics program, 'Paint' (**Start→Programs→Accessories→Paint**). Open a new file and hit ctrl v (or choose paste from the menu). An image of your computer screen will be pasted into this file. You can clip it till you have got the image you want. You can then paste it into a word processing document or a graphics file.

On the Mac hold down 'apple' and 'shift' and press 3. It will save the screen to a file on your hard disk called Picture 1 (later copies will be saved as Picture 2, Picture 3 and so on). Double click on this file and it will open a graphic image in 'Simple Text'. You can then click and drag to select the part of the image you want to keep. When you have done this copy it (apple c). Then open the graphics or word processing package you want to put it in and paste (apple v).

Escape sequences

Internet software strains many computers to their limits and it is common for computers to crash regularly when using the Net. If your computer stops responding there are a few measures you can take without resorting to the drastic measure of switching the machine on and off – a practice which computer technicians frown upon.

If your screen will not respond to the click of your mouse the first thing to do is wait a little while. Since Web software lumbers along so slowly you will often find it takes a couple of minutes to do a particular task during which you cannot do anything else on your computer.

If nothing happens after a few minutes hold down alt (on Macs the apple key) and hit tab to switch to your other programs. If the other programs are still responding then the problem is not with the computer itself but with one particular program. You just need to exit that one program and restart the program.

If you cannot switch between programs and your screen is completely locked (that is, if the cursor will not respond to the mouse at all) you should use the escape key sequences.

The escape sequence on PCs is **ctrl alt delete** (hold down ctrl and alt and hit the delete key). When you hit these keys you will get a message on the screen. If the problem lies with one program you will be given the option to close down just that program, which you should take. You should also be given the option to restart your computer without actually having to turn it off and on – this is called a 'soft boot' – or to shut it down completely.

On Macs use **apple alt esc** (hold down apple and alt and hit the escape key) to quit a program which is not responding. If this does not solve the problem hold down apple ctrl and hit the start button to restart without turning the machine off and on.

If you find that you have to use these escape sequences regularly then you have a problem which probably needs to be solved by your local computer support people.

Shareware and freeware

Most of the software you need for Internet research should already be on your computer, things like a word processing package, a Web browser and email software. There are several other items you will need which may or may not be on your machine. If they are not on your machine the first thing you should do is find out if they are available at your college or university, if your computer services people have copies which are easy for you to get access to. If they do, this is the easiest and fastest way to get access to this extra software. If not, you are going to have to learn a little more about freeware and shareware.

Freeware is free software. Freeware tends to be of two kinds, the big packages produced by big companies which are free because they encourage you to use other services they provide and the small packages produced by individuals.

Shareware is generally produced by small companies and they allow you to use it free of charge for a limited period of time. You then have to pay them a fee if you want to continue using the software. For these companies it is a way of publicizing their name and hopefully making some money from the honest users who pay for their shareware.

Freeware and shareware are very much an Internet phenomenon. The Internet makes it possible for companies to make new software widely available at very little cost while giving the user instant access to a huge range of small but useful software packages without having to deal with an intermediary like a computer shop.

Generally the big freeware packages, such as Web browsers, are made available directly by the companies at their own Websites. You will find links to this freeware all over the Web.

Shareware and the smaller freeware packages are easily available through big shareware and freeware archives. Among these archives are **www.winsite.com** (for PCs), **www.download.com** and **www.shareware.com**. These sites are huge and each of them is organized differently. You should not get bogged down in too much 'exploring' of what they have; you could spend days at this. The most efficient way to get what you need is to select your system (the type of computer and/or operating system you use) and then to look at the most popular current items. Virtually everything you will need for Internet research will fall into this category. If an item you need is not there hunt around a little in the software categories. For example, there will generally be a category for Internet-related software and another for graphics.

Note that many of these software archives do not screen for viruses. This is another good reason to download only popular packages. Popular packages are unlikely to be infected by viruses simply because, if they were, lots of people would have been infected and the package would have been removed from the site. In addition, if only a few people have downloaded a package it is likely that it is not very useful or is of interest only to a very specialized audience. Most archives have some sort of rating system and as there is so much shareware out there which is of little use I suggest that, where such a rating system exists, you only download packages which have been highly rated.

Software for uncompressing files

Lots of the shareware and freeware available on the Internet has been compressed or 'zipped' or archived to reduce its size and therefore its download time. You can recognize compressed files by their extensions. They end in **.bin**, **.zip**, **.hqx** or **.tar** or a number of other extensions depending on which software has been used to compress them.

Newer computers should automatically recognize and uncompress such files and if your computer does this you need not worry about them further. If that is not the case the first thing you need to get hold of is the software for uncompressing files. The principal shareware packages which do this are, for the Mac, Stuffit Expander (**www.aladdinsys.com**), and for the PC, WinZip (**www.winzip.com**). In both cases look for the most recent versions or a recent successor to these. One type of compressed file uncompresses itself automatically when you double click on it. This is called a self-extracting archive and will have the extension **.sea**.

Internet software

Web browser software is generally freeware. If your computer or your local network runs an older version of Netscape Navigator or Internet Explorer you can get the newer version straight from the Internet and install it on your own machine. At the Websites listed below you will get a list of sites you can download from. Choose one near you.

Netscape Navigator: **home.netscape.com**
Internet Explorer: **www.microsoft.com/ie**

As with all software, check if you can get it locally first from computer services. It will be a lot quicker and simpler if you can. If not, do note that these are huge monsters of programs which can tie up your computer for a few hours as they download. In addition they are very popular, so the sites can get clogged up and take even longer.

Some of the big freeware packages also have the useful feature that if downloading is interrupted and you start again, you do not have to download the entire package again, just the part that you did not get the first time.

Beware also of installing too many different Web browsers on your machine. When you uninstall them to make room for new or different versions you never seem to quite get rid of everything in the old version. It can get a bit messy. In addition, these programs are so huge that to have a few versions on your computer at the same time is quite a waste of space.

Finally, you should get a copy of the Adobe Acrobat reader. A lot of documents on the Web are in PDF (Portable Document Format) form. They include a large proportion of the academic articles out there. You can only read these documents if you have the Adobe Acrobat reader, **www.adobe.com/prodindex/acrobat/**.

Bits and bytes

Byte: the memory needed to encode a single letter or number such as **R** or **7**. There are 8 bits in a byte.

Kilobyte (K for short): about 1,000 bytes (1,024 or 2^{10} to be exact) and therefore about a thousand letters or numbers, the equivalent of almost a page of plain text. One small photo can easily take up 50 kilobytes.

Megabyte (megs for short): about 1,000 kilobytes (1,024 to be exact), equivalent to about 700 pages of plain text.

Gigabyte: 1,024 megs, that is about a million K or over 700,000 pages of text.

Documents will usually be measured in K, software packages in megabytes and hard drives in gigabytes.

Email

Introduction

There's a strong argument for saying that email is the most important and useful Internet application. Time after time, veteran Internet users stress that email contact with real people is the most useful aspect of the Internet. Despite the visual attractions of the World-Wide-Web many people find it much more convenient to have information emailed to them than to have to go and get it on the Web.

Getting a good email software package, learning how to use the features which are particularly important in research, and customizing it to suit your requirements are important preparatory steps before you undertake research on the Internet.

About email addresses

Email addresses are not case sensitive. You can write them in capitals, lower case or a mixture of both. It does not make any difference to the computer unless you have one of the few antique email packages which do make a distinction. If you do, get a new email package. Nearly all email addresses take the basic form of **person@place**. The part before the @ is the person, the part after is the address of the institution or organization which provides their email services.

Software

Your email package may not be a separate package but a part of a Web browser. The email part of the Netscape browser is called 'Messenger'. In Internet Explorer it is called Outlook Express. If this is the case, you will need to give your Web browser the address of your outgoing and incoming mail servers when first setting up. This is information which your own college or university will give you. If your email address is **me@mycollege.edu** your mail server address is probably **mail.mycollege.edu**. Alternatively your mail server may have been given a personalized name like 'skywalker' by the people who run it. In that case your mail server address will be **skywalker.mycollege.edu**. If your email is already working then these details have already been filled in for you, in which case you do not need to worry about it any further. However, if your college or university usually uses a separate email package I suggest you stick with this rather than use the Web browser email. It is likely to be quicker to use and there should be more documentation available locally. The problem about setting off on your own path is that there may not be too many people around locally to help you if you get lost.

A third option for email services is to ignore your local system entirely and use free Web-based email services. The number of such services has multiplied beyond count. It seems that every political party, newspaper and software company is now offering free email services. Among them are **hotmail, mailexcite, mailcity, bigfoot, rocketmail** and **goplay**. Just type the name of any one of these services in the bar at the top of your Web browser and you will get to their home page (unless you're using IE5 in which case add **www.** to the start and **.com** to the end). Netscape Web Mail is at **webmail.netscape.com**. Web-based email has the advantage of giving you a sense of independence from your college or university – you do not have to rely on it being up to date because you have a direct link to an international email service. It also has the advantage that you can log in and check your email from anywhere in the world. People also like the fact that even if they move, their email address will remain the same.

However, these Web-based services have distinct disadvantages. It can be hard to receive attachments. They are wasteful of time (your time) and energy. These services generally require that you open a bulky Web browser every time you check your email. Your local email software should open quickly and use little memory. Having a Web browser open for such a simple operation as checking email is overkill and it means you may have your Web browser open every day.

They are also slower to use. Checking an email takes extra seconds than it would on your local system, seconds which add up over the months to represent a considerable waste of time. In addition, in 1999 the security of one of the main free email services, Hotmail, was breached leading to a certain erosion of confidence in these services.

Finally there is the danger that at some stage, perhaps when enough users have become so dependent on and comfortable with these services that it is too much effort to change, these services will start to charge users a fee. As your research continues you will find that your email archives become an important repository of research information. If your free service starts to charge you may be stuck with it because it is too difficult to work out how to transfer these archives. You may also want to hold onto an email address which you have given to so many people. Some of these services already charge for 'extra' features which are standard in most email packages.

While these services are useful I strongly recommend that you keep your local email software and address as your primary one and invest your time in learning how to make optimum use of it. It is a far better long-term investment. In the long run it is probably a bad idea to become dependent on a commercial Web-based service.

Connecting to your email remotely

One of the great attractions of Web-based email is that you can log in easily and check it from anywhere in the world. The truth is that you can do this with virtually any email system if you know a few details about your home system. It is worth finding out these details locally and trying this out. Connecting remotely means connecting from another computer, whether it is thousands of miles away or just next door.

Your college or university may have made arrangements for you to connect to your email remotely and provide information about this. If so, they are the best source of information on how to do this. Even if they have not made such arrangements you can usually get access to even the most basic email systems remotely.

If your local mail server is a Unix server (and the vast majority of them are) the following steps provide a 'quick and dirty' way of getting access to your email when you are away from home.

Before you go: Ask locally for the telnet address of your mail server. Confirm that it will accept external connections. If it will not you cannot get your email remotely.

When you are away: Open telnet (for more on telnet see below). If you cannot find telnet, open a Web browser and type the address of your mail server in the bar at the top of the browser, putting *telnet://* before the address. When a telnet window opens give the login id and the password you use when you check your email at home. Type 'mail'. Type 'help' or '?' to get commands. Type 'q' to quit.

Email: basic functions

Sending an email

At the head of an email message are the following 'fields':

To:
cc:
Subject:

The 'To:' field, giving the email address of the person you are sending the message to, is the only one you really have to fill in. It is recommended that you also fill in the subject field with a word or two which briefly describes what the message is about. People get so much email that the clearer the detail you put in the subject line the more likely they are to give your message the attention it deserves. Make it short, though, because the person you send it to will only see the first ten letters or so of the subject line in their list of newly received email. 'Cc' is a pretty old-fashioned term. It stands for 'carbon copy', the old blue copies people made on typewriters. The message will also be sent to anyone whose email address you type in the 'cc:' field. It is somewhat redundant because you can put pretty much as many email addresses as you like in the 'To:' field, separating each of them with a comma or a semi-colon.

   In either case, the people who receive your email also receive a list of everyone else you sent it to. The only way to prevent this is to use a field which is available on a lot of email programs: 'bcc'. 'Bcc' stands for 'blind carbon copy'. People whose email addresses are entered in this field will receive the email without the addresses of the other people it has been sent to. This is useful if you do not want people to know they are part of a big long list or if you do not want to share your list of email addresses with everyone on that list. If someone receives that list it is a simple matter for them to paste it into the 'To:' field of their own email message and send a message to everyone on your list. You might be better not to present people with this temptation.

   If you are using special characters such as accent marks, ask the person receiving the email if they can read them. Often they will not be able to, but will not tell you this out of politeness.

Reply and forward

All email packages give you the option of replying to messages. It means you do not have to type out the address of the person you are replying to and the software will also put in the subject heading of the original message in your new message, though you may want to change that. When you use 'reply' you are given the option of including the text they sent you. Most people do this, thinking they might as well, but unless it is necessary it is probably better practice not to. It just clutters up the screen and clogs up email inboxes faster than necessary.

You can forward messages you have received to other people but note that, in strict legal terms (Lehnert, 1998: 472), you cannot do this without the permission of the person who sent it in the first place. Apart from the law, common courtesy suggests that you ask the person before you forward a private email which they intended for your eyes only.

Saving outgoing mail

Most email packages automatically save the email you send in an 'outbox'. If your package does not do this automatically, change the settings so that it does. Apart from building up an archive and record of what you have sent it also means that if a message you send 'bounces' and is returned to you, you can send it again by opening the outbox and 'resending' it.

Mailboxes/mail folders

When you first use your email you will have at least two mail folders or mailboxes (different terms for the same thing). All mail you receive goes into your inbox while everything you send should be saved in your outbox. You should try to keep the inbox clear so it just contains recent messages that you have yet to deal with. Particularly when you start subscribing to email lists you will find that you need to start organizing your email. You should start creating mail folders. In particular you should set up a 'lists' or 'subscriptions' folder in which you keep information about all the email lists you are subscribed to, especially information on unsubscribing. It can also be useful to set up separate folders for each list you have subscribed to, in which you store all the messages from that list that you want to keep. One method of organizing incoming email which I recommend strongly is extravagant use of the delete key, otherwise you will quickly find things getting out of control.

As time goes on you will find that a fairly large proportion of your research material will actually be stored in your email folders and that these folders are an important archive in their own right. You need to be sure that your email software allows you to search your email archives in some way and you need to learn how to use this search facility. In each of your folders you should be able to sort your messages not only by date but also by author or subject, a useful way of finding all your messages on one subject or from one author.

Filtering

When you have subscribed to a few lists you may find that you do not want to read messages when they come in but that you prefer to look at all recent messages from the same list once a week or even once a month. At this point you will want to start using filters. A filter allows you automatically to direct certain messages to folders, clearing them straight out of the inbox. You can filter according to the sender or the subject of messages so it is an easy matter to direct all the messages from a certain list into a folder for that list.

Address books/distributions lists

All email software allows you to build up lists of email addresses so that you can send email to everyone on the list just by typing the name of the list in the 'To:' field of your message. You should find out how to do this on your software and start building lists of people to whom you regularly send the same email.

You have to be careful how you use such lists. People can get very annoyed if they think they are receiving email from you just because they happen to be on a list which you casually included them on. It can feel very impersonal to the recipient and if you do it too often you can really irritate people.

Your address book, or whatever it happens to be called on your software, will also allow you to give nicknames or short names to people you regularly send email to. When you type the nickname in the 'To:' field of your email, your software automatically provides the email address.

You can usually add someone's address to your address book while viewing a message from them. There is usually a 'take address' or similar command available in the menu. If you 'take' the address it will be added to your address book and you will be prompted to give it a nickname.

Signature

All up-to-date email packages allow you to create a signature file. The information you put here will appear at the bottom of every email message you send. It should include your name and email address and your real-world address at work or college. You should turn off the signature file when you are sending commands to machine addresses like listserv and majordomo (that is, when you are subscribing to lists), otherwise you just get back a bunch of error messages, though it does no real harm.

Attachments

These are one of the great joys of email and one of the great torments – joy because you can attach almost anything to an email message (you can send people audio or image files as well as plain old words), torment because you will sometimes be sent attachments you cannot decipher. There are several possible reasons for this problem. The sender may have used an encoding your email software cannot deal with. In this case you should ask them to resend the attachment in a simpler form and you should consider changing to an email package which recognizes all encoding formats.

Certain email software refuses to deal with email over a certain length, over 1,000 lines in some cases (Lehnert, 1998: 97). The system will simply spit back anything which breaks this barrier. For this reason all very long text messages should be sent as attachments.

One peculiar feature of email attachments is that they can only consist of plain text. Attachments cannot be binary files like images. So, if you are attaching an image or other binary file to an email message your software converts it to text using a form of encoding called MIME. The recipient's email software will automatically decode the file back into its original form. All current email software is 'MIME-compliant' and if your software is not you will need to change it.

Attachments provide an excellent motivation for getting to know your computer's file system well. When you go to attach a file to an email message you will be allowed to choose from your file system and you can only manoeuvre to the files you want to attach if you know where they are. In addition, all attachments you receive are saved to an attachments folder which is often buried deep in your file system. You will want to save some of these attachments elsewhere and you can only do that if you can find them in the first place.

Web browsers

Introduction

This section deals with the very basics of using a Web browser. Many users have learned to use Web browsers with no formal training. They use the Web reasonably efficiently but often without a clear idea of how even the basic commands work. This section is aimed at such users as well as at those who have never used a browser. Use of the Web at a more advanced level is dealt with in detail in chapter 5.

Understanding your Web browser

Netscape Navigator (NN) and Microsoft's Internet Explorer (IE) are currently the two most popular Web browsers. In this section I refer to version 4 of NN for Macintosh. In the case of IE I refer to both IE4 and IE5 for the PC, two recent versions, because there are major differences between the two. Appendix 4 gives commands for Netscape 6 for Macintosh, the most recent version of the Netscape Web browser. Not all of the command sequences listed in this book will necessarily be applicable to the specific version number of the web browser which is running on your computer. There can be some variation in menu set-up between slightly different versions of the same browser. Thus versions 4.3 and 4.7 of a browser can be identical in all but a few menu options. Nonetheless, most of the options given here should be applicable to most readers of this book.

Although Netscape and Microsoft do their best to give the impression that these browsers <u>are</u> the Internet, they are not. They are just software packages which allow you to connect to other computers and look at material on them. Microsoft and Netscape ensure that it is very easy to connect to their Web pages and the Web pages of associated services through their browsers. Thus, menu items like 'netsearch' at the top of NN will link you to pages provided by Netscape. You do not need to use these pages – they are no more essential to Web exploration and no more the heart of the Web than thousands of other Web pages are. So the first thing to realize is that the menu bars on both NN <u>and</u> IE are there to direct you towards the parts of the Internet they want you to use. As an Internet researcher these are not really the areas of the Web that are most useful to you. The first thing you need to do is take a step towards breaking the Netscape/Microsoft connection.

Customizing your Web browser

Every time you start up NN or IE the company's page greets you unless someone has already altered this. The first thing you need to do is to change this 'start-up' page. If you're based in a college it may be that your college or university has already changed it to their home page. Even if they have it is worth knowing how you can change it to a different page if you want to.

NN: **Edit→Preferences→Navigator.** In the 'Homepage' box type the Web address of the page you would like to have as your start-up page.
IE4: **Edit→Preferences→Web Browser→Home/Search**.
IE5: **Tools→Internet Options→General→Home page**.

For the moment just change it to your college or university's home page if you're based in a college or university. Their pages are targeted directly at users on your campus and are generally your best starting point for exploration of the Web. Do not change it to a page which is slow to download. This will delay your browser opening every time. Note one thing in particular. There's no need to use the search buttons on NN or IE. They just bring you to a list of search engines. You can get directly to any one of the major search engines like Yahoo or AltaVista just by typing the name in the bar at the top of your browser. If this doesn't work add **www.** to the start and **.com** to the end.

Basic navigation

In one sense navigating the Web could not be simpler. Run the cursor over the blue-underlined text till the cursor arrow becomes a hand and click (just once). 'Ta da', you are downloading a document, you are surfing the Net – it is as easy as that.

Hyperlinks

The blue-underlined text is a hyperlink. Sometimes it is red or yellow because some Web page designer thought it would be nice to play with the colours, but it is generally blue, Behind every hyperlink there is a hidden Web address. Run the mouse over a hyperlink and look at the bar at the bottom of your browser. The Web address hidden behind the hyperlink will appear there. When you click on a hyperlink you are giving a command to your computer, the command 'get the document at the address hidden behind this link and display it for me in my Web browser'.

If you have recently viewed a particular page (usually in the past thirty days), the hyperlink to that page will appear dimmed in your browser, a duller shade of blue.

Home

No matter how deeply you have explored or how far you have strayed, clicking on this button will bring you straight back to your start-up page. It is useful during the early stages of Web exploration when you can get lost very quickly.

Back and forward

The back arrow brings you back through the Web documents you have looked at, following the sequence backwards, like Hansel and Gretel following the trail of stones back out of the forest. However, if you go back and then strike out in another direction it forgets the original trail and will only bring you back along your most recent trail. Forward can only be used if you have already gone back. If you have gone back 'home', forward will bring you out along the trail again.

History/Go

In NN and IE5 this is called 'history', in IE4 and Netscape 6 it is called 'Go'. This is a list of the Web documents you have just looked at. In fact, it is the list which the back and forward commands use to tell them what is 'back' and what is 'forward'. Once you go back a few steps and branch out on a new trail history forgets the old trail. You can click on any document in the history list and go directly to that document. It provides a much faster way of jumping back or forward a few documents.

Bookmarks/Favorites

For the beginner, bookmarks ('Favorites' in IE) are the best way of keeping a record of useful sites you would like to go back to, though they will very quickly need to be organized into folders. To add an item to your bookmark list on NN, click on 'add bookmark' in the pull-down menu under the little bookmark icon. In IE4: **Favorites→Add page to Favorites**. In IE5: **Favorites→ Add to Favorites**.

You can go back to the bookmarked page directly at any time by opening your bookmarks and clicking on that page. The titles which bookmarks are given are sometimes meaningless and you may want to change them to titles which tell you more about what the bookmark points to.

Open

If you have been given a Website address by someone or you have got it from a newspaper or magazine you can open it in two ways. Just click with the mouse in the bar at the top of your browser and type the address in, then hit the return ⏎ key. Alternatively, in NN: **File→Open→Location in Navigator** and type the address in the box which appears. In IE4: **File→Open location**. In IE5: **File→Open**.

Usually you do not have to type in the full address. You can leave out the http:// at the start of the address and the browser will automatically add it in. If the address begins in www you can leave that out and if it ends in .com you can leave that out too. Browsers automatically add all of these to incomplete addresses though IE5 does not. So, if you want to connect to **http://www.anysite.com** you just have to type 'anysite'. Effectively this means you can get the Web page of almost any very large commercial company just by typing its name.

Stop and reload/refresh

These may well be the two most important menu items for someone just starting to use the Web. It can take a long time for a Web document to download and often it seems to get jammed in the system. Half of the document downloads in a minute but ten minutes later no more of it has downloaded. This is the point at which new users can panic and start clicking all over in desperation. Don't panic (Adams, 1979: *passim*). You can stop a document downloading by clicking on 'stop'. It may take a second or two to respond but it will stop. You know your browser is downloading (or at least trying to download) because the little icon in the upper right is moving (in the case of NN, shooting stars, in the case of IE, a rotating globe or Windows logo). In addition the stop button will be red and highlighted. When you hit 'stop' the shooting stars or globe stop and the stop button fades to pink.

If a document is not downloading quickly there is one method which almost always speeds it up. Click on 'stop', then click on 'reload' ('refresh' on IE). Your browser will then try again to download the same document. Wait for a short time – ten to twenty seconds is usually my limit. Then click on 'stop' and 'reload' again unless the document is downloading more quickly. Do not be afraid to stop and reload even if you downloaded 90% of the document before it jammed. Generally most documents will start to download more quickly after a few stops and reloads.

Just one thing. 'Reload' will reload the document whose address is displayed in the bar at the top of your browser. If your browser has not even connected to the other machine the page's URL will not be displayed here and reload will just call up the last page you successfully downloaded.

If a document you are downloading includes Java or ActiveX it can be very reluctant to respond to the stop button. It will keep on trying to download long after a normal Web document would have stopped.

There are a few other things which will help to speed up the time it takes to download items from the Web. One is to switch off images. In IE4: **Preferences→Web Browser→Web Content→Show Pictures**. In IE5: **Tools→ Internet Options→Advanced→Multimedia→Show Pictures**. In NN: **Edit→ Preferences→Advanced→Automatically load images**. If you can deal with not having the graphics you can surf the Web at easily ten times the speed. A single little picture can take as much time to download as fifty pages of text.

You should also try to avoid peak surfing times in the USA when the Internet is at its busiest – that is, working hours in New York, Chicago and Los Angeles.

Find

You download a Web document. It is huge. You do not know where in the document you will find the information you are looking for. This is where you use the 'find' command. It allows you to do a simple keyword search of the Web document. 'Find' is a little crude and if you have a long Web document you want to search through, it might be a better idea to save it as text, open it in your word processor and search it there.

Understanding plain text

Plain text files are files which consist only of the characters you can type on a keyboard and see on your screen. They include letters, numbers and most punctuation marks. They do not include special characters like accents on letters. Neither do they include invisible things like tab. The technical term for plain text is ASCII (American Standard Code for Information Interchange).

Email messages are plain text. So are Web pages. Word processing documents are not plain text. They include all sorts of complicated coding for creating bulleted lists, columns, different fonts, underlining and all the rest. This coding is not visible to you, the author, unless you open a word processing document in a plain text editor. Then you will see just how much complex coding it includes. Two pages of plain text take up about 2K of memory, but two pages of a word processing document can easily take up 30K.

Saving and viewing documents

When you save a document from the Web you can save it as one of two types of document. You can save it as html (also known as 'source') in which case it will have an **.htm** or **.html** extension (in IE5 save it as 'Web Page, HTML only'). You will be able to view it within your Web browser by opening it from the browser menu (IE4: **File→Open File**. IE5: **Open→browse**. NN: **File→Open→Page in Navigator**) or by double clicking on the document itself (in most computers). It will look like it did when you viewed it on the Web except that all the graphics will be missing. In fact you can open any file on your computer in the Web browser in this way. If you open an html document in a word processor or a text editor it will be full of html code in angle brackets like these < >,< >.

Alternatively you can save it as text (also known as plain text). In this case your document will have a **.txt** extension. All of the confusing html code will have been removed and it will consist only of the text you saw on the screen when you first viewed it, minus any special formatting. The graphics will be missing from this version too. You can open this up in a word processor or text editor but it is no longer a Web document and if you open it in your browser it will be plain grey text. IE 5 also offers you the option to save files as 'Web page, complete'. This creates an exact copy of the page, graphics and all. In the course of doing that, however, it creates a new document which looks the same but does not have exactly the same html code as the original document.

To save a graphic from a Web document click on it with the right mouse button and choose '**save this image as…**' (in NN), '**Download image to disk**' (in IE4) or '**save picture as**' (in IE5). Any Web documents you save should be saved as source/html. You can always make a plain text copy of an html document but there is no way of restoring the html code later if you save it as plain text.

Printing

Printing Web documents is usually just a matter of clicking on the print button in the browser. Graphics and text will be printed together very much as they appear on the screen. However, there is one common problem which occurs on some Mac computers. Some Web authors specify that their documents should always be a certain width. If they do not specify this their document will adjust to fit your window. If they do specify the width it can make the document awkward to view. You will have to use the scroll bar at the bottom of your browser to scroll the document from left to right. It can make it even more awkward to print. You may find that your printer deals with the extra width by putting the overflowing text on to separate pages thus using twice as much paper to print the document. There are two ways to prevent this on a Mac. You can reduce print size to 90% or 80% of the original size (**File→Page Setup→Reduce or Enlarge** or **File→Page Setup→scale**). This reduces the size of the text making it slightly less comfortable to read but fitting it all within the margins of one page. Alternatively, print the Web document as a landscape view (printing across the length of the page) rather than the usual portrait view (printing across the width of the page) (**File→Page Setup→Orientation** or **File→Page**

Setup→**scale**). You keep the original text size though it uses up more paper than reducing text size does. (Thanks to Mike McCool for these tips.)

You should also make sure from the start that important information you will need for citation purposes is included on the printout, including date of printing, URL and title of the page. It seems both IE and NN automatically put this information on printouts unless otherwise instructed. You can change the settings on NN: **File**→**Page Setup**.

From this point on you should be saving copies of all documents that you are likely to use in your research and, within reason, printing out all documents you are reasonably sure you will use. Longer documents can be saved or bookmarked until you are sure you really need a printout.

Other tools

Telnet

Telnet was one of the core Internet utilities long before the Web came into existence. The Web has taken over a lot of the jobs which telnet used to do. For example, telnet was used to connect to online databases. Now most of those databases are on the Web and it is much easier to use them.

In a sense telnet is the technology of the past but for an old-fashioned technology it is remarkably persistent. A lot of those old databases have not yet gone onto the Web and telnet is still used to get access to them. This includes a large proportion of online library catalogues around the world. Some of the hyperlinks on the Web are actually telnet links. You will recognize them because they begin with **telnet://** instead of **http://**. When you click on a telnet link you will be presented with a new little window inviting you to log in. Sooner or later on your Web travels you will hit a telnet link. It is important to know how to deal with it when you do.

Telnet allows you to connect to other computers, usually to specific sections of those computers like an online database. You cannot download files but you can look through the sections of the computer they give you access to, using the keyboard commands they provide. Once you are within the telnet window forget about the mouse. In telnet only keyboard commands are recognized. You can only go back through text you have typed by using the delete key so be careful to type things correctly the first time. All telnet databases have their own set of commands which they recognize, so when you first connect to a site by telnet make a note of the basic commands, in particular the exit command. A pen and paper will come in handy at this point.

You should close telnet by using the exit command used by the particular database you are connected to or by closing it from the menu in your telnet software. Do not close it by just shutting the telnet window. If you do this the connection actually stays open until the other computer shuts you off, thus tying up resources at your end and the other end. If the telnet window absolutely refuses to respond to your keyboard commands to quit, the emergency quit command is **ctrl]** (hold down the ctrl key and tap the right square bracket key). Sometimes you will be asked when you log in to select a terminal type, sometimes by being given the prompt 'TERM'. VT100 is the most common terminal type. Try this first.

The simplest way to use telnet is from within your Web browser. Enter the telnet address you want to connect to in the bar at the top of your browser. Put **telnet://** before the address. If you find you are using telnet a lot, search through your files for the telnet software (it may be called 'NCSA telnet' on a Mac and 'WinQVT' or similar on a PC). Make an alias (on the Mac) or a shortcut (on PCs) so that you can get easy access to it without having to open your Web browser.

You will often find yourself waiting in telnet for a response to your commands from the computer you have connected to. When this happens, resist the temptation to enter a few alternative or extra commands in an effort to speed things up. Your commands will be stored and as soon as the computer is finished with your last command it will run all the other commands one after the other, with often confusing results.

If you have an account on a Unix computer which allows telnet connections you should be able to log on to your account from anywhere in the world and work on it just as you would if you were working on the computer itself. This can come in useful but unfortunately it means learning the basic Unix commands. If you want to explore this option further you will need to get a Unix account and start reading about Unix. For most users this is not worth the time and effort required.

FTP

FTP, File Transfer Protocol, allows you to connect to another computer for the purpose of doing one thing only, transferring files, either from that computer back to your own machine or vice versa. FTP was the main method used to transfer computer files across the Internet before the advent of the Web. You will still come across FTP archives on the Web, collections of files which you can download. You will recognize them because they will have **ftp://** at the beginning of the address. Unlike telnet these ftp sites do not require any special skills; you can move through them and save from them just as you would from an ordinary Website – pointing and clicking. You will find that many of the large collections of software online are actually FTP sites. An FTP site will often include a 'Readme' or index file which will give you details about the items available on that site. FTP sites will show you lists of files and folders with very little extra detail or help, so it helps if you understand how your own file system works. There is one symbol you will see which is probably unfamiliar to you. The double dots, ··, mean 'the folder above this one'. In other words, it will take you back up a level in the file system. Every folder on a Unix computer includes ··, providing a shortcut back to the folder immediately above it.

If you end up writing your own Web documents you may well find yourself using FTP to transfer them from your own computer to the Web server which makes them available to the world. This is something you cannot usually do through your Web browser. There is more information on this in chapter 10. If you plan to do this you will need to get hold of an FTP package such as WS-FTP (for PCs) or Fetch (for the Mac).

Gopher

Gopher is a kind of half way house between the old world of FTP and the new world of the Web. (See appendix 3 for more on Gopher.) When it came out it was the first tool to make it easy to search through other people's computers. The Web came out a year or two later and eclipsed Gopher. There are still Gopher sites out there, like ghost ships from the early 1990s, frozen in time, exactly as they were when they were abandoned sometime after the appearance of the Web.

Some organizations still use them because they are a simpler way of storing large numbers of plain documents than the Web is. You will recognize a Gopher site because the address will start with **gopher://**. Gopher uses menus. Each menu is a set of links and links only, no descriptive text. This link can be to one of several things but cannot be a link to a Web document. Once you go into gopherspace, as it is called, you are stuck there. You can get out on the Web again by using the back button or the history list on your browser. Links on a Gopher menu will point you either to a directory (that is, another Gopher menu), a file (graphic or plain text), a searchable database or a telnet link. These will each be represented by different icons which vary depending on which Web browser you use.

Newsgroups

Newsgroups are a distinct part of the Internet, quite separate from the Web and email. Newsgroup messages are posted to the newsgroups by anyone who wants to post. They are then distributed to news servers across the world. News servers are computers (or dedicated sections of computers) which are devoted solely to storing messages from the thousands of newsgroups in existence. There are so many messages that news servers hold onto messages for just a few weeks or even days before deleting them to make way for new messages. There are major problems associated with newsgroups and it seems possible that they will become ever less useful as a research resource. Nonetheless it is essential to a comprehensive research strategy that you do at least a cursory exploration of what is available on the newsgroups and learn how to read them. They are dealt with in detail in chapter 4.

It used to be that people read newsgroups through 'newsreader' software packages. But newsreader software is now included with the major Web browsers and this is probably the simplest way for you to read it.

IE and NN both include newsreaders. From the Netscape icon choose 'Collabra Discussion Groups'. In IE it is part of the 'Outlook Express' package.

It may be that the newsreader has been set up for you already. If it does not work straight away you will have to enter a few details, including your name and email address. You will also need to enter the address of your local news server. If your college's Web address is **www.mycollege.edu** it is highly likely that its news server address is **news.mycollege.edu** but you will need to check locally.

Your local news server will not carry all newsgroups partly because there are so many and partly because a lot of colleges and universities censor and block certain newsgroups, particularly those with strong sexual content. However, you will be able to get access to these newsgroups through Web-based services as outlined in the section on newsgroups in chapter 4.

Your newsreader will give you different options for viewing newsgroups. When you have decided which newsgroups you wish to follow, subscribe to these groups. It just takes a click of the mouse to subscribe; it does not commit you to anything. You can unsubscribe with another click of the mouse. Once you have subscribed set your newsreader to 'show subscribed newsgroups' (available under the options menu). Now whenever you open your newsreader you will only see those groups you have subscribed to. The newsreader will also give you the option to 'show active groups'. If you choose this option as well you will only see subscribed groups which contain messages you have not yet read.

If you have just started using your newsreader and you want to test it out by posting a few messages, post those messages to **misc.test** and **alt.test**. These groups were created solely for the purpose of receiving test messages. One last piece of advice. Give a false address in your Usenet posts, otherwise you will be deluged with junk email.

Keeping up with changing research tools

In the past few years new Internet research tools have emerged, most importantly the Web browsers. Existing tools like email, telnet and FTP have either changed beyond all recognition or become marginalized. The tools are immensely easier to use than they were a few years ago. At the same time some of these tools have become overcomplex, huge unwieldy packages which attempt to do too many things and which change so often that it is hard for a researcher to keep up with the latest version.

When learning about the tools for Internet research it is important not to let yourself become too distracted by the shiniest newest item of software available. Sometimes it can be wiser to let a few new versions come out before you update. Otherwise you can waste time and energy downloading and learning new software. In the end these tools remain precisely that, tools. Your job is research and the tools are important only to the extent that they contribute to your understanding of the topic you are researching.

Now that you have at least a basic command of the tools, the next chapter of this book deals directly with the first phases of that research.

3

Searching for books and articles

The growth of the Internet has sparked off a debate on the future of print publications. On one side of the debate it is argued that printed matter is being made redundant, that the future lies with hypertext books which allow you to read a book online in whatever order you choose, and that it lies with 'electronic newspapers', personal news-feeds via the Internet (Negroponte, 1996: 152–4). The cyber-sceptics, on the other hand, argue that printed books and newspapers are far superior to their electronic competitors (Stoll, 1995a: 142) and that it's awkward to read an electronic book in bed, never mind in the bath.

In the light of this debate it's a little ironic that over the past few years the Internet has become the central storehouse for information about print publications. Far from replacing books the Net has become the gateway to them. If the Internet contained nothing else but the databases of information about books and articles it would be a precious resource. The student setting out on that traditional first step of the research process, the literature search, has the sort of access to information about the world of books and articles that earlier researchers could only have dreamed of. Going online is now the best way to find out about what's offline. In beginning your online literature search remember the basic guidelines which apply to any literature search:

1. Find the most relevant materials as quickly as possible.
2. Avoid getting bogged down.
3. Get into the habit of recording information about sources in a form which you can understand when you go back to it later (Bell, 1993: 39).

This advice applies, to the power of ten, to an online literature sense where it's especially easy to become distracted and bogged down.

Starting in the real world

People

The Internet may be the best place to find out about printed materials but it is not the best place to start your literature search. The search has to begin offline and the best starting point is generally human contact. If you have a research supervisor they can play a vital role at this stage. They should be the person best placed to point you towards the core texts that you need to read at the very beginning. The databases and catalogues cannot tell you which books are central to your research, which are the best, which are absolutely essential. Throughout your research a supervisor should remain a valuable source of bibliographic information, capable at their best of pin-pointing immediately a source which it could take you hours of online searching to find. Above all a good supervisor will be able to assess two vital qualities which no databases have been able to quantify except in the crudest mathematical terms: relevance and quality.

Other human contacts are also important at this stage of the research process. If you are lucky enough to be based somewhere where other people are studying related topics, personal exchange of information about books and articles in the area adds an important element to the initial search.

Books

A prime 'real-world' source of bibliographic information is books and articles themselves. The footnotes and bibliographies of key works on the subject point you to works which are directly related. In many subject areas people have published bibliographies, books whose sole purpose is to create a catalogue of all published matter on a particular subject. In addition there are journals produced annually which are devoted to listing books published on a specific subject during the year just past. Look for journals whose titles begin 'Annual Review of…'. Finally, many journals see it as part of their duty, where no such bibliographic source exists, to publish in each issue of their journal a bibliography of recent publications in their subject area. These print sources are generally easier to use and are a richer resource than the online databases.

Before you ever tap a single key on a keyboard browse the shelves of a college or university library. Make a note of the classification numbers of the key works in the area, which can often be spread over a few different classifications. Have a look at the shelves where books with these class numbers are located. See what your own library has immediately available. There is no electronic means of assessing a book's usefulness to your research which can match the effectiveness of taking a book from a shelf and flicking through it. Using those traditional search engines for books, the index and contents page, you can usually judge very quickly whether it's worth exploring further.

The first online source you need to consult is your library's online catalogue. You will usually access this from a computer in the library or at home. In the case of most college libraries, it can also be used by anyone in the world who connects to it through telnet or the Web (see chapter 2 for more on telnet). In this sense your local catalogue is 'on the Internet'.

Doing a classmark search on the main classifications of interest to you will turn up those books which your library holds which were not on the shelves when you looked. It is also then worth doing a subject search (if the catalogue allows it) of the main subject headings which are relevant to you. The place to start your subject search is on the inside pages of key books in the area. Many academic books provide 'Library of Congress Cataloging-in-Publication Data'. This includes the subject categories the book belongs to. There are high-level categories such as 'Social Sciences' and sub-categories below them like 'Social Sciences – Computer Networked Resources'. The latter includes books dealing with Internet resources relevant to the social sciences. Many books are put under a few different categories. A book on the geography of the Welsh language can appear under several categories including 'Welsh language', 'Language policy-Wales' and 'Linguistic Geography'. Each of these categories may be worth exploring for related books. If your library uses these categories in its subject search it can be a useful way to turn up new classmarks and therefore new books relevant to you. When you connect to other library catalogues you can have a quick look at all the books in the subject categories or classmarks of most interest to you.

Journals

Academic journals are much more accessible through the Internet than books are and it can be tempting to go online to start your search for articles from these journals.

However, such journals can be searched much more quickly and efficiently by lifting the print copies and flicking through them. There are likely to be a few journals directly concerned with your subject area and a few others closely connected to it. If your library subscribes to the printed versions of these journals you should start by scouring recent issues of them for relevant articles. When you then go to do a keyword search of the article databases you can simply ignore all articles from these journals since you have already covered them. You will be able to concentrate on the articles from more obscure sources.

Most of the above adds up to one simple piece of advice. Exhaust your local print resources before you take a single step in your online literature search.

Searching for books

Online library catalogues

For several years past it has been possible to get access to hundreds of university and other online library catalogues through the Internet. It used to be that telnet was the only means of getting this access. Increasingly now libraries are putting their catalogues on the Web, making it considerably easier to use them. 'Library Web-Based OPACS' (**www.lights.com/webcats**) provides links to library catalogues on the Web organized geographically and by library type. The US Library of Congress also provides a search form for library catalogues (**lcweb.loc.gov/z3950/**). It is awkwardly named, z3950, but it provides a Web interface to hundreds of libraries in the USA and beyond. For many libraries, though, it's still necessary to connect by telnet. All of the libraries have their own passwords but it is possible to get access to all of them through Hytelnet (**www.einet.net/hytelnet/ START.TXT.html**).

Hytelnet provides a huge list of telnet links to library catalogues around the world, arranged geographically and alphabetically. When you choose a site to connect to, Hytelnet tells you the password and any other login details needed to use that site. Be careful when using Hytelnet. All of these libraries have their own keyboard commands which you will need to make a note of when you connect. You are connected by telnet and will have to exercise all the caution you would with any telnet link. Refer back to the chapter 2 section on telnet for details.

As libraries have begun to develop Web versions of their catalogues groups of universities and libraries have come together to create tools to allow the user to search several libraries simultaneously. It may well be that your library is part of such an arrangement. One such service is COPAC (**copac.ac.uk/copac**) which allows you to do a unified search of major university research libraries in the UK and Ireland, by subject and by author or title. You can also search it for journals to see which libraries hold the journals you want.

A larger and more elaborate service called 'WorldCat' is provided by OCLC. You can only get access to this service if your institution subscribes to it. It is one of a suite of services provided by OCLC, which is US based, and draws on the co-operative efforts of over 8,000 member libraries. If your college or university does subscribe they will provide a link on their Web pages directly to OCLC. This is the link you should use. You should only go to the OCLC home page at **www.oclc.org** if your institution is not subscribed and you want to learn more above the databases OCLC provides. WorldCat allows you to search simultaneously a 'Union Catalog' of the collections of thousands of libraries world-wide. A 'Union Catalog' is the US term for a catalogue which brings together all or part of the catalogues of two or more libraries. WorldCat includes not only books but a huge range of other materials which have been catalogued. It is weighted very heavily towards North American libraries and, to a lesser extent, towards English-speaking countries in general. If you have a very specialized query this can be a great resource, pulling out a handful of obscure items for you from most of the biggest and best libraries in the world. If you are doing a broad initial search, forget it. You will be swamped.

WorldCat has one interesting feature which may be of interest to anyone who has ever written a book. A curious author interested in how far their book has spread can search for a particular book and get a list of all of the libraries which hold that book.

You may be wondering at this stage why you would bother searching all of these catalogues. Certainly it would be a monumental waste of time to try and search all, or even a dozen, library catalogues just to ensure you had a comprehensive list of books in your area. Rather it can be useful for very specific purposes.

If your research concerns a specific place and your library is not based in that place (whether it be a country thousands of miles from you or a city a hundred miles away) it is well worth checking through the catalogue of a library located in that place. Libraries tend to have large collections related to the place they are located in, often including relatively rare material. It is also worthwhile searching catalogues at universities which are home to specialized research institutes or centres in your broad subject area. Such institutes either will have ensured that a large specialized collection of materials on the subject are available in the library or might even have their own library with its own online catalogue. When you connect to libraries through library catalogues and university Websites you will find that many of them provide additional bibliographic resources. Some libraries will provide an option to search only through their latest acquisitions. Others will provide select bibliographies on certain topics or specialized catalogues dealing only with material in a particular subject or a special collection which they hold. They are not necessarily even catalogues of printed materials: 'Visual Information Access', for example, is a catalogue of visual materials at Harvard and Radcliffe Universities which includes photos, slides and objects (see the Harvard online catalogue at **hplus.harvard.edu**). There is no systematic list of such unique online bibliographic collections and resources but keep an eye out for these unique catalogues when visiting library sites.

Certain libraries have now begun to catalogue Websites and to include them in their online catalogues. This, however, takes us away from the world of print into the area of searching for pure Internet sources. It is dealt with at length in chapter 6.

There will be certain key people who have written important works in your research area. It is generally easy enough to find out where they work, if they are alive. Wherever they are based they will generally teach quite specialized courses related to their writings. You may well find that they have built up an extensive collection in your area of interest and that it might include items that are a little more obscure or rare.

In all of these cases your best guide to moving through these other library collections is the classmark numbers for your subject which you gathered in your own library, providing they use the same system. Alternatively you can search by subject, where that option is available.

In many cases libraries catalogue items which are put on desk reserve or course reserve (two terms for the same thing). If course or desk reserve lists are available they should be a main menu item on the catalogue, though they may be obscurely named. If you connect to a catalogue at an institution where your subject is very important these lists will show you what texts are being used in teaching the subject. In certain universities course/desk reserve items are listed under the name of the professor who teaches the course. If you strike lucky you may be able to see what texts the main experts in the area are using to teach classes on the subject.

There is one final type of library whose catalogue is worth searching. These are the big copyright libraries, those which aim to collect every single published item from a certain country or set of countries or in a certain language. These libraries aim for a complete collection. In certain cases they also have specialized collections of printed materials which are extremely rare. Details of a few of the larger of these libraries in the English-speaking world are given below.

The US Library of Congress (**www.loc.gov**) As its name would suggest, this is the official library serving the US legislature in Washington, DC. The Library of Congress is not a place for casual searching. If you just want to check quickly the date of publication or author of a book do not wander in here. It provides quite a complicated set of options for searching its catalogue which is called LOCIS. The advanced search allows you to go beyond the book catalogue and to search the library's collections of manuscripts.

The British Library (**opac97.bl.uk**) OPAC 97 is the online catalogue for the reference and document supply collections of the British Library in London. One of these collections is the humanities and social sciences collection which includes unique resources on particular areas of interest. The catalogue is worth exploring to see if there is a specialized collection or archive of interest to you. If, for example, you are interested in British colonialism you will find much of interest that can be found nowhere else.

In addition to these library catalogues there is a major database concerned solely with books.

Booksinprint.com (**www.booksinprint.com**) is perhaps the most comprehensive database available of books currently in print. It also includes over 500,000 book reviews. It is only available to subscribing institutions and traditionally its use has been restricted in many institutions to library staff.

Creating a bibliography

In the course of your research you will have to build up a bibliography of your own. There is no need for you to type anything directly into your bibliography. Just copy and paste directly from an online catalogue (ctrl c and ctrl v in case you have forgotten, apple c and apple v on the Mac). All the better if you can find an online catalogue which presents book details in the format that you plan to use in your bibliography. This minimizes the time you spend editing. There is commercial software available which helps you to organize your bibliography, allowing you to reformat your references automatically in different citation styles. ISI Research Soft (**www.risinc.com**) provides a range of such packages, including ProCite and Reference Manager.

Online bookstores

After trawling through libraries the online bookstores may seem like overkill. Most of them are not directed specifically at academics. Nonetheless, nearly all of them carry academic titles. The online bookstores have certain drawbacks. They're only concerned with selling you books and as a result most of them are concerned only with books which are in print. In this sense they are a much less comprehensive source than the large library catalogues. Just because a book is out of print does not necessarily mean it is either old or useless. Many academic books have a very limited print run of maybe a few hundred copies. If they all sell out in a year or two the publisher may not bother to re-print them.

The online bookstores focus on the new. It is in their interests to promote and publicize and thereby sell new books. Online bookstores are effectively huge searchable book catalogues which are heavily weighted towards what is new. Some of them provide searchable collections of reviews and short descriptions of books. The latter is something you generally won't find through a library catalogue. Some of the bookstores have added features which allow you to do novel sorts of searches for books. They are the sort of searches not possible on most library catalogues and they provide another way into the literature which can turn up unexpected results.

Amazon.com (**amazon.com**)   is one of the original online bookstores. When you have found a book on the Amazon site you have the option to view a list of books which readers who bought this book also bought. In the best-case scenario this takes you along a trail of useful sources which you might never have found otherwise.

Amazon allows readers to review books. Undoubtedly some of these reviews are valuable but there does not seem to be the level of quality control or organization necessary to make this a truly useful research resource.

Waterstones Online (**waterstones.co.uk**)   A British bookstore chain. You can ask it to search for out-of-print books. Books are organized by categories. There are a huge number of sub-categories within the category 'social science'. You can restrict keyword searches to a particular sub-category.

The Book Pl@ce (**www.thebookplace.com**)   The online bookstore of Dillons, a British chain.

Books.com (**www.books.com**)   A US online bookstore.

Borders.com (**www.borders.com**)   A US bookstore chain.

Old books

Older books which have gone out of print and are no longer on sale in book-shops can be harder to get hold of than newer books. Library catalogues are the best way to find out about them but if you actually want to get hold of a copy for yourself there is one online service which is very useful.

Bibliofind (**www.bibliofind.com**)   is a database of old, used and rare books held by second-hand booksellers world-wide. You can order books via the Web and the individual bookseller is responsible for shipping the item. It is a good source of information on rare and obscure items but it does seem to depend on individual booksellers ensuring that records of their stock are kept up to date.

New books

The means by which researchers traditionally found out about new books in their area of interest remains the most important means of keeping up: book reviews in newspapers, journals and magazines, personal contact/word of mouth, and for those who are involved in teaching, publisher's catalogues. For graduate students it could be much harder to get hold of publisher's catalogues and they are effectively shut off from this source of 'advance warning' of new books.

The Internet has provided several means of supplementing these traditional sources. The first is by allowing direct access to publishers. Publishers generally try to concentrate their efforts on certain subjects and you will often find that a relatively small number of publishers publish the main books in your area. Most publishers now run Websites. They are primarily designed to promote sales but they often allow you to browse their catalogue by subject or by keyword and to look at information about forthcoming titles. It would be a sheer waste of time to search the sites of a lot of publishers but it can be useful to look at the sites of a few of the major publishers in your field.

The Publishers' Catalogues Home Page (**www.lights.com**) provides links to the Websites of over 6,000 publishers, organized geographically.

Several publishers offer an email 'alerting' service. You can subscribe for free and they will send you an email notifying you of new and forthcoming books in the areas of interest you have specified. Below is a list of some of the larger British and US academic publishers online:

Association of American University Presses Online Catalog (**aaup.uchicago.edu**)
The AAUP allows you to browse books by subject or search by keyword. It provides descriptions of books and you can buy books through the site. It has a new releases section, organized by subject. If you subscribe (for free) to the new release notification service AAUP will send you information on newly released books in your areas of interest.
Princeton University Press (**pup.princeton.edu**) The press provides an email list to update you on its latest publications, by subject.
The University of California Press (**www.ucpress.edu**) provides electronic editions of over fifty of its books (**www.ucpress.edu/scan/books.htm**). You can read the full text online but you can't download or print them.

Oxford University Press (**www.oup.co.uk**) You can search the press's catalogue and order online. If you do a keyword search for the title of a book, results will be arranged by subject category.

Sage publications (**www.sagepub.co.uk**) Search Sage's publications by author, title, date and descriptions of publications.

Routledge (**www.routledge.com**).

Blackwells (**www.blackwells.co.uk**).

Addison-Wesley (**www.awl.com**).

Simple searching

Searching the databases of publishers and bookstores requires very different techniques to searching sophisticated library databases. They tend to have a much simpler search facility, although it may be beautifully designed. They generally reward simple searching techniques. Use broad terms, the broadest possible. These databases will often only index the titles of books so the more specific your term the more likely it is that your query will return no results at all. Use variations on your search term. On simple databases 'politics' may bring up no results while searching for 'political' brings up dozens. You can miss everything relating to your subject if you do not use the exact spelling of the word which most commonly appears in titles. Simple databases can be utterly unforgiving of minor mistakes. If you are searching by title it is often better just to enter one or two words if you are not certain of the full title. If you get one word wrong it may spit back the request.

The services below are devoted to providing information on new books from a wide range of publishers.

Baker and Taylor Academia Online (**www.baker-taylor.com/Academia/ Academia.html**) A monthly newsletter listing upcoming academic books by subject. It provides details on books being published in the current month and the following month. Thus, a July issue will have information on books to be published in July and August.

Books-in-Reveal This is one of several services provided to paying subscribers by CARL Uncover, of which more in the section below on journal articles. Subscribers are alerted by email to new books in their subject area. As with other such pay services your library will have a link to it if you are subscribed. The only reason to go to the Uncover home page (**www.carl.org/ uncover**) is if you want to get more information about its services.

Book reviews

The Internet is an important new source of book reviews. Internet book reviews are often longer than printed reviews. Lack of space is not a restricting factor. For this reason the best of these reviews constitute a new form of academic writing, engaging in deep debate with the argument of the books they review. The worst are meandering and self-indulgent. In some cases Internet book reviews offer the author of the reviewed book a right of reply and therefore put into the record the sort of debate between author and reviewer which is not that common in print.

Many email discussion lists commission and distribute reviews of books and a good list can be a prime source of useful reviews. Detailed information on email lists is provided in chapter 4. There is one email list, H-Review (**H-net2.msu.edu/reviews**), which is entirely devoted to distributing reviews of academic books in the humanities and the social sciences. Membership of the list is dominated by academic researchers. Reviews are of generally high quality.

Searching for articles

Understanding academic articles

Academic articles are the articles which appear in academic journals. They are marked out by certain features which are designed to ensure high standards of accuracy and quality. They have to be properly referenced, acknowledging and providing proof of sources through footnotes and a bibliography. They are subject to peer-review. That is, they have been reviewed by working academics familiar with the subject. An academic journal is, almost by definition, one whose contents have been subject to peer-review. It is particularly important to understand this when going online. Some databases mix together articles from academic journals with those from magazines, making no distinction between the two genres. When you get the results of a search part of your task will be to distinguish between them. Many of the established journals have set up electronic versions while at the same time new 'electronic journals' have been established on the Web which have no printed version. Some of the new electronic journals are peer-reviewed and are of high quality. Others are not and it is necessary to be able to distinguish one from the other.

Understanding databases of articles

Databases of academic articles are a phenomenal research resource and their accelerated development since the advent of the Web is playing a major role in transforming the practices of researchers. These databases were initially accessible only through telnet and provided only bibliographic information and abstracts of articles. In the past few years they have started to provide, via the Web, the full text of journal articles. In some cases articles are provided just as they appear in the journals – diagrams, maps, photos and all. While the full text of articles is only available for certain journals, for very recent years and, of course, only to paying subscribers, it is likely to become ever more common for journals to provide full text online.

It is likely that your library has chosen to subscribe to one or perhaps two of the major database providers described below. It is most important for you to learn how to use these locally available services well. There is a huge overlap between services but enough differences that it would be a mistake to rely on just one. In the summer of 1999, for example, I ran a search on the words 'ethnic', 'conflict' and 'territory' on two of the biggest social science article databases. They each gave me back six articles but they only had three of these articles in common.

The databases of articles are a labyrinth of overlapping and competing collections. There is a big hefty print publication called Full Text Sources Online (**www.infotoday.com/fso/default.htm**). The full text is not available online, just information to entice you to buy the printed version. It is devoted to listing exactly what each database holds. It reveals a certain chaos produced by the competition between database companies. A particular journal may well be indexed in a dozen different databases. Database A will index it from April 1984 onwards and provide full text articles from June 1998; Database B will index it from 1989 and provide full text from June 1997. In addition they will each provide a slightly different set of searching options and results which are organized a little differently. The result is that searches on both databases may well bring back quite different sets of articles. Add to this the fact that, while they index many of the same journals, none of the databases indexes exactly the same set as any other. There is a massive overlap. To confuse things further, the services which give us access to the databases and which our libraries pay their subscription fees to are not always the creators of the individual databases within the range they offer. Thus, the exact same database can be available through several different subscription services. It would be a major research job in itself to figure out just exactly what the differences in holdings between the databases are.

You would be wasting your time to try. It is important simply to realize that none of the databases is comprehensive. It is important not only to scour more than one database but to explore other sources of information about journals. Your library will contain journals which are not on any of the databases. Most of the databases are interested in the bigger and more prestigious journals. Hundreds or even thousands of smaller or more specialized academic journals are not included in any of these databases.

The databases also tend to be extremely shallow in historical terms. In most cases they hardly index anything before the late 1980s. Neither is there much consistency in the periods they cover. A database will cover one journal from 1985 and another from 1992 and unless you do a bit of research into the database you have no way of knowing what its coverage is. It means that if you were aiming to plug the gaps in the database by going to the printed versions of the relevant journals you would have to do a bit of work to figure out which years you needed to check in which journals. It is far easier to do it in reverse: go to the main journals in your field and scour them before you ever go near one of these databases.

If your library is subscribed it should provide hyperlinks to these services, often allowing automatic access without the need for a password to users within your institution. If you are based in the UK you will find yourself using BIDS a lot. This is a database provider, of which more later, whose services are available free of charge to researchers in British universities.

Databases

A database is made up of individual records. All the items relating to a single document (author name, title, other citation details, abstract and perhaps the full text of the document) go up to make one record, the record for the particular article. However, each of these items is a separate 'field' in that record. Every record in the database will contain those same fields. When a record is broken into fields like this it makes it much easier to search. You can search just the author fields of all records, for example. This is exactly what you are doing when you 'search by author' on a library catalogue or article database. It is something which you cannot do on the open Web where the search engines cannot really tell one part of a document from another, cannot tell which is the author name, which part is the abstract and so on. An emerging standard, XML, is intended to allow Web documents to be split into clearly labelled fields so as to allow more sophisticated Web searching in the future, to allow us to search the Web like we search databases (see chapter 5 for more on XML).

Searching article databases

Article databases provide a lot more information about articles than libraries do about books and consequently there is a lot more text you can search than in a library catalogue. They require development of a new set of keywords more specific than those used to search library catalogues, but less specific than those you will later develop for searching the great open spaces of the Web. They share with library catalogues a rigid database structure of fields and records (see inset on databases) which allows much more targeted and effective searches than you can carry out on the open Web. You should hone your keywords and search phrases on one database, experimenting with ways to squeeze out every last item relevant to your research. You can then use these terms to do 'mopping-up' operations on other article databases, getting items not available on the first database.

Searching by keyword A standard keyword search will usually search several items relating to an article including the abstract, title and sometimes a list of keywords chosen by the author of the article. In a way these searches are quite crude, not distinguishing between author and place. For example, a search on Washington can bring up articles by authors called Washington as well as those with Washington in the title.

Searching by subject You will be familiar with this option from library catalogues and as a result will have built up a set of subject categories relevant to your research. On some databases you can carry out subject searches specifying that articles have to fit into all of the subject areas you specify. This has the advantage of allowing you to restrict the search very tightly. If you search for all items in one broad subject area the list of results will usually be unmanageable.

Searching by title   This is extremely restrictive as it is quite normal that no keywords relating to a subject will appear in an article's title. It can be useful if there is a tendency in your field to use a certain term in titles. It is really useful to a researcher who knows the title or part of the title of an article and is looking for more details on it.

Searching by date   You can restrict searches to a certain time period. This is particularly useful when you are returning to a database you have previously searched. You can limit your search to articles added in recent days or months.

Dealing with results   Some databases contain only academic articles. Others make no distinction between them and magazine articles. In most cases magazine articles will not be of much use to you. You will need to learn to distinguish between the two to save time spent on following useless links. Particularly if a magazine article is very short, a page or two, it is unlikely to provide much new and original information and can usually be avoided.

Saving searches   Several services offer you the option of saving your search. Avoid the temptation to do this at the early stages. Wait until you have found the most effective search terms. The advantage of saving your search is that you can then run it regularly against new additions to the database. This provides a painless way of keeping up with new articles relevant to your research. At least one service provides this function in the form of an 'automated alerting service', Uncover Reveal (**www.carl.org/uncover**).

Uncover Reveal sends you email at regular intervals listing new articles which match your search terms. It might seem like a researcher's dream, like those cassette tapes which supposedly allow you to learn languages in your sleep. You can now just sit back and relax as all the latest research is delivered to you by email with no effort on your part. This is where you have to give yourself a shake, wake up and remember that the Uncover database is not by any means comprehensive and that your search terms can never be perfect. If you rely totally on one service like Uncover Reveal you can almost be guaranteed that you are missing out on important new articles in your field.

Getting hold of the articles   In the case of most articles the databases can still do no more than provide you with the sort of bibliographic detail which will allow you to order the articles through your library. Some of the services allow you to order a copy directly from them, for delivery by fax or mail, but this can be an expensive way to get hold of an article. It can be cheaper to use your own library's interlibrary loan service.

Where your library is subscribed to a service which provides the full text of at least some of the articles on the database you will be able to download those articles to your own computer according to the arrangements made between your library and that service. The proportion of articles whose full text is available on these services is increasing rapidly.

It may well be that interlibrary loan will continue to be a useful way of gaining access to articles simply because of the high prices charged by the online services. Interlibrary loan is being transformed by electronic inter-library loan. In the USA many universities perform interlibrary loan via the Internet. The library supplying the document scans it in and sends it by email. The library receiving it can forward it by email to the researcher who requested it or just tell them it's available at a specific web address.

It may seem a weak competitor for the big databases at first glance but electronic interlibrary loan in fact gives you access to a vastly larger selection of articles than the databases do since their collections are so limited.

There is one development which raises huge questions over the future of these article databases: the appearance of electronic journals from the major academic publishers. These provide a new and competing avenue of access to the fulltext of many of the same articles. It may well be that in the next few years access to articles may be redirected away from these databases and through the journal publishers. Even as the databases expand into offering the full text of articles there are countervailing forces which may ensure that they never become complete or comprehensive storehouses of full text articles.

The major article services

This section is organized by company. Each of these companies provides a suite of databases most, but not all, of which are article databases. It is organized by company because libraries have to deal with companies. They will often deal with only one or two of the companies, selecting a range of databases from one company because it is cheaper and simpler than just taking one or two databases from each company. If your library deals primarily with OCLC, for example, you will have access to a cluster of databases from this company. For this reason it makes sense here to deal with the article databases company by company.

The services below, unless otherwise stated, are only available if your library has subscribed to them. In many cases, however, you can perform limited searches or get access to a limited selection of databases even if your library is not subscribed.

FirstSearch Electronic Collections Online (from OCLC) (**www.oclc.org**) The FirstSearch Collection from OCLC include several databases of relevance to social scientists. You can search all of these databases simultaneously. The advanced search offered by OCLC for all its databases is easy to use, consisting of a series of clear and simple options. It allows you to specify in great detail which words should appear in the different fields. You can specify the author, the date, the keywords which should appear in the abstract and words which appear in the article title, all in the one search query. It allows you to create very narrow and focused searches. ArticleFirst is a database of abstracts and citation details for articles from over 10,000 different publications. These publications cover a huge range of subject areas and you will get a much more diverse set of results than you would get from searching one of the social science article databases. It does not distinguish clearly between articles from academic journals and magazines and it can be a lot of work to tease the two apart.

ContentsFirst is a specialized service searching only the table of contents of over 10,000 journals. Because it pulls out tables of contents for individual issues of journals, rather than details on individual articles, it can be especially useful in the early stages of research for identifying journals of use and individual issues of journals which might be particularly useful. Journals often devote an entire issue to one subject, for example, and by removing the articles from the context they were published in the databases can actually make it more difficult to find related articles. This is, of course, a case for simple searching, looking for one or two keywords likely to appear in the titles of relevant articles. It also provides a means of looking through the contents pages of recent journals if you do not have access to the CARL Uncover services (mentioned below).

OCLC hosts specialized databases in a variety of social science subjects some of which you will also find on other online services. These allow you to search smaller and more focused collections which include a higher proportion of leading academic journals. They include:

SocSciabs: Social science abstracts
Socio Abs: Sociological abstracts
ContempWomenIss: Contemporary women's issues
EconLit: An index of economic literature
PsycFIRST: Psychology abstracts
Dissabs (Dissertation Abstracts Online): A database produced by Bell and Howell Information and Learning and also available from its online service Proquest Direct, which is dealt with below.
Book Review Digest: Summaries of reviews from academic journals.

There are also specialized databases under the category of 'Arts and Humanities' which may be of interest to social science researchers.

BIDS (Bath Information and Data Services) (**www.bids.ac.uk**) BIDS is of most relevance to UK users. Access is free of charge to researchers at UK institutions but is not generally available to researchers outside the UK. However, researchers outside the UK can search some of its databases and view abstracts of articles. BIDS provides access to a range of academic databases which include several databases which US users can access via the private US services. UK users will, for example, be used to accessing the ISI Social

Sciences Citation Index not through ISI's online service, Web of Science (see below), but through BIDS.

IBSS (International Bibliography of the Social Sciences) is described by BIDS as one of the largest and most comprehensive social science databases in the world. It covers the social science disciplines of economics, sociology, politics and anthropology. The full text of some of the articles on the database is available.

Ingenta Journals includes only articles for which the full text is available. It covers several hundred academic journals from a small number of major publishers. Anyone can search the service and view abstracts. Researchers whose library is not subscribed can pay for individual articles by credit card. The journals cover a huge variety of disciplines with the result that this is not a very focused collection.

Uncover Web (**Uncweb.carl.org**) Uncover is a database of academic articles which includes articles going back to 1988. When you have perfected your search terms you can enter those terms in Uncover Reveal. You will then be sent regular email alerts giving you bibliographic details for new articles which match your search. It is a perfect example of the Internet being most useful when it takes the form of email.

Reveal also has a table-of-contents alerting service. You can select up to fifty journals of interest to you and the table of contents of new issues will be emailed to you shortly after they are published.

ISI's Web of Science (**www.isinet.com**) In many senses the Web of Science is just another article database allowing you to search huge collections of article abstracts and bibliographic information about articles but it has slightly different origins to the other services listed above and as a result provides a different and uniquely useful way of searching its databases. It represents the online incarnation of citation indexes, those huge volumes crowding the library shelves which were concerned to record who had been citing who. You could use them to see how many times and by whom a particular academic article had been cited – an entire publication devoted to tracking the footnotes of academia. It provides a unique 'back-door' search which allows you to explore the literature along the tracery of links which connect articles to one another through their footnotes.

The Social Science Citation Index (SSCI) is the main Web of Science database relevant to the social sciences. As is the case with virtually all of the article databases it is shallow in terms of historical coverage, covering the SSCI back to around 1990. Previous years of the SSCI are available in hard copy only, though historical coverage may be deepened in the future. The SSCI contains details not only on articles but also on book reviews. You can restrict your search to certain types of items to, for example, exclude book reviews. You can restrict your search to particular languages and by time period. The broadest search you can do is to search by topic. This searches the titles, abstracts and keyword lists of articles for the keyword you enter. The SSCI also allows unusual search options which reflect its citation origins. You can search by author of course, but also by cited reference allowing you to bring back every article which cites a particular author or a particular article. This produces a list of articles which are related to each other but which it might be extremely difficult to assemble through the conventional article services. You can search by author affiliation, that is by the university the authors are located at, allowing you to build lists of people at particular universities who are working in your area. This can suggest institutions and departments whose library catalogues and Websites might be of use to you.

SSCI also allows you to save queries. You can then return at regular intervals and restrict your search to recently added items, producing a list of new articles relevant to your research.

ISI also provides a service called Current Contents Connect (**connect. isihost.com**), a one-year rolling service. That is, it searches only articles published in the previous twelve months. It provides a few special features such as publisher and author email addresses.

Proquest Direct (**www.bellhowell.infolearning.com/proquest**)   These are online article databases from Bell and Howell Information and Learning (previously UMI), a company which was perhaps best known for its database of dissertation abstracts.

Bell and Howell also provides Pro Quest Course Packs (**www.proquestpack. com**) access to collections of full-text articles designed to service college courses. The instructor can customize them by eliminating articles they don't wish to use.

Northern Light (**www.northernlight.com**)   Northern Light has very different origins to any of the services mentioned above. Other services moved existing databases onto the Web and then adapted to the Web. Northern Light was born and raised on the Web, an entirely new service which is much more geared up to serving users through the Web. Thus Northern Light from the beginning gave researchers a very flexible 'pay-per-article' option. It is not necessary that your library be subscribed. You can set up your own user account and download individual articles, paying by credit card. Northern Light searches both the open Web and its 'Special Collection', an article database. One of the major drawbacks of Northern Light's special collection is that a huge proportion of its articles are from magazines or newspapers rather than academic journals. Many articles are from very obscure magazines. There are certain gems available from high-quality journals but it seems to be a lower proportion than on most of the online services.

Anyone can search Northern Light and look at abstracts of articles. You only have to pay if you want the full text. Northern Light organizes your search results into what are called 'custom folders' which cluster the results by subject and by source. This is unique to this service and can save you a lot of time sorting through results. Thus, if the search pulls back a dozen items from one Website they will be grouped together in a single folder.

Looking for old articles

When it comes to the Internet, anything before about 1990 is 'old', reflected in the fact that most of the online databases do not go back much further than that. It is not beyond the bounds of possibility that an article from before 1990 might be of use in your research. The services below are working from the opposite end to most databases, beginning at the beginning and reaching forward into the 1980s and 1990s.

PCI Web (Periodicals Contents Index) (**pci.chadwyck.co.uk**)　PCI Web indexes the contents pages of thousands of periodicals in the humanities and social sciences. It has concentrated on indexing journals from their very first issues up until 1990–1 and is gradually moving forward. It provides only tables of contents, no abstracts, no full text, but PCI Web is one of the few sources of searchable information about earlier journal articles. You can only get access if your library is subscribed.

JSTOR (**www.jstor.org**)　JSTOR provides the full text, in PDF form, of articles from a range of journals. PDF preserves the original look and page numbering of the articles so it is simple to cite them. The collection includes important key journals in the social sciences and humanities. It is concerned with older issues of journals and its arrangements with many journals specify a time-gap before they can put newer issues on the service. So, it seems it will not become a source of current articles but always act as an archive which is a few years behind the times. It fills an important gap and at the time of writing was the only major service devoted to providing the full text of older issues of journals. You can only get access if your library has subscribed.

The big commercial databases

Far back in the mists of time, when academic article databases were but a gleam in some publisher's or librarian's eye, the business community was already using powerful online databases which provided the full text of articles from a vast number of sources. These were the days before the public had ever heard of the Internet. The databases were accessed via telnet. They were so expensive and so complex to use that companies hired specialized searchers just to search them and only business companies could pay the sort of fees the databases charged. Many university researchers did not even know they existed. Known as 'proprietary services' they were, and still are, immensely powerful database services. They are distinguished by the fact that they are very up to date. Often the full text of articles is available online within hours of publication. They also allow very sophisticated searching. Articles are split into separate fields which can be searched separately allowing for very specialized searches by researchers who feel it is worth the effort it takes to learn how to make optimum use of these search options. For further detail on these services see Basch (1998: 138–51).

Some of these services are so directly focused on business that they are of minimal interest to social scientists, services like Dow Jones News Retrieval or Dun and Bradstreet. Others are now broadening their coverage, moving onto the Web and deliberately targeting the academic research market. They are not concerned primarily with citation details but with providing fully searchable full-text articles. In addition, they are more concerned with news articles than academic articles. Although now targeting an academic audience their business roots are visible from the strong focus on business news. In addition, their Websites were not particularly user-friendly in the early stages and had very much the feel of big business ventures dipping their toes in the unfamiliar waters of academia. The legacy of catering to highly trained and highly paid professional researchers was visible in the rather sparse instructions for use and the complex overlapping and intertwining of the various pricing options. I deal below with two of the largest of the proprietary services.

Lexis-Nexis (**www.lexis-nexis.com**)   Lexis-Nexis provides the full text of articles from literally thousands of newspapers in addition to specialized materials such as news broadcast transcripts which are extremely difficult to get hold of by any other means. Lexis-Nexis now provides a range of services targeted directly at academic users and marketed under the banner 'Congressional Information Services'. One such service is 'Academic Universe' which among other things provides news transcripts, foreign language news, political news, country profiles, general reference and a lot of business-related news. The service is not restricted to published articles but includes working papers. Another service, 'Congressional Universe', is a database of US government documents. CIS Statistical Universe provides a guide to statistical sources both on- and offline, in particular to statistics produced by the US government.

Dialog Knowledge Index (**www.dialog.com**)   Dialog provides access to about 900 databases spanning disciplines from medicine to marketing. Many of these databases are vast universes of information in their own right. The databases are described in the Dialog Bluesheets which are available via the Web. They include databases of newspaper and magazine articles, and databases on psychology and sociology. At least some of these databases are also available through some of the other services dealt with above.

Dialog Select is the service which provides Web access to selected databases. It provides pull-down menu options for searching which are very easy to use.

Electronic journals

Electronic journals are a much more recent phenomenon than the article databases. They provide an alternative and, in the long run, a competing mode of access to the full text of academic articles online. They are introduced after those databases because the universe of full-text online academic journals is still a relatively small one. Searching the electronic journals means searching a very restricted selection indeed: only the biggest publishers, only the biggest journals. The end result is the same as the article databases, searchable collections of articles, but their origins mean that they are organized very differently.

In the first place, they are not conceived of as databases but as the online counterpart to printed journals (except in a few cases where there is no printed counterpart). Access to them is regulated in the same way as access to journals is. Your library must subscribe to individual electronic journals and you will have access just to those journals, not to the full output of a particular publisher. If you have access to one issue of a journal you have access to all issues. A few publishers are experimenting with charging per article viewed but the dominant system is library subscription (see Cline McKay (1999) for more details). In general libraries which subscribe to the printed version of a journal will get free access to the electronic version, or access for a small extra fee. Libraries can also choose to subscribe only to the electronic version. Usually this costs almost as much as the printed version but allows libraries to save on storage space.

In most cases it is the publishers themselves who have taken the initiative to create electronic versions of the journals and it is possible to get access directly through publishers' Websites, if, of course, your library has subscribed. Some of the major publishers produce so many journals that they are marketing their sites directly. A huge number of publishers now provide free email alerting services, sending out the tables of contents of new journals. A few of the larger publishers are described below.

Science Direct (**www.sciencedirect.com**)   This is a pay subscription service from Elsevier Science containing the full text of more than 1,000 of their science and social science journals. At the time of writing it provided back issues of journals from 1996 onwards. You can restrict your search to journals in the social sciences and can search by author, title or abstract, or search the full text of articles. You can get article summaries and subscribers can get the full text of articles either in PDF (so that it can be cited easily) or plain text (for quicker downloading). The collection is huge but of course it is restricted to the output of one publisher. Even if you are not subscribed you can search descriptions of the journals, abstracts of articles and tables of contents. It also provides an alert service to email you details of new articles which match your search terms.

Johns Hopkins University Press (**www.muse.jhu.edu/journals**)   Project Muse provides access for subscribers to the full-text online versions of over forty journals published by JHU Press. It is expanding to provide access to journals from other university presses.

Cambridge Journals Online (**www.journals.cup.org**)   This gives free access for anyone to tables of contents, abstracts, search facilities and alerting services, and access for subscribers to the full text of articles. If your university has a subscription to the printed edition of a CUP journal you are entitled to free access to the online version. Visit the site or ask in your library for details.

Routledge Journals (**www.journals.routledge.com**) Several journals are available online to paying subscribers. Modest collections of earlier issues of the journals are available free of charge to anyone.

Sage Contents Alerting Service (**www.sagepub.co.uk**) will email you the tables of contents of new issues of the journals you select.

SARA (Scholarly Articles Research Alerting) (**www.carfax.co.uk**) Carfax Publishing provides this email alerting service which sends out the tables of contents of new issues of its journals.

Aggregator service-providers It is not only individual researchers who find it a nightmare to deal separately with the databases and Websites of a myriad different publishers. Librarians trying to manage subscriptions must have been tearing their hair out. They probably still are. It is still impossible to find one source which gives you access to all the available electronic journals. However, there have emerged several 'aggregator service-providers' (Cline McKay, 1999). One of their prime purposes is to allow libraries to manage their subscriptions to electronic journals. None of them deals with all the journals and there is a huge overlap between all of them. One spillover effect of these aggregators is to provide large searchable databases of information about current journals from large numbers of publishers. Non-subscribers can search these huge databases and find out what a particular journal provides online, whether it provides tables of contents, abstracts, or the full text of articles. Subscribers can search as they would search ordinary article databases by author, title, keyword, and a variety of other options. Two of the main aggregators are Blackwell's Electronic Journal Navigator (**www.blackwells.com**) and Swetsnet (Europe: **www.swetsnet.nl**; North America: **www.swetsnet.com**).

Purely electronic journals A few years ago it seemed the Internet might greatly reduce the cost of academic publishing. The development of the Internet was seen by many as an opportunity for academics to bypass the publishers. They could 'publish' their own work on the Web for no cost. Other researchers could access it with no charge. This dream of free circulation of academic work has not materialized. To organize peer-review, the hallmark of an academic article, takes organization. To 'publish' on the Web is not an effort-free endeavour. At the same time, academics rely on recognition from other academics to further their careers. Articles on the Web have not gained anywhere near the same status as printed articles and thus academics have little incentive to publish on the Web. There are some attempts currently in progress to organize Web publishing by academics independently of the big publishers. However, as of now, the publishers remain king.

The vast majority of electronic journals are simply supplements to a print counterpart. There are very few purely electronic peer-reviewed journals, those which actually do avoid the cost of print and distribution.

There are quite a lot of purely electronic journals on the open Web. Many have low standards, lack peer-review and deserve their poor reputations. Others maintain high academic standards. One initiative seeking to promote the development of free academic journals is the ICAAP. The International Consortium for Alternative Academic Publication (**www.icaap.org**) provides a database of free full-text peer-reviewed online journals intended to make it easier for researchers to find these journals. The future of such initiatives will depend in the long run on the academic community accepting the validity of work that is 'published' online without any print counterpart.

The future   It may be that in the coming years the way academic journals are published will be transformed. The 'hard' sciences have already shown the way. Take JAIR, the *Journal of Artificial Intelligence Research* (**www.cs.washington.edu/research/jair/home.html**), founded in 1993 as one of the first electronic journals. Articles submitted to JAIR have to follow strict layout requirements. Essentially they have to be in a form which allows them to be put immediately on a Website. They are reviewed quickly and as soon as they are accepted are put online. When a certain number of articles have been built up on the Website they are published as a volume of the journal. The online version has thus become the primary version of the journal and the first one available. The printed version is secondary. Other trends are also threatening to disrupt the existing power of publishers, notably the moves being made in some medical research centres to distribute research results via well-organized, peer-reviewed Websites rather than through expensive printed journals. It may be that electronic journals will gain in status as a result of such developments, in which case academics will be more willing to publish in them and they will begin to provide a serious alternative to printed journals.

Government publications

Many governments have strong incentives to put their publications on the Web. It provides a cheap means of distributing information which in many cases they are legally obliged to distribute. Printing this information is expensive and certain government publications in the USA are now only made available via the Net. For the researcher outside the USA the Internet provides the sort of access to US government documents that was previously possible only by visiting the USA.

I say US government because its output on the Web dwarfs the output of all other governments combined. It is a universe of information in its own right. The bulk of this section deals with US government publications.

US government

The US government has the biggest Web presence of any government but it can also lay claim to being one of the most chaotic and confusing. There are several different ways of getting access to this information, most of them overlapping but never covering the exact same set of data. I'll deal first with the services provided directly by US government agencies, the official services, and then with the various other services which allow you to search US government documents.

GPO Access (**www.access.gpo.gov**) This is the online service of the US Government Printing Office which is legally responsible for printing US government publications. It is thus the 'official' site for US government publications on the Web and you would expect this to be the obvious place to start a search. The GPO is not, however, responsible for either the Websites of US government agencies or for much of the output of the US Congress. In addition, some US government agencies publish their own materials and these do not come under the care of the GPO. Thus it provides access to a huge range of US government documents but not by any means to all of them.

GPO Access provides several databases of which one of the most important is MOCAT, the Catalog of US Government Publications (**www.access.gpo.gov/su_docs/dpos/adpos400.html**). Many of the GPO Access databases are also available elsewhere on the Web, sometimes in a form that's easier to search and with more comprehensive coverage. In particular, GPO Access overlaps with the official site for the US Congress, THOMAS.

THOMAS (**thomas.loc.gov**) Named after Thomas Jefferson, this service of the Library of Congress provides information related to the US Congress, including information about bills, transcripts of debates and the reports of congressional committees. The committee reports deal with a vast array of subjects and draw on the testimony of experts. They can be a valuable source of information on issues of political debate in the USA.

Fedworld (**www.fedworld.gov**) This is the official gateway to all US government information online, from official publications through catalogs to government Websites. It allows you to search a range of government databases. One of the more useful of these is the NTIS (National Technical Information Service) database. This is a database of US government reports, or reports funded in part by the US government, including reports produced by university researchers (Basch, 1998: 184). You can search summaries of the reports and order hard copies of those you're interested in. To emphasize how chaotic things are, you can not only get access to this database through Fedworld but directly through the NTIS Website (**www.ntis.gov**), through the private service DIALOG and through a service called **'usgovsearch'** which is dealt with below.

Fedworld allows you to search US government Websites but you can generally do a more precise and complete search of these sites by going directly to them and using their own search options. Fedworld is good for identifying useful sites in the first place but then you should go directly to those sites.

US government search engines

The services listed here are not responsible for publishing or providing documents on the Web. They merely allow you to search materials produced by the US government. The largest such service is 'usgovsearch' (www.usgovsearch.northernlight.com). Great controversy surrounded it when it first came out because it required users to pay a subscription to search US government documents, most of which are freely available on the Web. It allows a combined search of what is said to be a complete and comprehensive index of US government and military Websites and of a huge number of related periodicals from the Northern Light database. It allows you to search Web material by agency and organizes material by subject area.

This service illustrates a very significant trend. It provides very little information which is not available for free on the Web. What it charges for is the service of allowing you to search that information more quickly and efficiently and comprehensively than you can do by any other means. Better, more complete, searching has now been quantified in dollar terms.

This suggests that while the Web may remain a 'free' resource, to search it efficiently will cost you. If this can be done for one type of material on the open Web, there seems little doubt it will be done in other areas too. Researchers may find increasingly that the best, the most specialized and comprehensive search engines will be pay services.

Google US Government Search (www.google.com/unclesam)   Google is one of the big keyword search engines out there on the Web. It allows you to do a search restricted to US government and military Websites. It is not as complete or comprehensive as **usgovsearch** but if it is US government publications you're looking for it does you the favour of excluding any non-government documents from your search. As it happens you can do this from most keyword search engines in any case.

Searching for US government sites on any keyword search engine

The US government and military were deeply involved in the birth of the Internet. As a consequence of this they each got an entire domain name to themselves, **.gov** for the US government, **.mil** for the US military. Most search engines allow you to restrict your search of the Web to include or exclude certain domains. On AltaVista (www.altavista.com) add **+host:gov** to the end of your query to ensure you only search US government sites; add **+host:mil** to restrict it to military sites. Most other search engines use 'domain:' or provide this as an option in a drop-down menu. See chapter 7 for more detailed information on using this command.

Govbot (**ciir2.cs.umass.edu/Govbot**)   is a database of over 1.5 million US government and military Web pages from the Center for Intelligent Information Retrieval (CIIR).

Government resources on the Web (**www.lib.umich.edu/libhome/Documents. center/govweb.html**)   This guide from the University of Michigan Documents Center provides links to information by and about the US federal government. (**www.lib.umich.edu/libhome/Documents.center/federal.html**), US state governments (**www.lib.umich.edu/libhome/Documents.center/federal. html**) and local government (**www.lib.umich.edu/libhome/Documents. center/pslocal.html**). They link to sites about government as well as to official government sites.

Other governments

There is huge variation in the amount and type of materials which governments make available on the Web. Many wealthy western governments have adopted the Internet enthusiastically and put vast amounts of well-organized and valuable information online. This is often aimed primarily at their own citizens, a part of a wider aspiration towards provision of more efficient services to citizens (see Hoff *et al.*, 2000). By contrast, many of the poorest governments aim their Websites exclusively at the outside world rather than at their own citizens. The agencies which are online tend to be those such as tourist boards, industrial development agencies or government information bureaux which have a vested interest in contact with foreign investors, tourists and journalists.

Unlike the US government most other governments do not have entire search engines or directories devoted to searching their documents. Among the notable exceptions are the UK government which provides 'Open Government' (**www.open.gov.uk**), a list of UK government Websites organized by subject and by function.

Several governments have their own domains: **gov.uk** for the UK, **gov.au** for Australia, **gov.jp** for Japan, **gov.at** for Austria, **fgov.be** for the federal government in Belgium. Not all government documents are to be found in the official domains in all countries owing to inconsistent policies on Web addresses in some countries. Nonetheless you can use the domains to do a search on any search engine restricted to the domain of the government you're interested in as outlined in relation to the US government in the inset box above. Thus on AltaVista **+host:gov.uk** will ensure that your search only brings back documents from the UK government domain.

Foreign government resources on the Web (**www.lib.umich.edu/libhome/ Documents.center/foreign.html**) The University of Michigan Documents Center provides this excellent guide. It provides links, organized by country, to official government documents and Websites and to Websites relating to governments around the world. This is a good place to find out whether the government you're interested in has a specific domain. You can then use the domain to search for that government's official documents through the search engines. It is not by any means comprehensive but it provides a good starting point.

Theses and dissertations

Theses and dissertations used to be almost impossible to find out about, let alone get hold of. The only place a record of their existence was kept was in the library databases of the universities where they had been completed. In recent years they have become much more accessible and have become a major new research resource. Note that the words thesis and dissertation can be used to describe both Masters- and doctoral-level work, depending on the university or country concerned.

Huge numbers of high-quality dissertations are completed but never published perhaps because their subject matter is too obscure to tempt a publisher or because, although packed with information, they are written awkwardly.

There are a number of online services now devoted to providing not only bibliographic details about theses and dissertations, but to making the full text available, for a fee.

ProQuest Digital Dissertations (**www.bib.umi.com/dissertations**) ProQuest is one of the big online article services but the jewel in the crown of its services is the Dissertation Abstracts database. This database can also be accessed through a number of the other online services previously listed. It is a searchable database of abstracts, keywords chosen by the authors and basic citation information like title, date of submission and author. It provides abstracts for doctoral dissertations from 1980 onward and for Masters theses from 1988 onwards. While only subscribers have access to the complete database anyone can have 'guest' access which allows them to search citation details and abstracts for all titles from the last two years. Complete copies of dissertations can be ordered via an associated service.

The database is described by its creators, UMI, as 'the one central authoritative source for information about doctoral dissertations and master's theses'. Certainly no database is more entitled to make such a claim but the database is limited to items from universities which have arrangements with UMI. While virtually all North American universities are included, coverage is much patchier elsewhere in the world and is far from comprehensive. Its time coverage is also relatively shallow and it is still worth checking the online catalogues of institutions where a lot of graduate work related to your topic has been done.

Aslib Index to Theses (**www.theses.com**)   This is a database of abstracts and citation details of Masters and doctoral theses accepted by universities in the UK and Ireland. It grew out of a print publication and it covers the period from 1970 onwards. Thus it has deeper historical coverage than Dissertation Abstracts while covering only the UK and Ireland. As a result it contains much material not found in any other database. Once again it is not to be regarded as comprehensive, even within the limited realm which is its concern. You can only get access if your library is subscribed.

Networked Digital Library of Theses and Dissertations (**www.theses.org**)   This service draws on collections of 'Electronic Theses and Dissertations' archived online at a number of universities and a few larger commercial services. It differs from the services just dealt with in that it provides the full text of dissertations, downloadable as PDF documents, for a modest fee. It differs too in allowing very sophisticated searching based on XML standards (see chapter 5). Quite a limited number of theses and dissertations are available.

Dissertation.com (**www.dissertation.com**)   This commercial service includes a 'dissertation library' which provides the full text of dissertations via the Internet, for a small fee. It is part of the NDLTD mentioned immediately above. It also allows you to order theses and dissertations as bound copies via amazon.com. You can search for dissertations by keyword or browse through lists of dissertations grouped by subject.

MIT Theses and E-Theses Online (**www.theses.mit.edu**)   Searchable by author, title and abstract, this service provides the full text of a selection of Masters and doctoral theses from all MIT departments.

News

Newspapers and other news sources such as magazines and TV and radio broadcasts are not academic literature. They are, however, often heavily used by academics in the course of their research, not only for keeping up with broader current trends which are related to their work but as both primary and secondary research sources. As primary sources news items illustrate social attitudes and political concerns; they provide examples of principal arguments in major debates. As secondary sources newspapers chart on a day-to-day basis many of the same phenomena which academics trace over longer periods of time. They allow the researcher to construct a more complete chronology of events relevant to their research.

It was time-consuming enough for the researcher to read one daily newspaper, watch one daily TV news show and listen to the radio news a few times a day. The Internet provides access to many more news sources. Certain of them allow specialist researchers to focus narrowly on current news more directly relevant to their research topic and/or to the broad subject area they are working in. The Internet also provides easy access to news archives which were often difficult to access.

Current news

Current news is available everywhere on the Web. The main advantage it presents to the researcher over the current news they read in the newspaper is that it is searchable by keyword, allowing you to pull out only stories related to your topic. Virtually all of the big Internet search engines and subject directories, from AltaVista to Yahoo (see chapters 6 and 7), provide current news stories. Most of them draw on the wire services, newspapers or TV news and there is a huge overlap between them. They focus on current news, often not providing archives of older news. A huge proportion of newspapers and magazines have set up their own Websites and independently provide access to their own archives. Obviously if you want to search all the news in the world it can be very time consuming to visit the archives of each newspaper individually. However, it may be that your searches of the big newspaper article databases will reveal quite a small number of newspapers which seem to pay particular attention to topics relevant to your research. Alternatively you might be aware from other sources that a particular newspaper is likely to be of use to you, perhaps because of its location or its political sympathies. In either case you may well want to visit the archives of individual newspapers which in many cases will be more complete and will be searchable in very different ways from the articles from those papers which form part of larger databases.

The online versions of newspapers present certain problems for the researcher. In many cases they do not include all of the articles carried in the printed edition, meaning that a researcher might miss out if they rely solely on the online version. In some cases the contents of the two versions are dramatically different as newspapers hire people to write solely for the online version. This is an important issue you will need to address if you are relying very heavily on one particular paper as a source. Some newspapers have begun to charge fees for access to their archives, an unsurprising development.

Below is a series of sites which maintain large collections of links to the individual Websites of newspapers, magazines and broadcast media:

AJR Newslink (**www.newslink.org**) Links are provided by the 'American Journalism Review' to newspapers, magazines and broadcast media.
Internet Public Library: List of Online Magazines and Serials (**www.ipl.org/ reading/serials/**) Links are organized by subject and alphabetically by title and are searchable by keyword.
Yahoo: News and media category (**www.yahoo.com/r/nm**) This is the News category of this major Internet guide (more in chapter 6). It links to a huge variety of news sites, organized by media type, by subject and by country.

The Internet Public Library: List of Online Newspapers (**www.ipl.org/reading/ news/**) Links to the Websites of newspapers, organized by country and alphabetically by title. You can search the list by keyword.

E&P Media Links (**www.mediainfo.com/emedia**) This is a database of links to media Websites, organized by media and by location.

These listings can be of limited use, particularly because they usually make little attempt to distinguish between the higher quality newspapers of record which place a lot of importance on accuracy and the ideal of objective reporting and newspapers which place less emphasis on these ideals. If you are looking for newspapers from a particular country a better starting point can often be a general Web guide to resources on that country which will almost always include annotated links to that country's media (see chapter 6).

Clarinet   is a current news service which is made available as a collection of Usenet newsgroups (for more on Usenet see chapters 2 and 4) and via the Web (**www.clarinet.com**). This service is only available if your institution or ISP subscribes to Clarinet. Newsgroups in Clarinet are devoted to distributing up-to-date news organized by topic and by place from a variety of sources. If a news item is relevant to several different groups it will be posted to all of them. If you read only one group you can be reasonably sure you are reading everything relevant to that topic.

Newspage (**www.newspage.com**)   is one of a number of services which offer to provide you with personalized news updates at regular intervals. You can create a customized news feed tailored to your needs by selecting the topics you are interested in. It provides news from a variety of sources including newspapers and the wire services. You can visit the site and check recent news stories related to the topics you ticked, but if you want to have these stories regularly sent to you by email you will have to pay.

The wire services   News stories from the wire services are all over the Web. You will recognize most of them by their abbreviations, for example AFP, PA, UPI. They have become a principal source of news information on the Web because even before its advent they were geared up to rapid and flexible world-wide delivery of news items. If you take a look at most newspapers you will see that the wire services are not restricted to the Web. Most newspapers have taken stories from these services for decades, using them for coverage of countries where they themselves could not afford to have a full-time reporter. Now the wire news feed which once came into the offices of newspapers is available to anyone through the Web and the wire services have made all sorts of deals to provide searchable up-to-date news via almost every search engine, portal and news site on the Internet.

It is important to note that the wire service news you get through search engines or portal pages comes from a few large agencies who also provide much of the world news you read in your daily newspaper. In addition, they seem to have made non-exclusive deals with the various Websites. That is, any given wire agency is providing the same news to several search engines and portals. If you searched the news of all these services you would get a huge overlap. Below is a list of some of the major wire services:

AFP: Agence France Press, France (**www.afp.com**)

AP: Associated Press, USA (**www.wire.ap.org**)

PA: Press Association, UK (**www.pa.press.net**)

Reuters, UK (**www.reuters.com**)

TASS, Russia (**www.itar-tass.com**)

UPI: United Press International, US (**www.upi.com**)

Xinhua, China (**www.xinhua.org**)

One final word of warning. You will find news reports all over the Internet forwarded by email or placed by individuals on their own Websites. Beware of news items delivered second hand. Always try to find the official version. It is a simple matter for someone to crop or alter a text to suit their own political purposes before they send it on or put it on the Web.

News archives

While many of the sources of current news also give access to older news stories they are not set up explicitly as news archives. The focus is on 'now' and the services they offer reflect this. Below are a few services which are more concerned with archiving news stories, allowing the researcher access to collections with more historical depth. Some of them are provided by the same online services which provide databases of academic articles. The major commercial services, Dialog and Lexis-Nexis, are not covered here as they were dealt with earlier in this chapter. They provide a vast array of databases of newspaper articles targeted in particular at business researchers.

News Library (**www.newslibrary.com**)   This is an archive of articles from a huge number of US newspapers, including large numbers of local and regional newspapers. Coverage in terms of time varies greatly from one newspaper to the next. Flexible search options allow you to search one or all or any combination of newspaper titles in the archive. Anyone can search for free but if you want to see the full text of an article you have to pay by credit card.

ProQuest Direct: Newspaper Abstracts (**www.bellhowell.infolearning.com/ proquest**)   This is just one of the databases provided by this online database service. 'Newspaper Abstracts' covers a relatively small number of newspapers but among them are many of the major US daily papers including the *New York Times*, the *Los Angeles Times* and the *Washington Post*. Records for most papers go back no further than 1987 and this is, for the most part, a database of abstracts only. For the most recent years of some newspapers you can get the full text of articles but you pay for the privilege. Information from the larger newspapers can be on the database within 24 hours of publication.

Think-tank policy papers

US-based think-tanks devoted to producing research which will feed into government policy, and generally informed by a particular political ideology or agenda, have always sought to spread their views as widely as possible. For this reason quite a few of the big think-tanks make the full text of their policy papers available via their Websites. One source of information about these papers is the 'current awareness' page of the Scout Report for Social Sciences (**scout.cs.wisc.edu/scout/report/socsci/metapage/**) which lists think-tank sites. To find out about older think-tank papers search the related Scout Report archives (**scout.cs.wisc.edu/archives**). The Scout Report is dealt with in detail in chapter 4.

4

Making contact

Human contact: the Internet at its best

In the mid 1990s veteran online researcher Reva Basch conducted interviews with dozens of people who made their living from finding information online (Basch, 1996). Time and again these experienced researchers mentioned in their interviews that the most valuable resource on the Internet was other human beings. In the midst of the massive databases and the powerful search engines, the fact that the Net allowed increased direct contact between individuals was seen as its greatest contribution to research. Many of the researchers had stories of how a faraway expert in one particular field was able to answer their question more quickly than they could ever have hoped to have answered it by searching the Web or the online databases. It is a good reminder of just how useful a research resource other people can be. Neither the printed word nor the Web can ever provide information as up to date, as comprehensive or as detailed as the information which people keep in their heads. Not only that, but if people do allow you to 'search' what is in their heads you can do the sort of searches and get the sort of results that Internet search engine developers can only fantasize about: flexible and open-ended queries delivering precise, personalized answers, to use the language of the databases.

The dream of a never-ending world-wide conversation

In the early years there was a lot of utopian fantasizing about the potential of the Internet to advance human knowledge and even to promote world peace through increased communication and understanding. The Internet was described in a famous US court judgment rejecting censorship as a 'never-ending world-wide conversation' (quotation in Grossman, 1997: 94). It was hoped that some day anyone who wanted to know the answer to anything would be able to pose their question in the midst of this conversation and receive an answer relatively quickly. This would certainly make the research process a whole lot easier.

To a great extent that dream has evaporated over the past few years. This is partly because of the way in which the potential of email and newsgroups was abused, by people trying to publicize themselves or their products or, unthinkingly, by new users. Many new Internet users, 'newbies' in the derogatory terminology of veteran users, had no idea how the email lists and newsgroups operated and would ask questions which they could have answered themselves by just checking an encyclopaedia or their computer manual. The response to new users asking basic questions on email lists was summed up in the terse abbreviated answer, RTM, Read The Manual, or the even less polite, RTFM.

In the early days, up to about the mid 1990s that is, most of the discussion lists and newsgroups prided themselves on their egalitarianism and lack of censorship. Famous experts would participate in discussions and anyone could argue with them. As the open lists began to clog up with junk, with stupid questions and uninformed rants, those experts began to melt away. One result of this was that the open lists were drained of expertise, drained of the very people best able to answer the questions being posed in this continuous world-wide conversation. The open lists are far less useful to researchers than they were a few years ago although newer Internet users still contribute enthusiastically. Another result was that new lists were set up, closed lists. New lists for serious discussion often decided not only to monitor, edit and restrict postings but to limit membership to certain groups, to academics, graduate students and librarians, for example.

In any case, despite all the talk about the virtual community and vigorous online debate email lists were never really great popular forums. The vast majority of list members never contribute anything to a list, not a single question or answer, let alone an eloquent contribution to debate. One survey of list users showed that 83% of list members had never contributed anything. Only about 6% had sent more than one or two messages (Kitchin, 1998: 83, citing Kawakami). The 'lurker' who reads but does not contribute is actually the typical list subscriber.

The dream may have almost evaporated but there are still some useful wisps of that dream about. As a researcher you will be able to get access to the restricted lists in your area of interest. And while people have become less active on these lists in discussing things, the lists are now heavily used to distribute information about conferences or publications or job vacancies.

Email mailing lists as a research resource

A good email list is useful to a researcher for a specific set of purposes, including:

- *Providing a forum for initial research queries* This does not mean asking questions like 'please tell me everything you know about the American economy' but rather asking questions about the most useful books on your topic or asking whether there are less obvious sources you should be using.
- *Providing a point of contact with other people*, be they graduate students or academics, currently working in the same area. It can be the starting point for co-operation and sharing of information on a one-to-one basis.

- *Information about academic happenings related to your subject*, such as announcements of conferences, publications, scholarships and research projects.
- *Access to reading lists and syllabuses for courses at other universities*, particularly useful if you also have to teach in your subject. Academic email lists are often used for exchange of such materials.
- *Providing a forum for very specialized research queries* This is one of the functions of a good email list which at its best is almost magical. There are certain questions which are not very easy to answer through library research. Perhaps there is a quote you once read but whose author and exact wording you cannot remember. I am not saying you can answer every such query on an email list but it provides the sort of resource which had no real counterpart before the Internet. For one example see the inset box below.

Using an email list for very specialized research queries: an example

Browsing through a library years ago as an undergraduate student I came across an article about St Patrick's Day parades in a US city. It showed maps of how the routes had changed over the years. I made no note of the article. I was just looking at it out of curiosity. Six or seven years later I was doing some research into political parades in the north of Ireland. I still vaguely remembered the article I'd seen years before and thought that the US article might throw an interesting light on the controversy over parades in Ireland itself. Not only could I not remember the name of the article or the journal it appeared in, but also I didn't even know if it was a history, sociology, politics or geography journal. I couldn't remember the name of the city dealt with.

In September 1995 I sent the following message to the H-Ethnic list: 'Does anyone know of an article which was published a few years ago on the patterns of change in a St Patrick's Day parade in (as far as I remember) a small town in New England? It included maps of the gradual changes to the route, which eventually took in the town centre.'

Within days I had received several different replies. The replies gave me details not only of the article I had seen but of several others on very closely related topics. Prior to the existence of the H-Ethnic list finding this article might well have proven impossible. The list meant that this vague query, based on scant and scarcely remembered knowledge, could be answered rapidly thanks to the generosity and helpfulness of members of the H-Ethnic list.

Making the most of lists

There is a certain skill involved in using email lists for the purposes listed above. These guidelines on effective use of lists draw in part on 'The art of getting help' by Phil Agre (1996b).

Check the real world first Do not ask a question on the Internet which you could easily answer using other sources.

Make sure you are in the right place This is probably the key to making effective use of email lists. Somewhere out there is a list where people will take your query seriously, consider it appropriate and be in a good position to answer it. Conversely there are thousands of lists where none of these will apply and your query will just disappear into a black hole. Your central task is to find the list for you.

Watch the traffic Apart from the obvious way, reading a description of the list, the best way to find out if it is the right place to ask your question is to subscribe to the list and watch the traffic on it for a while.

Check the FAQ A lot of lists and newsgroups have an FAQ (Frequently Asked Questions), a document which can often run to fifty pages and answers the questions most commonly asked on that list. Before you ask a question check to make sure it has not already been answered in the FAQ.

Be sceptical Do not automatically trust the answers you receive. People can be wrong, even on email lists.

Give something back The ideal of a 'virtual community' (Rheingold, 1995) may be a little tarnished but email lists still do constitute communities of a certain kind. The more you contribute to helping others the more likely that others on the list will be prepared to help when you have a query.

Guidelines for good practice

The term 'netiquette' is used to describe a loose set of standards for behaviour on the Internet, particularly directed at preventing aggressive and insulting behaviour. What follows is practical advice on polite behaviour online, essentially advice on how to avoid annoying people. Email allows instantaneous responses of the kind previously only possible in conversation, where tone and inflection provided a wealth of extra information about the meaning of the response. Email messages are often sent off carelessly and hastily by the sender and misinterpreted by the recipient. Before you send an email:

Think twice Never send a message without re-reading it at least once to check content and spelling. Sometimes you will be amazed to read the things you have typed in haste.
Think of the tone It is easy to sound abrupt and unfriendly in an email. Without being pedantic about it, it is important to keep to a polite tone with people you do not know. Sarcasm and irony travel notoriously badly via email. Avoid them. Too many people will think you are being serious. Don't type in capitals: IT REALLY ANNOYS PEOPLE.

Be very careful of what you write Email is not private and it is not secure. Unless you or your college or employer have taken steps to secure the privacy of your email, your messages can be read by lots of other people. Not only can your email be read by the authorities at your own institution and scanned by intelligence agencies (see chapter 5), but it can also be read by people at the computers it was routed through as it travelled from you to the recipient. It will be automatically stored by some of those servers and kept for years to come. There are measures you can take which at least ensure that it cannot casually be read by anyone whose server it passes through. Outlook Express, the email package in Internet Explorer allows you to encrypt mail for these purposes. There is also freely available software called PGP, 'Pretty Good Privacy' (**www.pgp.net**), which provides quite strong protection. It can take a bit of effort to use encryption, though. It is far simpler not to use email for confidential communication.

When you are mailing to public discussion lists there is an added danger to your privacy. Many lists and newsgroups now have searchable archives. Employers can easily do Internet searches of these archives to see what employees or prospective employees have been posting to the Net. You may find that the intemperate message you sent in haste in a bad mood one Monday morning will join an archive and linger out there for decades to come, forever attached to your name.

Sign your messages Make sure every message at least includes your name, preferably using a signature file (as outlined in chapter 2). Your identity is not always obvious to the recipient of emails you have sent.

Being careful out there

Flames, trolls and pigs

Wendy Grossman has compared the Internet to the Babel Fish described by Douglas Adams in *The Hitch Hiker's Guide to the Galaxy*. This was a tiny fish you could stick in your ear which would instantly translate any language for you. The Babel Fish, 'by effectively removing all barriers to communication between different races and cultures, has caused more and bloodier wars than anything else in the history of creation' (Adams, cited in Grossman, 1997: 195). The flame wars which have raged in email discussion lists and newsgroups illustrate the point that instant contact is as likely to facilitate conflict as co-operation.

Flames are abusive email messages. They often evolve from disagreement in an email discussion which escalates rapidly into mutual abuse, fits of screaming, threats of violence and finally a full-scale flame war which drags other subscribers to the list into the conflict.

Fascinated by flames in much the same way that arsonists are, some mailing list subscribers deliberately try to provoke flame wars. For some it is a form of recreation to post messages which are so provocative, so filled with hate and invective that other subscribers get whipped up into a frenzy. Those messages, posted just to see what reaction they provoke, are called 'trolls'. You do not want to waste your time responding to trolls.

Phil Agre suggests that, holding off until all of the anger is out of your system, you respond politely and carefully (Agre, 2000a). An alternative is simply not to respond. 'Never wrestle with a pig. You both get dirty, and the pig likes it', as one Net saying puts it (Grossman, 1997: 108). You do not have to respond to all email messages and a good place to start is with abusive messages.

Online harassment

Most flamers are just letting off steam. Some email participants are grimmer, more obnoxious characters. Increasingly, it seems a small minority of people are using email to harass individuals or groups of people.

People have used email to send racial abuse and to sexually harass. This can be scary if the abuse is being sent by someone in the same physical location as you, if it is another student at your college, for example, which has been the case in some well-known email harassment cases.

The first thing to bear in mind is that email contact is subject to the same laws as other forms of contact. If you are being harassed via email by someone at your college, report it. If you would not answer an abusive note slipped under your door by them then do not answer their abusive email either. The structures in your institution which deal with any form of harassment, whether it be student advisors or counselling services, are the appropriate first port of call.

Bear in mind, however, that email addresses can be forged and people's accounts can be used by other people who know their password. It is always possible that the person whose address is on the message may not be the person who wrote it.

There seems to be a widespread illusion that email contact is not subject to the law in the same way that other forms of communication are. It is. A threat is a threat whether you email it or say it. It is not so long ago that a high-school student in the USA who casually, and probably jokingly, threatened Bill Clinton in a newsgroup found himself being interviewed by the FBI (Lehnert, 1998: 463). Ultimately if a person does not stop harassing you by email the courts may be the place to deal with the matter.

Spam

The longer you have had your email account and the more visible your address is, on Websites or in email discussions, the more likely you are to get spam. Spam is junk email, advertisements usually.

In the USA in particular it has become a plague. As lists of email addresses are harvested from Websites and email lists by companies which sell them to advertisers, mailboxes have become choked with garbage. Users outside the USA are in less danger because US-based advertisers generally do not devote as much energy to targeting people outside North America. No matter where you are, though, it is only a matter of time before you receive your first spam. You can reply to the spammer and ask them not to send spam to you again, but many spammers falsify their email address so you cannot reply (a practice which the US government is in the process of making illegal). In this case you can get their current real address from the full header of their email. Most email packages allow you to look at this header which is full of technical detail.

You can report spammers to the postmaster in charge of their email. If the spam came from **spammer@anywhere.com** you can report them to **postmaster@anywhere.com**, sending them a copy of the spam you received (see Lehnert, 1998: 101–5).

If this gets no response you can send your email to a server which will try to forward your complaint to the right address. Just send your complaint to **domainname@abuse.networks.net** where domain name is the second part of the spammer's address. Thus, **spammer@anywhere.com** should be reported to **anywhere.com@abuse.networks.net**. Your message will be forwarded to the address which deals with complaints related to that domain. You can find out more about this service at **www.abuse.net** (Lehnert, 1998: 102).

If you find yourself deluged by spam you can set up filters (see section on email in chapter 2) which will redirect much of the spam into a folder you can call 'spam' or 'garbage' or whatever you like. You can empty this folder regularly, making sure before you delete that your trap has not caught genuine email messages.

Wendy Lehnert, adapting rules developed by Adam Boetinger, an anti-spam activist, suggests the following filters are pretty effective at detecting spam (Lehnert, 1998: 137):

Subject contains: !!!
Body contains: $$
Body contains: OPPORTUNITY
Body contains: FREE
Body contains: MONEY

Viruses

One of the most common means of spreading viruses is by email. If you have been using email for more than a few months you have probably already been hit by one relatively harmless virus, the 'hoax virus', email warnings about viruses that do not exist. You will recognize them because they will ask you to forward it to everyone you know and it will not come from a recognizable official source. As a rule you should only pay attention to warnings with some form of authority behind them, sent by your computer support people, for example. People send out these hoax virus warnings for the same reason that virus writers create and distribute viruses – to see how many people they can fool and how far their message or virus can travel. The effect is to generate huge amounts of unnecessary email and to waste a tiny bit of everybody's time.

Other viruses are more serious. Among the most common are macro viruses. Your virus-screening software should pick these up and they are not too difficult to get rid of, but they are annoying. They are transmitted in word processing documents, in particular Word 6 and Word 7 documents, and in Excel files. You activate the virus by opening and working on the document. You will know you have the virus because some of the documents you are working on will suddenly have **.dot** extensions and you will have trouble saving them. If you have virus-screening software your computer will refuse to open the document. You should let the sender know the document is infected. Often they will not even realize they have a macro virus.

You should always be extremely wary of any executable files sent to you by email unless you trust the source absolutely and you can also be sure they are not unwittingly passing on a virus. An executable file, recognizable by the **.exe** extension, is a program. The vast majority of viruses are transmitted as programs or hidden inside programs.

Do not worry about opening an email message, though. You cannot get a virus from just looking at your email, unless you're using certain versions of Outlook Express. Viruses can only be passed on if you open an attachment which is infected.

Mailing lists

Email mailing lists are probably the most popular and most useful form of group communication on the Internet. They are sometimes called listservs, after one of the most popular software packages used to provide them. The spread of email to virtually all university staff and students has contributed to their popularity and usefulness. The archives of email discussion lists are an entirely new kind of research resource, like having access to tape-recordings of thousands of conversations stretching back over several years. There are certain disadvantages associated with mailing lists such as the fact that their archives are often difficult to search or do not exist at all. The archives of newsgroups by contrast are easily accessible and searchable.

Issues of authority

There are several different types of mailing lists, each with different sets of rules. The hand of authority rests much more firmly on some types of lists than others.

List subscribers are often unclear about who is responsible for the list they are a member of or even what 'being responsible' might mean. There really is no set pattern for this. It is a simple enough matter for an individual or an institution with a bit of technical knowledge to set up an email list. Now that there are several free Web-based services which allow you to set up a Web-based email list it is possible for almost anyone to set up a list. Just because someone sets up a list does not mean they are an authority on the subject the list deals with. It does not even mean that they keep an eye on what happens on the list.

At the other extreme there are lists which are set up by experts in the subject area and are administered almost as tightly as a print publication, with an editor and an editorial board.

Moderated discussion lists

These are lists in which a list moderator, a real human being, plays some role in filtering or editing messages posted to the list. Most moderators do not use a heavy hand, but merely stop abusive and irrelevant email from being posted to the list.

At the other extreme from the lightly moderated lists are the lists which are very tightly controlled, such as the suite of lists under the authority of H-Net (**h-net2.msu.edu**). Each H-Net list has an editor and an editorial board and is controlled almost as tightly as a print publication. Membership of the lists is composed of academics, graduate students and other interested groups such as journalists and librarians. See the inset for more on H-Net.

H-Net (h-net2.msu.edu)

H-Net was initially concerned only with history but has broadened out to deal with the humanities in general. There is plenty to interest social scientists and many of the historical lists are much concerned with politics, sociology, economics and related social sciences. The H-Net lists are among the most valuable academic resources on the Net, the email discussion list at its most focused and useful. It is also the discussion list at its most controlled and most restrictive. The lists are managed by editors who actively contribute to the lists themselves, powering them along and ensuring that the lists never die from inactivity. They use the lists to inform members of useful Internet resources and of academic events relevant to their subject. Editors also monitor and sometimes edit and rearrange contributions from members, gathering together several answers to a particular query, for example. Even if you don't join you can access the H-Net Website and the sites for individual H-Net lists and search their archives. If you find the right list the archives can be a very focused and therefore useful collection of high-quality material in your subject area. Many of the lists have a very strong focus on the USA.

Unmoderated discussion lists

These are lists which are not controlled by anyone – no moderator, no editor. There will still be a list owner, the person who set up the list in the first place or who has taken over from the person who set it up. In the beginning the great majority of lists were unmoderated. It was part of the political philosophy of Internet users that there should be no censorship. In many cases unmoderated lists developed into moderated lists as the owners responded to pressure for increased control from subscribers fed up with the poor signal-to-noise ratio. Even unmoderated lists are subject to some level of supervision. The list owner may send occasional messages reminding people of the subject area the list is devoted to and asking them not to send email on completely unrelated topics. They may issue guidelines as to what sort of material is most welcome or unwelcome on the list. They will perform occasional policing duties, removing particularly obnoxious contributors from the list.

The key feature of unmoderated lists which marks them out from moderated lists is that action is taken after the fact. Anyone can post anything to the list, anything obnoxious, offensive, irrelevant or hateful. It is only afterwards that action is taken against them.

Many unmoderated lists have become clogged up in recent years with irrelevant, ill-informed, self-indulgent messages or have been engulfed in flame wars. They are often of more interest as an illustration of human interaction on the Internet than as a serious research resource.

Distribution lists

These are one-way mailing lists. You subscribe and are sent regular messages by the list owner. This is the sort of list you are signing up to when you ask to be sent regular information about new books by a publisher or when you subscribe to an email newsletter. You are not invited to contribute nor are you expected to. Such lists are extremely common. They range from low-volume lists which might send out a message once a week or a few times a year to high-volume lists which send you messages almost every day.

There are numerous distribution lists which are devoted to a particular current issue, subject area or country. Such lists typically distribute a mix of news stories, statements and documents relating to the issue or country they are concerned with.

An exemplary list of this kind is the 'Red Rock Eater News', a list devoted in large part to social and political issues around computing in general and the Internet in particular. Phil Agre, an expert on the subject, sends out an eclectic mix of materials relevant to the topic. If you can find such a list in your subject area it can be absolutely invaluable. To subscribe to the 'Red Rock Eater News' send a message like this:

To: requests@lists.gseis.ucla.edu
Subject: subscribe RRE

Do not put anything in the body of the message.

Another useful type of distribution list is the newsletter or bulletin devoted to a particular subject which is sent out at regular intervals, weekly or monthly. Perhaps the best such newsletter relevant to the social sciences is the Scout Report (**scout.cs.wisc.edu**) which is devoted to reporting on new Internet resources relevant to social academic researchers. See the inset below for more information.

The Internet Scout Project (scout.cs.wisc.edu)

This project was established in the early days of the Web to serve the research and education community in the USA, funded by the US government's National Science Foundation (NSF). It produces the Scout Report. It used to produce and the three subject-specific reports, on business and economics, on science and engineering, and on the social sciences but these have been discontinued.

The Scout Report on Social Sciences (**scout.cs.wisc.edu**). To subscribe send an email to **listserv@cs.wisc.edu**. In the body of the message type 'subscribe SCOUT-REPORT'.

This report is one of the most valuable social science resources on the Internet. It provides descriptions of major Internet resources relevant to researchers focusing on new resources.

Scout Report Archives (**scout.cs.wisc.edu/archive**) is a database of the descriptions of Internet resources which have appeared in the Scout Report. The archives include several thousand entries and allow for very detailed searches. They are dealt with in detail in chapter 6.

Listserv, listproc and majordomo – understanding mailing lists

A university or other institution which hosts mailing lists will manage them through a piece of software called a list server. This software can manage subscriptions and other commands to large numbers of lists, including commands used to search the list archives. The three main list server software packages are listserv, listproc and majordomo. They all do roughly the same thing: manage a limited number of tasks for a large number of mailing lists. When you subscribe to a list you do not email the address which existing list subscribers send messages to. You send a message to the list server software asking to be subscribed. Only afterwards do you start sending email directly to the list itself. The list server address will take the form **listserv@ anycollege.edu** or **listproc@anycollege.edu** or **majordomo@anycollege.edu**.

Your message is being sent to a piece of software which just recognizes a specific set of commands (see inset box for subscribe and unsubscribe commands for all three). It is just as well to remove your signature file when you send to one of these addresses. Your signature file will cause it to send you error messages. List servers are also unforgiving of spelling mistakes.

Once you have subscribed you send all your messages to the list address. This address will usually take the form **listname@anycollege.edu**. You will notice a lot of lists which end in the letter L. This just stands for list. In the early days people thought it was a good idea that a list address should be instantly recognizable by that L.

Subscribing to and unsubscribing from a mailing list

List servers are not case sensitive. Commands can be in lower case, upper case or both. Don't put anything in the subject field of your message.

Listserv

Send commands to listserv@*anycollege.edu*
Subscribe
Subscribe *listname yourfirstname yourlastname*
Unsubscribe
Unsubscribe *listname*

Listproc

Send commands to listproc@*anycollege.edu*
Subscribe
Subscribe *listname yourfirstname yourlastname*
Unsubscribe
Unsubscribe *listname*

Majordomo

Send commands to majordomo@*anycollege.edu*
Subscribe
Subscribe *listname*
Unsubscribe
Unsubscribe *listname*

Trouble with unsubscribing

You may experience problems in unsubscribing from a mailing list at some stage. What follows are instructions on what to do if you find yourself in this situation. They are based on an article by Stephanie and Peter Da Silva (1999).

If you have kept the message you received when you first subscribed to the list you should have no problem. It will tell you how to unsubscribe. If not, look at a recent message from the list and see if it provides details of how to unsubscribe.

If that fails, find out the address of the list, which will be in the header of any message from that list. If the list address is *listname*@**anycollege.edu** the 'Request' address for that list will usually be *listname*-**request@ anycollege.edu**. This address may be monitored by a human. Write them a short polite note asking to be removed from the list. Be sure to give the name of the list and your email address.

Alternatively this address may be looked after automatically by the list server software so you should also send a message directed at this possibility. Type 'unsubscribe' (and nothing else) in the subject line of your message and in the body. Turn off your signature file.

If this does not work it will at least result in your being sent a help message or an error message which will often include instructions on how to unsubscribe. If it does not it will at least provide the list server address for this list. This will usually start with **listserv@**, **listproc@** or **majordomo@**, depending on the software used for that list.

Once you have this address just refer to the inset box above for details on the standard unsubscribe commands for the different types of list server.

There is one final complication which may arise. You may get a message saying you are not subscribed to the list. The list server software is checking your email address against its list of subscriber addresses and cannot find an exact match. This may be because it recorded a slightly different version of your address when you first subscribed. Assume your address is **me@mycollege.edu**. Assume the computer that hosts your email account is called '**bart**'. Its full address is **bart.mycollege.edu**. You will have been told that your address is **me@mycollege.edu**. All mail sent to that address will reach you without difficulty. However, your full 'real' address is **me@bart.mycollege.edu** and this 'real' address will be included, unknown to you, in the header of every message you send. This is the address some list servers store as your address. When they get an unsubscribe request they take the short version of your address and try to find it without success because it does not match the longer version they have stored. The way to get round this is to add the long version of your email address to your unsubscribe message:

unsubscribe *listname* **me@bart.mycollege.edu**

In this case it may take a few days for the request to be processed. If this fails just try again a few days later.

In the worst-case scenario you can write a personal note to the 'postmaster' for the machine the list is hosted on, **postmaster@anycollege.edu** in the example given. Do not do this unless you have tried everything else first.

Other list commands

Apart from subscribing and unsubscribing there are a range of other commands you can send to a list server address.

   When you subscribe to a list you are automatically added to a list of subscribers which is available to anyone who requests it.

   To request a list of subscribers, ordered alphabetically, to a list called SOCSCI-L:

   REVIEW SOCSCI-L BY NAME

To request that your name is not included on this list:

   SET SOCSCI-L CONCEAL

To put it back on again:

   SET SOCSCI-L NO CONCEAL

When you go away for a while you can stop mail being delivered:

   SET SOCSCI-L NOMAIL

To turn it on again:

   SET SOCSCI-L MAIL

One of the best ways to judge the value of a list is to look at the statistics for the list, how many subscribers it has, how many messages are sent.

   To get statistical information about a list called SOCSCI-L:

   STATS SOCSCI-L

Many mailing lists generate a lot of messages every week. If you want to receive all the messages from a list called SOCSCI-L together once a week (in the case of some lists, once a day) as a single message:

   SET SOCSCI-L DIGEST

(On listproc: SET SOCSCI-L MAIL DIGEST).

   To cancel the digest and go back to the original method of delivery:

   SET MAIL SOCSCI-L

(On listproc, SET MAIL SOCSCI-L ACK).

   The digest will have an index of the individual messages at the start. The disadvantage is that it is a bit more awkward to save or transfer individual messages that you want to keep. For more details about the digest option check the welcome message you received from the list. Some lists require you to unsubscribe from the regular list and then subscribe to the digest.

Searching for mailing lists

Finding the right list or lists for you can take a while, not least because it can take a few weeks of being subscribed to decide whether a list is really useful to you or not. Do not be afraid to subscribe to several lists at the same time. Just be sure to keep the details they will send you on how to unsubscribe. Do not be afraid to subscribe and unsubscribe rapidly if you find a list is not useful to you. You are not hurting anyone's feelings, usually.

The good news about searching for a list is that once you have found a few good lists in your subject area you should be able to end your search. A good list moderator will be concerned to keep you updated about happenings in your area and if a new list on a closely related topic is set up you should hear about it on your list.

There are an increasing number of search services on the Web which search for mailing lists. Many people automatically turn to these sources first when looking for a list. There are, however, quicker ways to find a high-quality list relevant to you. One of the quickest ways is to look at the H-Net lists and see if there is one relevant to you (see inset).

Another shortcut is that trusty old resource, personal contact. Ask people doing related research what email lists they find useful. If you find the right people this can be a spectacularly fast and efficient way to find a good list.

Web subject guides are dealt with in detail in chapter 6. These guides gather together links to useful resources on a particular subject. They will often point you to the major mailing lists in the subject area and provide a much quicker way to find them than the mailing list search engines.

Mailing list search engines

There are several search engines which search for lists. They generally search only the titles of lists and short descriptions of them. None of them is any-where close to providing a comprehensive database of lists. New lists are created every day. It often takes quite a while before the list search engines learn about them. Even many well-established lists are not included on these databases. Some of the list search engines will return several references to the same list. To top it all, list descriptions can sometimes be inaccurate or too short to be informative.

These search engines respond to simple searching, the broadest terms and every variation on those terms. If it is matters Scottish you are interested in, for example, be sure to search for Scot, Scots, Scotland, Scottish and any other variation you can think of. Each will bring up an entirely different set of results on most list search engines.

Liszt (**www.liszt.com**) This search engine sorts results into 'Liszt Select' lists and others. The Liszt Select lists are those judged to be of higher qual-ity. Liszt also allows you to browse through mailing lists organized by sub-ject. Only some of the lists have been categorized by subject and you will miss a lot if you only browse by subject. At time of writing it was often difficult to find exact subscription instructions for lists via Liszt. However, virtually all lists have a standard subscription procedure which you can follow once you know the list address and the list server address (see inset on subscribing to and unsubscribing from a mailing list).

TileNet (**tile.net**) Tile Net indexes far fewer lists than Liszt but doesn't seem to bring up such a high proportion of private lists and local lists. It provides clear subscription instructions for every list as well as details on list owners.

Reference.Com (**reference.com**) This list search engine emerged from a project at Stanford University. It provides a detailed FAQ on how to use the service. It differs from most of the search engines listed here in that it also archives the full text of messages from all of the mailing lists it has permission to archive. You can search the archives of individual lists although you cannot search all of the archives together. You can design an advanced search on this site and it will email the latest results of that search to you regularly.

CataList, the official catalog of LISTSERV lists (**www.lsoft.com/catalist.html**) This only includes lists which use the listserv software. A huge proportion of lists use this software and CataList provides the best searchable database of these particular lists, one which, according to CataList, is kept constantly updated. It searches the titles and short descriptions of lists and you can arrange lists by the number of subscribers they have. It also tells you if lists are archived on the Web. It seems only a small minority are.

PAML, Publicly-Accessible Mailing Lists (**www.neosoft.com/internet/paml**) This excludes the private lists which other search engines sometimes bring up. The database is updated monthly and can be searched by keyword and by subject. It provides descriptions of lists and subscription details.

Egroups (**www.egroups.com**) Egroups is very different from any of the search engines listed above. Egroups allows people to set up mailing lists which are Web based. That is, all email messages are posted to a Website. Egroups allows you to search the full text of recent messages from Egroup lists, but you can only search list archives, the 'vaults' as they call them, if you are a member of that list. You can also search a database of list titles. These searches give you access only to Egroup lists, which are quite distinct from lists run using the major list server software packages. They represent only a tiny fraction of the mailing lists available. Search results give you the number of members on each list and the total number of messages.

Mailbase (**mailbase.ac.uk**) This is a collection of over 2,500 lists serving the academic community in the UK, although not restricted to that community. You can search by keyword for lists of interest to you. You can search the archives of individual lists or, even better, choose the option to 'search many lists'. This allows you to search the archives of all of the lists in a particular subject category or, alternatively, to search the archives of several lists together. In the latter case you need to type in the names of all the lists yourself so you really need to know which lists you are interested in. It is great to be able to search the archives of several lists together. It is a pity you cannot do this in most list search engines.

Meta-List.net (**www.meta-list.net**) searches a database of over 230,000 mailing lists.

Lists to avoid

Some of the list search engines do try to select and highlight high-quality lists but in general they are unable to distinguish lists by quality and useful-ness. They also include a range of different types of lists without distin-guishing between them. They make no distinction, for example, between discussion and distribution lists. Neither do they distinguish between lists which are open to everyone and those such as the H-Net lists which restrict membership. There are certain types of lists which you should learn to iden-tify and avoid, as follows.

Lists which are dead or dying   Some of the list search engines tell you how many subscribers a list has (or had the last time they checked). Since only a tiny proportion of list subscribers ever contribute it stands to reason that a list with under 100 subscribers is likely to have very little traffic. If the num-bers have dropped below about twenty it is highly likely that the list is dead or dying. A list with so few subscribers can become disused for long periods and die without ever being pronounced dead. There are other lists which are stone dead, no traffic for months or years but which still exist as a list server address. You can subscribe and get a welcome message but you will never receive another message. Constantly active discussion lists by contrast will generally have over 1,000 subscribers and you will usually discover that there are quite a limited number of such discussion lists in your area of interest.

Private lists   Many of the list search engines make no distinction between private and public lists. Private lists are lists set up by an organization or group of individuals connected by work or a co-operative venture of some kind. Membership is restricted to those at the organization concerned or actively involved in the venture. They were never intended to be publicized at all but large numbers of such lists are picked up by the list search engines and it can be difficult to distinguish them from public lists. They tend to have extremely specialized titles. There is often nothing to stop you trying to subscribe to them but there is no point. They are not intended for people out-side a particular project or workplace.

Local lists   Huge numbers of lists are devoted to discussions between people in a certain geographical location on a particular topic. You might for exam-ple have a California waste recycling list which will be dominated by discussion of local recycling programmes and state-wide debates. It may also deal with broader issues around recycling but this may be such a small proportion of the traffic that the list is really not of much use or interest to those outside California. You will recognize local lists because almost invariably the name of the list includes the name of the local place they are concerned with.

Searching list archives by email

The great drawback of using email lists as a research resource is that it is extremely difficult to search the archives of email discussions. Some lists do not even keep archives, others keep them only in a format which means you have to search by sending email commands. It is still the case that the vast majority of list archives are not searchable through any of the search engines described above.

As a consequence the best approach to searching email archives is to identify the specific lists of interest to you. These may include lists which are not currently useful but whose archives may reveal a 'glorious past' rich in discussion and information from those early enthusiastic days. You will then have to search their archives individually so you might want to limit yourself to two or three major lists in your field. There is too much out there to even attempt to be comprehensive. Most lists store their archives on their list server. To access the archives you send commands to the list server address, that is the listserv, listproc or majordomo address. In general only list subscribers are allowed to search the archives of a list.

Below are a few basic commands which apply both to majordomo and listserv lists. Say, for example, you want to look at the archives of a mailing list called 'SOCSCI-L' which is hosted by **listserv@anycollege.edu**. To get a list of all of the material held in the SOSCI-L list archives send the following message:

To: listserv@anycollege.edu
INDEX SOCSCI-L

This will return a list of the files in that archive, documents which can consist of a single message, a collection of messages related to a single topic or a log (a collection of messages from a specific time period). The name of the files will be on the left of the screen, in some cases appearing after the name of the list. Short descriptions appear on the right. If you want a file called DEVIANCE from the SOCSCI-L list send this message:

To: listserv@anycollege.edu
GET SOCSCI-L DEVIANCE

Log files should be called something like LOG9803 or LOG9901 (logs for March 1998 and January 1991 respectively).

You can also search for a particular word or words in the full text of all the messages in a list's archives. Assume you want to search for the phrase 'general chaos' in the archives of the SOCSCI-L list. Send the following command:

search 'general chaos' in SOCSCI-L.

To search for the word chaos on its own send the command:

search chaos in SOCSCI-L.

You will receive a list of numbered messages which contain the phrase or word you searched for. Assume you want to get message 91 from that list. Send the command:

getpost SOCSCI-L 91.

There are more advanced methods for searching list archives by keyword but they are a little complicated. You can get details on these methods in the case of listserv by sending the message 'Info DATABASE' to any listserv address. You will get back a document about fifty pages long.

Discussion groups

Email mailing lists deliver to your mailbox. Other Internet forums for discussion and information require slightly more effort on your part. These discussion groups have one great advantage over email for the researcher: good archives which can be easily searched.

Newsgroups

In many ways newsgroups are very like unmoderated discussion lists. Anyone can post a message to the group, anyone can reply. Anyone can join. There is no censorship, no control, no restrictions. People who repeatedly send abusive aggressive messages can, however, find their access to Usenet suspended. Newsgroups differ from email lists because they use a different technology to distribute messages and this means messages are accessed and archived very differently (see chapter 2 which describes how to use the news server software and explains some of the technical detail about how the newsgroups work). Messages are usually referred to as 'articles' or 'postings'. Newsgroups are also called 'news' or 'Usenet news' or are just collectively known as Usenet (User's Network). Despite the fact that they are called 'news' they are generally used for discussion rather than for passing on news. Because newsgroups are so uncontrolled, they suffer from all of the problems which unmoderated lists suffer from, only worse: spam, flames, irrelevant and abusive postings and excessive cross-posting (when people post the same message in several newsgroups simultaneously, something which the technology makes it easy to do). Because they are so uncontrolled newsgroups have become a prime target of censorship in several countries (see Grossman, 1997: 96–7).

Things have become so bad that many newsgroups have been abandoned by everyone but the spammers and flamers and are utterly worthless as research resources. Of course, if you are an anthropologist, sociologist, political scientist or psychologist the newsgroups do provide fascinating evidence of online community and communication in action.

Understanding the newsgroups

According to Basch (1998: 54) there are over 50,000 newsgroups. The key to identifying those which are useful to your research is understanding how they are organized. Newsgroups are arranged in hierarchies. Below is a list of the top-level hierarchies which are likely to be relevant to social scientists:

Alt – alternative
Biz – business
Clari – news stories from Clarinet, a pay service
Comp – computers
K12 – US schools (kindergarten to 12 years of age)
Misc – miscellaneous
News – about newsgroups and the Internet
Rec – recreation and hobbies
Sci – science
Soc – society, culture, religion
Talk – discussion, focused on current issues

Each of these top-level hierarchies is home to hundreds or even thousands of individual newsgroups. The top-level hierarchy it belongs to is the first part of every newsgroup name. There will be at least two parts to the name of every newsgroup, so, for example, **soc.culture** belongs to the soc hierarchy. It is for discussion of culture in general. **soc.culture.indian** also belongs to the soc hierarchy and is for the discussion of Indian culture. **soc.culture.indian.kerala** is for discussion of the culture of the Indian state of Kerala.

Each of these is a distinct and independent newsgroup, none of them dependent on the other, each devoted to a more specialized discussion than the one before it. Because they are so closely related many messages will be cross-posted to all of these groups. If you find one newsgroup relevant to your work you will find that it receives a huge number of messages from related groups and that there is therefore no real need to look at closely related groups.

Most newsgroups of use to social science researchers belong to one of half-a-dozen top-level hierarchies, described in further detail here.

Soc Perhaps the hierarchy most useful to social scientists, this was intended as home for groups concerned with society, social issues and socializing (Pfaffenberger, 1997: 261). Major sub-hierarchies within soc which are relevant to the social sciences include **soc.culture**, **soc.religion**, **soc.history** and **soc.feminism**. **soc.culture** includes newsgroups on virtually every country in the world from **soc.culture.albanian** to **soc.culture.serbia** and onwards. The **soc.culture** groups, focused as they are on individual countries, can be a rich mine of information for those studying an aspect of a particular country. They are also the forum for a large proportion of the political discussion which takes place on Usenet.

Talk is devoted to discussion and argument, which can be ferocious at times. It includes many newsgroups concerned with current controversies, heavily weighted towards issues topical in the USA, from abortion to gun control. It is a useful source of information about the main arguments in these debates and includes a hierarchy **talk.politics**, which includes several newsgroups devoted to political issues.

Alt is the 'alternative' hierarchy. It was set up by people who believed that users should be free to set up their own groups without having to deal with the administrators of Usenet. While these administrators did not control the content of newsgroups or the articles posted to them, they had the power to decide whether a new newsgroup should be added or not. In the alt hierarchy, however, which is beyond this control, anyone can set up a newsgroup, give it any name they like and devote it to any subject they like. The result is a 'hierarchy' which is utterly anarchic, where groups are born and die every day. A huge proportion of all newsgroups are alt newsgroups. These groups include many which are dedicated to the utterly obnoxious, to subjects well beyond the bounds of general acceptability. They also include groups dedicated to the obscure and the marginal and, depending on how obscure or rarefied your topic is, there is always a chance that there will be an alt newsgroup devoted to your topic. Sub-hierarchies within alt which are especially relevant to the social scientist are **alt.society**, **alt.religion**, **alt.politics**, **alt.activism** which is heavily used for political campaigns, **alt.current-events**, **alt.culture** and **alt.feminism**.

While all servers are obliged to carry the main hierarchies, including soc and talk, which themselves include articles which are inflammatory and offensive to many, no news servers are obliged to carry any alt groups at all. You will be able to search and read the alt hierarchy through the newsgroup search engines.

Misc, for miscellaneous, is an official top-level Usenet hierarchy which includes all of the groups which administrators could not classify under the other official hierarchies. It is always worth checking out if a group relevant to you might have been filed under miscellaneous.

News is not for the distribution or discussion of 'news' but for discussion of the newsgroups and Usenet itself. It includes groups which are devoted to discussion of the future of the Internet, of interest to those concerned with studying social, political or economic issues surrounding the Net.

Clari is the one major Usenet hierarchy which charges for access. It is run by a commercial company, Clarinet, and is given over entirely to the distribution of news. It's now also available via the Web (**www.clarinet.com**). You can only get access if your university or service provider is subscribed. Cross-posting is used to great effect here, stories being posted to all groups which they are relevant to.

Others In addition to these groups there are many top-level hierarchies specific to certain regions, including **de** (Germany), **au** (Australia) and **uk** (United Kingdom), which provide groups which will be of interest to users dealing with these particular areas or countries. **uk.politics**, for example, is a sub-hierarchy for discussion of British politics but note that not all discussions on UK topics take place in groups in the UK hierarchy and not all groups in this hierarchy are devoted to discussion of UK-specific topics. Note also that some newsgroups, particularly in the USA, are restricted to certain regions, for discussion of matters relevant to those regions. They usually will not appear on news servers outside the region.

Usenet II (**www.usenet2.org**)

Usenet II is an attempt to create a new Usenet where newsgroups are moderated and where excessive cross-postings, flames, trolls and spam are excluded. There is a classic political dilemma called 'the tragedy of the commons'. The 'tragedy' is that any resource shared by several people without any controls on its use will inevitably be destroyed. While everyone knows that Usenet will eventually be destroyed if it is full of spam, flames and trolls, individuals have no incentive not to flame or spam because no one person on their own can do anything to stop the 'tragedy'.

Usenet II was brought into existence on the assumption that Usenet is fast succumbing to the tragedy of the commons. You can only get access to Usenet II newsgroups if your university or college is subscribed (free of charge). Subscription details are provided on the Web page. Every newsgroup in Usenet II begins with the word 'net'. All top-level hierarchies therefore have two parts to their name. There is a very limited number of Usenet II groups but given how confusing the vast array of Usenet groups is this may not be such a bad thing. Among the top-level hierarchies of interest to social science researchers are **net.current-events**, **net.history**, **net.media**, **net.religion**.

Finding a newsgroup

The key to effective use of the newsgroups is to find one or two which are relevant to your work. You can conduct keyword searches of all of the recent messages from every newsgroup but with tens of thousands of newsgroups out there the results are so numerous they are scary. You might start your search for a newsgroup in **news.groups.questions**, a newsgroup where people ask which newsgroup would be the right place to ask a particular question. You might browse through the Usenet hierarchies at 'Usenet Info Center Launch pad' (**metalab.unc.edu/usenet-i**) to see what groups are available under the top-level hierarchies most relevant to you. This Info Center also provides statistics about groups, including the number of readers and messages they have. Alternatively the AltaVista discussion group search (**www.altavista.com**) will return a list of newsgroups which match your search term, rather than just a list of individual messages. You should use the broadest search terms here. You can also identify useful newsgroups by doing keyword searches of Usenet as a whole.

Searching the newsgroups

The main newsgroup search engines allow you to search individual newsgroup messages. When choosing keywords to search newsgroup postings you should bear in mind that the vast majority of postings are informal, original, personalized messages. They are not as formal as the sort of document you will find on the Web and are less likely to contain the key phrases and buzzwords used in more official documents. Given the sheer volume of messages it is important to avoid the sort of terms which come up regularly in messages in your subject area.

The search results will show a list of individual messages. They will include the newsgroup the message was posted to and you can usually connect to the newsgroup itself by clicking on its title.

Note, however, that the search engines are usually set up just to search recent messages (from the last two weeks or months) unless you specifically ask them to search further back.

Results will also include the thread a message is part of. A thread is a topic of discussion within a newsgroup. All messages belonging to the same thread will have the same subject heading. Some threads will continue for months and attract dozens or even hundreds of contributors. Others fizzle out from lack of interest after one or two messages. In most of the search engines you can see all of the recent messages from a particular thread just by clicking on the name of the thread. Most newsgroup postings make little sense in isolation and can only be understood in the context of the thread they belong to.

As was mentioned briefly in chapter 2, newsgroups are distributed via news servers. The newsgroup messages you look at will most likely be located on a computer, a news server, at your college or university. Because there are so many groups and so many messages they are wiped after about two weeks. You will be able to follow current discussion in a newsgroup through your newsreader software in Netscape Navigator or Internet Explorer. To search for older messages and to search the newsgroup archives you will need to use the big newsgroup search engines which archive newsgroup postings and allow you to search those archives. These archives are accessible through the search engine Websites, not through the news reader software.

Google Groups (**groups.google.com**)   This service originated with the purchase by the search engine Google (see chapter 7) of the accumulated archives of Deja.com, the original newsgroup search engine. It is an archive of Usenet discussions dating back to 1995. You can browse through the hierarchies and carry out searches restricted to certain hierarchies or to particular newsgroups.

The 'Advanced Groups Search' allows you to search for messages by a particular author, and to search the full text of messages, restricting your search by language and date. You can limit your search to particular newsgroups.

Your keyword search will also bring back a list of the main newsgroups associated with the keywords you have searched on, a good way of identifying useful groups.

Searching by author allows you to find all of the messages posted by a particular person. This can be abused, to build up a profile of a person's attitudes which might some day be used against them. This reinforces the point that when you post messages to newsgroups you are laying out a trail which you cannot erase. If you are concerned about this, there is one step you can take to cover that trail by preventing your newsgroup postings from being archived. Just put 'X-No-Archive:yes' in the header of your posting or as the first line in the body of the posting. Several of the big newsgroup archives such as **reference.com** will respect this request that your posting not be archived. However, there is no guarantee others will not archive it. Of course this means that a researcher can never be sure if a newsgroup archive provides a full record of what has gone on in the newsgroup. You need to be particularly aware of this if you are trying to analyse a discussion thread. It may be there are pieces missing that you will never find.

RemarQ (**www.remarq.com**)   searches Usenet newsgroups only.

Talkway (**www.talkway.com**)   This is another newsgroup searcher.

AltaVista (**www.altavista.com**)   This is one of the big keyword search engines but it also allows you to search the newsgroups using the 'discussion group' search. It provides one particularly useful feature, placing all of the messages from an individual thread together on a single Web page making it easy to download and/or print the contents of an entire thread. A little confusingly it refers to threads as 'topics'.

Reference.com (**www.reference.com**)   is primarily a search engine for mailing lists but also allows you to search newsgroup archives.

Liszt (**www.liszt.com/news**)   is best known for searching mailing lists, but will search newsgroups and also try to link you to the FAQ for groups, where they exist.

Tile.net (**Tile.net**)   is another email list search engine which also searches newsgroups.

Behaviour in newsgroups

The same guidelines which apply to behaviour when writing email also apply to newsgroups. If anything flames, pigs, spam and trolls are more plentiful in the newsgroups. There are a few pieces of advice particularly important in newsgroups. It is easy to cross-post your posting to lots of newsgroups at the same time. Avoid excessive cross-posting. It annoys other users. Be sure also to read the group FAQ. Newsgroups are where FAQs originated and there are several archives of FAQs including **www.faqs.org/faqs**, **www.arc.nasa.gov/enhanced/faq** and another at the Usenet Info Center, **metalab.unc.edu/usenet-i/**.

Bulletin board services (BBSs)

Bulletin boards are very like newsgroups. People can post to them and read the messages other people have posted there. They are quite an early method of Internet communication and they differ from Usenet in that they are locally or regionally based and you get access not through the Web or Usenet but by a direct dial-up connection. They are very much intended to serve a specific geographic area. When Howard Rheingold talks about 'virtual communities', he draws a lot of his hopeful examples from the BBSs (Rheingold, 1995). They are widespread in the USA where there are over 100,000 of them (Kennedy, 1998: 19) but rarer elsewhere. If there is a BBS in your local area it may be of interest if you are doing research on a local topic.

AOL and CompuServe discussion forums

AOL and CompuServe are big US-based Internet service providers (ISPs). As well as providing access to the Internet to people with computers at home they provide a lot of online content, access to which is restricted to these subscribers. This includes huge discussion forums. Since most students and academics have access to the Internet through a college or university they do not need AOL or CompuServe to get access to the Net and consequently are not as likely to participate in these forums as on the open Internet.

Web forums

Web forums are also called message boards or online forums or Web boards or Web bulletin boards. In many ways they are just newsgroups which are based on the Web. They are a much more recent form of communication than newsgroups or email lists. They are also much more numerous. They are not like the newsgroups where, with the exception of the alt hierarchy, all new newsgroups must receive official permission to come into existence. Anyone can set up a Web forum. As a result there were over a quarter of a million forums at the last count. A Web forum is often attached to a particular Website, the idea being that it will host discussion about the material on the Website. Many news Websites have set up forums for discussion of current events, 'salons' which include discussion of current political issues. Among these is Café Utne (**cafe.utne.com/cafe**). In addition major search engines such as Yahoo and Excite have set up large collections of Web forums on every topic under the sun. They often refer to them as the 'discussion area'. A single news site can often have dozens of Web forums attached to it. In general anyone can connect to a forum through the Web, read the messages which are already there and post their own messages. In some cases messages can only be posted by registered users. When you connect to a Web forum you will see a list of messages, each message an underlined hyperlink. Just click on the link to get the message.

The advantage of Web forums is that they provide much the same service as the newsgroups but without the need to learn how to use a news reader. On the down side the fact that you have to go to a Website to contribute probably cuts down on participation. Web forums also suffer from a lot of the same problems which afflict Usenet. Particularly because they are easily accessible through the Web, new users often stumble across them and take the opportunity to pose questions which really do not belong in that particular forum. I have come across forums which consist entirely of inappropriate questions, not one of which has been answered.

Forum One (**www.forumone.com**)   According to Forum One, it indexes over 270,000 Web forums. It allows you to search the titles of forums or to browse a listing of them, arranged by subject. It also provides a useful list of the biggest forums. Many forums are so tiny that it is not worth paying attention to them. They generate five or six messages and then quietly fade out of existence. As with newsgroups the best research strategy is to identify a few forums relevant to your subject and to go and search their archives individually. If you do a 'discussion search' through the big Web search engine, HotBot (**www.hotbot.com**), it will search the Forum One index.

Reference.com (**www.reference.com**)   also has a directory of Web forums which you can search.

There are big questions over the value of Web forums and their long-term future. Vast numbers of forums contain only one or two messages and even those are from new users who have wandered in by mistake. It may be that there will be a weeding out process or a consolidation in the near future and the number of forums will diminish drastically. For researchers interested in current events the forums attached to news services do illustrate some of the current debate on these issues. However, a forum will need to have generated quite a lot of correspondence to make it worth the researcher's while to search it.

Making contact with other researchers

Departments, research centres and individuals

When you have read a lot of the secondary literature and have some of your fieldwork behind you, you will often want to contact other people who have written in the area and to begin to make them aware of your work. You may be interested in knowing whether other people working in the area have recently published something that you might have missed or are working on an article or book relevant to your research. There are many points of contact with other researchers and this section details how to search most effectively at those points of contact.

A small minority of social science academics have set up sophisticated personal Web pages detailing their research work and interests. A smaller group still have taken to putting up the full text of articles they have written. In some subject areas people have compiled lists of such pages and it is worth checking to see if such a list exists in your subject area. Many more academics have a Web presence through their university department's Web pages. Probably the quickest way to get more information about an academic is to find out where they work and go to that university's Website. Every university Website should provide either a list of departments or schools or allow you to search the site by keyword. The Yahoo 'Colleges and Universities' list (**dir.yahoo.com/Education/Higher_Education/Colleges_and_Universities/**) provides links organized geographically, by country and region. They are very good on US institutions but their footing is a little more uncertain in other countries. They include many institutions which have the word 'college' in their title but are very small and specialized and are very different from mainstream colleges and universities.

Braintrack (**www.braintrack.com**) lists over 5,000 higher education institutions around the world, organized geographically.

Research centres can be a little trickier to locate than universities and there does not appear to be a consolidated list of research centres comparable to the Yahoo list of universities and colleges. However, SOSIG, the Social Science Information Gateway (**www.sosig.ac.uk**, see chapter 6 for more detail), provides short lists of research projects and centres as part of its subject categories.

The best way to find research centres is through the Websites of the universities they are affiliated to. They come in all shapes and sizes. In some cases the 'research centre' title is just a term of convenience used to describe the fact that several members of staff are working in the same broad area. At the other extreme a research centre can be a huge operation with its own buildings and full-time researchers whose only job is to work on the centre's long-term research projects.

University Websites will often provide searchable directories of staff. These databases cannot be searched by the big Web search engines and you run the danger of missing out on this information if you just rely on a key-word search of the Web. However, the Web can be a good place to start a search for an individual academic, provided they have a reasonably distinc-tive name. Just search for their name as an exact phrase; '*exact name*' will work in most search engines. For more detailed information see chapter 7. If you know the name of the university too, search for both in the same query (+'*exact name*' +'*university name*' in most search engines).

Doing this once in a search for a US academic and thinking how clever I was, I pulled up a bunch of reports on a funeral. It seemed the man I wanted to contact was dead, although people I knew were hoping to invite him to a conference. I had to read quite a bit about the funeral before I could confirm that the dead man just happened to have the same name and be based in the same place as the man I was looking for. Our man was still alive, buried in the second screen of hits.

There are a number of projects to create online databases of researchers in the social sciences. One of the biggest of these is run by UNESCO, the United Nations Educational, Scientific and Cultural Organization. UNESCO infor-mation services (**www.unesco.org/general/eng/infoserv/**) provide a range of databases concerned with education, sciences, culture and communi-cation. One of these databases is DARE (**www.unesco.org/general/eng/ infoserv/db/dare.html**), a directory which covers institutions, periodicals and specialists in the social sciences. It provides very sophisticated search options allowing you to restrict your search by country, type of institution, name of individual, or a subject keyword. Information about people is noto-riously difficult to maintain as it goes out of date so quickly. People move, they write new things, they develop new interests. For this reason databases like DARE are extremely difficult to keep updated. It is also important to note that this database is not in any way comprehensive. Google (**www.google.com/universities.html**), one of the major keyword search engines, provides a university search which restricts searches to documents from specific university Websites.

Scholarly societies/professional associations

Academic professional organizations are known as scholarly societies in North America and as professional associations in the UK and Ireland. They are the organizers of conferences and the sponsors of journals. They vary in how enthusiastically they have taken to the online environment. Some use their Websites just to provide membership and subscription information.

Others have used the Web to increase their importance as a central focus for their subject. It is an essential part of your research that you identify the relevant professional association for you and that you check out their Web presence. Just how useful the Website of the relevant professional association will be to you will depend on how well it has used the Web.

In the case of the American Political Science Association (APSA) (**www.apsanet.org**) each section of the association runs a distinctive Website within the APSA Website. Some of these sections have set up email discussion lists which are dominated by APSA members. Some of these lists are full of discussions of research, teaching materials, scholarships and jobs. If the professional association in your area does have a discussion list you may find it is one of the most useful Internet sources you can find, comparable only to a good H-Net list relevant to you. These lists often do not have the robust structures of H-Net lists, however, such as editorial boards and well-developed policy on postings.

You can search for the Websites of professional associations through an excellent site, the Scholarly Societies Project, based at the University of Waterloo, Canada (**www.lib.uwaterloo.ca/society**). Over 1,400 scholarly societies/professional associations are organized by subject category. You can also search them by keyword.

Conferences and current events

There are several major sources of information about upcoming conferences and events in the social sciences. Information about conferences is not as well organized and available in the social sciences as it is in other areas like medicine where there are pay databases which consist solely of conference information. The following services do have information about CFPs (Calls for Papers inviting people to propose papers for conferences), conference announcements, registration forms, conference programmes and related information. Conference sites will sometimes provide drafts of the papers to be read, but you usually cannot cite them without the direct permission of the author.

Meeting/conference announcement lists (**www.lib.uwaterloo.ca/society/ meetings.html**)   This covers links, organized by subject, to the conference announcement pages of professional associations. It is part of the Scholarly Societies Project mentioned above.

H-Net events (**h-net2.msu.edu/events**)   contains information about upcoming conferences, lectures and other events. The listings can be a little sparse and like most such services it is far from comprehensive, but it underwent a major overhaul in late 1999. It allows you to search for conferences by date, location and subject.

Contacting postgraduate students

While mailing lists and newsgroups devoted to your subject are a great way to find out about postgraduate students working in your area, there are a few forums given over entirely to the concerns of postgraduate students. H-Grad (**h-net.msu.edu/~grad**) is an H-Net list devoted to exchange of information and discussions between graduate students, and membership is limited to currently active postgraduate students.

There is a newsgroup called **soc.college.grad** which has a slightly different emphasis, focusing on sharing information about opportunities for postgraduate study and heavily focused on the USA.

The H-Net lists are open to postgraduate students and new subscribers are invited to contribute short biographies describing their research interests. You can search biographies in the archives of the list relevant to you to pull up a very focused list of people carrying out research on related topics.

Other ways to search for people

Apart from the methods outlined above of finding academic researchers there are more general people-finding services available on the Internet. You will find it difficult to avoid them. Virtually every major search engine and portal site has linked up with a people-finder service or developed their own service. Many of the search engines link up to the same people-finder services such as Four 11 (**www.four11.com**), Big Yellow (**www.bigyellow.com**) and Bigfoot (**www.bigfoot.com**). You will find links to these directories everywhere on the Web. They provide email addresses and sometimes real-world addresses and telephone numbers. Do not start your search for other researchers here. These services are often out of date. They have contact details for universities but often do not have work contact details for individual academics and they can be time consuming. As Reva Basch has pointed out (1996: xxiv) the quickest way to find a person's email address is to phone them up and ask them for it. These services are good, though, for quickly finding people you lost track of years ago, provided they live in North America and provided they have a reasonably distinctive name. Unlike print telephone directories you can search for a person's phone number and email address without needing to know anything about where they live.

Collaboration

The links you build through contacts with other people working in the same area may eventually result in collaborative work with them, whether it be jointly applying for research funding, writing articles together or carrying out a joint research project. Collaboration between academic researchers was increasing even before the emergence of the Internet, but it appears to be rapidly accelerating now, partly because Internet technologies make collaboration so much easier.

Simple collaboration

This requires neither elaborate software nor advanced knowledge. By simple collaboration I mean the capability for two or more people to work on the same document. The basic skills necessary are to be able to use email, send attachments by email and use the 'revisions' capabilities of your word processing software. Email has already been covered in detail in chapter 2; revisions have not. Most recent word processing packages have a facility to mark revisions. If you receive a document from someone else via email you switch on revisions (in Word 6, for example, **tools→revisions**). Then every change you make will appear, in a different colour, as a revision to the original. When you send it back as an email attachment your collaborator will be able to see which bits of text you deleted and which bits you added. They can then make further changes of their own and send it back to you. These will be in a different colour and you will be able to see the original document, the changes made by you and the changes made by your collaborator.

In order for this to work you must be sure that both of you have the same, or a very similar, word processing package and that you both have versions which allow revisions. If you find that your collaborator is using a word processing package which can't read your files, find out what package they have, what version it is and what platform it runs on (PC or Mac). Then see if you can save your document in that format. Just click on 'save as' in your word processor and look at the different options.

Advanced collaboration

You can probably get through your entire research career without needing to know how to use the technology dealt with briefly in this section. If you ever use this technology it will probably be with technical support and advice and you will not need to learn a great deal about it. There are many developments in this area which have taken place simply because the technology has made them possible. Some of the tools for communication currently available are of dubious value and it may be that in a few years' time they will look like dinosaurs. There are certain technologies which there is just no point learning how to use until their value has been proven.

A range of collaborative tools, including video and teleconferencing, are available through the two big browsers, Netscape Navigator and Internet Explorer. In IE4 they are gathered together as Microsoft Net Meeting. Net Meeting includes audio and video conferencing capabilities. To use these you will need extra hardware including speakers, a microphone, a soundcard which you slot inside your computer and, for video conferencing, a camera. You can get the cameras quite inexpensively these days. In addition to this the collaboration software provides a whiteboard. It is a simple graphics package on which several people can write and draw at the same time. It also has application sharing which allows you to work on a file on your own computer and let others watch or even make changes to the file themselves even if they do not have the software the file is open in. Document editing provides the same facilities as the revisions feature of your word processor. You can also transfer files by FTP (see chapters 2 and 10 for more on FTP). If you are dealing with large files, say big collections of statistics or very long documents, sending them by FTP is more efficient and faster than sending them as email attachments. You can do this through the collaboration software but you can just as easily do it by using ordinary FTP, if collaborators have somewhere they can receive files. You will have to ask locally whether you can use FTP but it is a lot more likely that your collaborators will be able to receive files by FTP than that all of you will be able to use the complex conferencing software. Netscape 4 includes a similar package called 'Conference' which has many of the same functions.

Think twice before trying to use such a package. It takes quite a bit of learning, not only to get used to the software but to learn how to use it effectively. The quality of voice and video transmission is still not of high quality. It is also not particularly flexible. It only lets you collaborate with others if they have the same or very similar software and if they have taken the trouble to learn how to use it. This is all very well if researchers in your field are keen computer users but in many of the social sciences such people are thin on the ground. You may sink a lot of effort into the software and find you can only use it to work with one or two other people in your field.

Collaboratories

At the most advanced end of the scale scientific researchers have been developing 'collaboratories'. These are online spaces for shared work which only people connected to the project can get access to. They are much more sophisticated than the communications packages available through the Web browsers because they are customized to the needs of a particular project. Thus a collaboratory might include joint databases, different sections of which are updated regularly by different parts of the research team. Those different parts could be located thousands of miles away from each other. It might also include software, for data analysis, for example, which has been developed specifically for the project and can be used by all participants. Collaboratories have been developed in the scientific research community in the USA. Intended to allow specialist research teams scattered across the USA to work together on a single project, they have facilitated the development of this model of a research project and partly as a result of this it is becoming more common for a single research project to involve widely scattered teams. It is likely that such collaboratories will gradually become more common in the social sciences, particularly at the quantitative end of disciplines where large shared databases make particular sense.

Human contact: a last word

Collaboration has been made much easier by the Internet. Email, on its own, has immeasurably strengthened communication between researchers not only internationally but nationally, locally and within individual university campuses.

Collaboration rests ultimately, though, on human willingness to co-operate over long distances. Often there is no explicit guarantee that your collaborator will deliver on their end of the bargain. One thing that makes 'delivery' more likely is real human contact, contact which allows trust and a certain level of mutual commitment to develop. It is important always to be aware that the sense of community, camaraderie and solidarity which email contact can inspire is quite fragile. It is easy to join an online community but it is also easy to leave, to sever those connections without a word of explanation. Beware of depending too much on any network or one-to-one contact which exists only via email and where there has never been personal contact. There seems little doubt that most people feel less obligation to respond to an email message than to any other type of communication. Perhaps it is because they are aware that it requires so little effort to send. Whatever the reason, be wary of trying to organize a co-operative endeavour via email contact alone with people you have never met and are never likely to meet. People will find it easy to drop the email-based project if they come under increased pressure from other commitments which involve face-to-face relationships. The corollary of this is that if you do wish to co-operate with someone you have contacted by email then try to arrange to meet face to face.

5

The Web

Out on the open Web

This is the first of four chapters dealing with research on the World-Wide-Web, or the Web as it's more affectionately known. More particularly these chapters deal with what I will call the 'open Web' (a term used by Basch, 1998). That does not include the big pay databases of articles and books dealt with in chapter 3. Although you use the Web to get access to these sources there are high gates and thick walls which clearly mark them off from the open Web. The open Web, as I am defining it here, does not include the discussion forums dealt with in chapter 4 either, from email lists to Web forums to newsgroups. These forums for discussion and contact belong to a clear and distinct genre, of direct contact between human beings. The walls between this realm and the open Web may not be as thick and strong but it is usually quite obvious when you have passed from one to the other.

To a great extent the open Web is that world of documents which you explore when you ask a search engine to search 'the Web'. The search engines do not search everything which is available through the Web. They do not search the pay databases, the newsgroups (unless you specifically ask them to) or the email lists.

The open Web, thus defined, has certain key characteristics. It is a realm of chaos. It is the realm which people are referring to when they talk of the difficulties of using the Internet for research. It is the dark and bottomless pit from which the search engines dredge up hundreds and thousands of 'hits'. It is all those documents which we view out of context and in isolation, which bewilder and confuse us. It is on the open Web that we first really encounter difficulty in evaluating and assessing or even in understanding documents.

This first chapter on the open Web is directed at developing an understanding of how things are organized out there. Documents on the open Web may be organized less clearly than on the pay databases but they are organized all the same. There is a certain order to the chaos.

Before you start

Before you start on a search of the open Web, take time to answer the question 'why on earth would I want to do this?' The open Web can be a frustrating and time-consuming place in which to conduct research. The returns for your efforts are often paltry. This is not to say that you should not use the Web. Every researcher will have occasion to do this. However, many of them will use the simple and sensible approach of visiting Websites which they have heard about through human contact or print publications. This is quick and easy, and a world away from systematically scouring the open Web for information relevant to your research. As outlined in chapter 1 the Web is particularly rich in certain types of material and poor in others. If your research concerns a topic of current debate in the USA the Web will be an essential resource. If it deals with events prior to the early 1990s no matter where they took place, it may well yield very little that isn't covered in published works. If in doubt as to whether you should bother with a major search of the Web have a look again at the section in chapter 1 on what the Internet is good for. If the type of materials mentioned there are of little interest to you perhaps you should give the open Web no more than a quick cursory glance to make sure you haven't missed anything important.

As your research continues, an important aspect of your work will be to make your questions more specific and this sort of narrowing is particularly important in your research on the open Web. The great danger of heading out on the open Web without a clear idea of what you are looking for is that it is so much easier to be distracted and diverted than when you are dealing with print literature. Since so many thousands of documents are just an 'instant' click away you will be strongly tempted to look at anything that is vaguely interesting. In principle this is a great idea, allowing you to explore serendipitously a huge variety of materials related to your subject. The danger of this is that you can find yourself very easily diverted far away from your subject area to materials which are of minimal quality but which had interesting looking titles.

A related danger is that you will allow the material you come across to play an undue role in shaping your research. Some people have actually devoted themselves to studying how researchers choose the materials they will carry out research on. Their results suggest that researchers tend to follow the path of least resistance to use as sources those materials which it is easiest to get access to (Dervin and Nilan, 1986; Hewins, 1990). Materials on the Internet, taken as a whole, are of low quality but are extremely accessible. If you begin to depend too heavily on Internet sources there is a danger that this will reduce the quality of the work you produce. A classic example of the dangers of relying on Internet sources is the way in which some undergraduate essays draw on Internet sources. Students can be drawn to easily accessible Internet sources which are directly related to their assignment, regardless of their quality. As a result students can end up quoting from people who know less about the subject than they do themselves, quoting from an essay by a school kid or another student.

When you have formulated a question which you would like to find an answer to on the open Web, the first thing you should do is a 'reality check'

(Basch, 1996: xxiv). Ask yourself whether the material you are looking for is likely to be out on the open Web. The key to answering this question is the same as the old-fashioned detective's key to solving any murder: motive. Ask yourself, why would anybody put the information I am looking for on the Web? Who would have reason or motive to put it there?

If you can provide even a sketchy answer to the question of motive not only do you have good reason to launch a search but you also have a head start in your search because you will have a broad idea of what kind of site you are looking for.

If, for example, you are looking for information about financial donations to the highly controversial Popular Corruption Party you might take an educated guess that these will not be available in a clearly organized accessible form on the party's own Website. You might reasonably surmise too that they will not be prominently displayed on the sites of major donors to the party. It might well be, however, that such information is made available by groups opposed to the party.

You might guess also that these donations are a source of public debate and argument and that they might well be mentioned in forums for such debate. Regardless of whether these guesses are correct or not, they provide a range of leads which will alert you to the sort of sites you need to look out for when you start your search.

Chaos

It is important to understand exactly in what ways the Web is chaotic. This will help you to bring your own sense of order to it. It is no great surprise that the open Web is more chaotic than the article databases, but even compared with the anarchy of the newsgroups the Web is chaotic. There is a deep-seated reason for this disorganization: the lack of agreed universal standards for the core elements that a Web document should include. In email the software forces the key identifying marks of sender and recipient address and date onto every email. In the newsgroups, even though people can use aliases, every message contains a sender's address, a subject title, a date, and the newsgroup they were posted to. All of these can be used to set items in their proper context, as part of a particular discussion at a particular time. Web documents, by contrast, share only one universal identifying mark, their URL, the Uniform Resource Locator which usually starts with http:// and which is also referred to as the Web address or even the Internet address. (For those who are worried about making an embarrassing *faux pas* when pronouncing URL, be assured that both 'You-are-el' and 'Earl' are valid pronunciations.) Even the URL can shift and change. If the person in charge of a particular Web document decides to rename the document or to move it around on their own computer, the URL changes. All that is solid melts away. To confound the problem, Web documents change, unlike printed matter and newsgroup and email messages. The same document at the same URL with the same title and author can have very different contents depending on when you look at it.

In addition it is often difficult or even impossible to get ordinary citation details. Out on the open Web it can take some serious detective work even to identify the author of a document. Finding out when it was written is often impossible and identifying the wider site or collection it is part of can require a fairly advanced understanding of the different ways in which Websites are organized. Even major organizations often neglect to stamp their authority clearly on the documents they put on the Web. You will often read about the lack of central authority and control on the Net but it is this lack of agreed standards at a fundamental level which is perhaps the most deeply rooted source of the chaos. Standards which outline the basic components which every Web document should include, such as author, title, date of writing and last updating, are being developed. They are described in detail at the very end of this chapter but it seems likely that it will be some years before these standards spread to the four corners of the open Web.

If there is a lack of structure governing the Web as a whole it does not mean that things are entirely disorganized out there. For one thing the bulk of well-established organizational Websites, be they universities, governments, political parties, businesses or others, are constructed clearly and coherently. Their sites are stable and authoritative. The Web around may be a swirling mess and you may reach such sites by a tortuous and confusing route, but once you are there you will generally find that documents are well organized, and will all have key identifying marks like author and date. These thousands or even hundreds of thousands of organizational sites stand out from the rest of the open Web, like neat and tidy islands of order rising out of the murky waters around them. While such sites are well structured they are often structured very differently to one another. To search the open Web effectively requires you to understand the concept of a Website, as opposed to a Web page, to learn to recognize the boundaries between sites and to do much of your searching 'by site' rather than by keyword or subject. This is dealt with in detail further on in this chapter.

Shifting chaos

It is bad enough that the Internet is chaotic. What is worse is that the chaos is regularly reshuffled with important and often negative effects on the Net's usefulness as a research resource. The speed at which the Internet itself changes is one of the best illustrations of the impact which it has on the pace of technological change. The Internet allows the rapid circulation of new ideas and new technologies. Within days the latest cool thing can have spread out from the most advanced computer research centres to the furthest reaches of the Net. Not surprisingly a large proportion of those fast-spreading ideas and technologies are related to use of the Internet itself. For a few years, back in the mid 1990s, it seemed there was a major new development in Internet technology every month or so. New Internet technologies became immediately visible to the user as people in charge of Websites and search engines raced ahead to try and keep up with the next big thing.

The speed of these changes has had very serious implications for researchers. It meant that researchers had to adapt to a host of new technologies because they changed the way in which documents were searched and viewed. New means of presenting documents disrupted older means of researching them.

A classic example of a purely technical change which had a huge knock-on effect on researchers was the introduction of frames, the scrollable panels on Web pages. When frames were introduced lots of Websites were restructured to make full use of frames. In many cases they were restructured just because frames were the hot new thing. A Webmaster could prove how up to date they were by changing to frames. Researchers using older browsers which did not support frames found that they could no longer get access to sites they used. They had to get the new, and bulkier, browsers. For some people this meant getting more memory or even buying a new computer. In reorganizing sites for frames many Webmasters shuffled all their files and renamed them. All over the Web links and bookmarks became obsolete. Researchers need to know the URL of a page, not only to learn more about the page but for citation purposes too. Frames obscured the URLs of individual documents. It meant researchers had to do more detective work to find a page's URL.

The appearance of frames is just one of a series of developments on the Web which have had a direct practical impact on researchers and which have disrupted methods of research which had been developing. Phil Agre has written of how the computer industry went through 'a long series of intense manias during the 1990s' and has pointed out the potentially disruptive effects of these 'wasteful storms of intellectual fashion' (Agre, 2001). It might be argued that the speed of change on the Internet, the impact of the desire to keep up with the latest developments, has a directly damaging impact on the end-user.

It is to be hoped that the pace of change will start to steady as people providing Web services realize that regularly changing their structures places regular burdens of relearning on the people who use those services. If the pace of change and innovation at the level of basic site structure begins to slow down it will have a beneficial effect on the work of Internet research, removing one major element of the chaos.

'I've got no memory...'

The Internet has a notoriously short memory. Earlier chapters of this book highlighted the historical shallowness of article databases and of the Web in general. Material from the 1960s is almost as inaccessible through the Net as material from the Middle Ages.

The open Web's memory problems go deeper than that. Part of the reason for this is an attitude that all that matters on the Web is 'now', this instant, today. It is reflected in the feverish concern of people to include the latest thing on their Website. It is reflected in that little phrase at the bottom of Web pages, 'last updated on…' as though the value drains out of a document if it is not constantly updated. Coupled with this idolization of the current moment is a certain disregard for the past. Many people who run Websites will 'update' pages by trimming out blocks of 'out-of-date' information and putting them straight into the wastebasket. The focus on updating promotes a culture of throwing away any information which is not completely current. When a Webmaster throws away old information they are often destroying the only copy of that information in existence anywhere.

Even if a Webmaster wants to preserve older versions of documents there are no well-established and widely used standards for archiving out-of-date Web documents. As a consequence those archives of Web documents which do exist vary greatly in their organization and structure.

The result of this lack of concern for memory and archiving is that a huge volume of information is wiped off the Net every day, mainly through the updating of pages, and disappears entirely from the historical record.

One major project, the Internet Archive (**www.archive.org**), is attempting to ensure that these materials are saved. Organizing them coherently so that researchers can use them as a source is another matter entirely.

Understanding Web addresses

Given that the URL is the one and only identifying component which all Web documents are guaranteed to have, understanding these addresses is an essential prerequisite to research work on the open Web.

The address of a document can quickly reveal information about a document which it would take much longer to find out by other means. It is also the key to understanding Websites, the topic of the next section of this chapter.

Protocol

The first part of any Web address is the protocol. The protocol used for Web documents is the HyperText Transfer Protocol (http), so all Web document addresses begin with **http://**. The :// just separates the protocol from the rest of the address. The other major protocols you will encounter, and which were dealt with in more detail in chapter 2 are: **gopher://**, **telnet://** and **ftp://**.

The vast majority of links on the Web are to Web documents, those which begin with **http://**. In recognition of this the main browsers will automatically add **http://** to the start of any address you type in if you have not done so already.

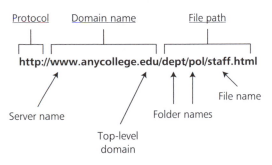

The structure of a Web address

Domain name

The domain name is the main part and the most important part of any Web address. It is the address of the computer you are connecting to or, more specifically, the Web server you are connecting to.

The domain names are intended to be descriptive and to provide information about the computer you are connecting to. Not so long ago you could be guaranteed that every domain name was the address of a distinct computer but things have become a little more complicated. Several different domains can be hosted on one machine.

The domain name shown in the example illustrates the way in which these addresses are composed. The domain name is the first part of the Web address after the protocol. The last part of the domain name is the top-level domain, **.edu** in the example, indicating that this is a US university. The middle part, **anycollege**, is the name of the university. The first part, **www**, is the server name or host name. It is the name of the actual Web server which hosts all of the Web documents at this university. You will notice a lot of domain names beginning with **www**. It just seemed like common sense to call a Web server 'www' so everyone would know what kind of server it was, that it was not a Gopher server for example. It could just as easily be called 'Fred' or 'Matilda'.

Note that while the domain name is not case sensitive, the file path which follows it is.

IP addresses

Every computer which is connected to the Internet directly (that is, not through another computer via a modem) has a unique IP address consisting of four sets of numbers like **127.131.10.176**. The computer's domain name is just an alias for this number. In routing messages and requests across the Internet it is these numbers which are used. They are the 'real' address.

When you make a request for a Web page at a certain domain the first thing your computer has to do is look up its 'real' address. It has to check the nearest DNS (Domain Name System) server which keeps tables of the IP addresses.

Top-level domains

The very last part of a domain name is the top-level domain. It tells you what country the computer is registered in or, in many cases, what type of organization runs the computer. Country domains are often easy to guess, like **.ca** for Canada, **.jp** for Japan, **.ru** for Russia. There is a top-level domain for every country in the world and a list is provided in appendix 1 of this book. They always consist of two letters. As well as country domains, there are also several 'category' domains. They all have three letters and tell you what type of organization runs the Web server you have connected to. They reflect the US origins of the Internet. Because the Internet was initially confined to the USA it seemed redundant to put **.us** at the end of domain names. It must have seemed like stating the obvious. The US government, US universities and the US military were heavily involved in the development of the Net at the initial stages. As a result, they each got their own top-level domain.

Thus **.mil** is the top-level domain for the US military and the US military alone. **.edu** is short for educational institution but the only educational institutions which use this top-level domain are US universities. **.gov** stands for government, US government. Things are a little less clear-cut in the case of the other category domains. **.com** stands for commercial sites and while the vast majority of **.com** computers are US based not all of them are. **.org** is the domain for organizations. It is unclear exactly what sort of organizations it is restricted to. It includes political parties in countries outside the USA as well as international organizations and NGOs. **.int** is theoretically for international organizations but some of the largest of these are in the **.org** domain, including the United Nations and the OSCE (Organization for Security & Co-operation in Europe). NATO, on the other hand, uses the **.int** domain. **.net** is for organizations concerned with the administration and development of the Internet, largely, but not exclusively US-based organizations.

It is important to note that **.com** is the domain which virtually all Internet Service Providers and all free Web space providers are confined to. Lots of small organizations use Web space provided by one or other of these sources and therefore the Web addresses end in **.com**. Just because their Web addresses include **.com** does not mean that they are commercial sites.

There is a country domain for the USA. It is **.us** as you might have guessed, but the vast majority of US sites do not use this domain.

While computers all over the world can register in the domains **.int**, **.org** and **.com** it seems the great majority outside the USA register in their country domains. The country domains are complicated as well. Just because a computer is registered in a certain country does not mean it is located in that country. Certain poorer countries which have domain names which are commercially attractive have taken to selling names to the highest bidder, no matter where they are based. There is no guarantee that a domain ending in **.tm** is actually located in Turkmenistan, for example. The small Central Asian republic has been selling domain names to US companies who treat the **.tm** as short for trademark. Likewise, the tiny Pacific island of Tonga is not actually home to the many Websites which have registered there simply for the purpose of having a domain name ending in **.to** such as **come.to**, **welcome.to** and so on.

It is a bit like all those ships cruising the ocean waves which are registered in Panama or Liberia simply because of the favourable terms for registration. There is no guarantee that a site is located in the country whose top-level domain it is registered in.

In addition, political preferences can play a role in determining which country domain people choose to register under. Ireland provides an interesting example. Northern Ireland is legally part of the UK and one would therefore expect Northern Irish sites to come under the **.uk** domain. However, many organizations in Northern Ireland which aspire to a united independent Ireland outside the UK choose to have a domain name ending in **.ie**, the country domain for the Republic of Ireland.

Several countries outside the USA have set up organizational domains of their own within the country domain. Thus the UK has **ac.uk** (academic community, that is universities), **co.uk** (commercial companies) and **gov.uk** (the UK government). In Australia **edu.au** is for universities, **org.au** for organizations. Japan has **go.jp** for government sites and **ac.jp** for universities.

Port numbers

Sometimes you will come across a domain name which includes an odd-looking number, like **www.anycollege.edu:80**. This is a port number. A Web server can allow access through several different ports. When you connect to the domain name on its own with no number you connect through the default port (which is usually port 80). Some Webmasters used to add the port number to their Web address to make doubly sure people could connect, but that is not done much anymore.

The path

After the domain name comes the path, **/depts/pol/staff.html** in the example given above. The path, as its name suggests, gives you directions to the particular file you want. If you cast your mind back to chapter 2 and the file structure of your own machine it will make it easy to understand. Each / separates one folder from another until the last item, which is the name of the file you want to retrieve, in this case **staff.html**.

When you connect to the Web server address in the example above your computer essentially asks the Web server: 'Please open the folder **depts**, then open the folder **pol** which is inside it. In that is a file called **staff.html**. Please send it to me.' You can often tell quite a lot from the path. Here, for example, it seems likely that **staff.html** is a list of staff in the politics department.

In one important respect the path is not like your own file system because on Websites most folders will have an index page. If you just type in the path as far as the end of a folder you will usually get the index page for that folder. Thus **www.anycollege.edu/depts/pol/** will get you the index page for the politics department.

Understanding Websites

Carrying out research on the Internet requires an understanding of how Websites are organized. The Website which a document belongs to provides the context within which that document can be understood, situating it as part of a collection of related documents. To use a Web document without knowing what site it belongs to is a bit like using a photocopied page without knowing anything about the book it is copied from. It is bad research practice to use a document with no understanding of its context, whether you are dealing with the Net or with printed materials.

Defining site

'Website' is not as simple a concept as 'book', however. A Website may well be the online equivalent of a book, the various chapters organized as separate Web pages. It might equally be the equivalent of a magazine, a journal, an archive or a collection of any of these. A site may take full advantage of the potential of hypertext and be organized in a way for which there is not even a remote equivalent in print. A broad definition of Website might describe it as consisting of all of the materials placed on the Web by a particular organization or project or individual. In this definition site is described in terms of authority. The central question is 'whose' site you are looking at. Sites, thus defined, can be massive. The Boston College site (**www.bc.edu**), the Irish government site (**www.irlgov.ie**), the US House of Representatives site (**www.house.gov**), all contain numerous sub-sections. It can also mean a tiny collection of documents put on the Web by a single individual or even a single document if it is genuinely not part of any larger organizing structure. The key element is authority.

Identifying authority is one extremely important aspect of identifying a site and thus understanding the context your document exists in. The problem for the researcher is that just defining a site by whose site it is often places it in a context too broad to be meaningful. Most large organizational sites consist of thousands of documents organized in many different sub-sections of the site. A researcher needs to be able to locate the particular sub-section of a site a document belongs to in order to understand it fully. Thus to understand a document on the '**anycollege**' site called 'list of courses' it is necessary to know if it is part of the law department section of the site, or the department of history sub-section, or if indeed it is just part of the 'anycollege' site as a whole, providing a full list of courses for the entire college.

A more narrow way to define site is to say that a site is a clearly distinct collection of documents. That is, although it may be part of a larger site, although it may have no independence or separate authority, it does have a distinct identity. By this definition, site is the lowest level of the organizing framework within which a document is located. This is the level which provides most information about the context in which a document exists.

Higher levels of organizations are included in the name you give to the lowest level of organization. For example, if an article on human rights law in East Timor belongs to a collection called 'human rights archive' run by the law department at 'anycollege' then the site the document belongs to is 'human rights archive of law department, anycollege'.

Both definitions of site are valid and useful but for the researcher site at the lowest level is crucial and when I use the term site in this section I am referring to site at this low level unless I state otherwise. Site, defined as the lowest level of the organizing framework, has certain key characteristics. It must have a home page which provides information about that site and provides access to an index of documents on that site. A site will have its own title clearly stated on its home page.

Site and URLs

The key to understanding sites is URLs. They are the most accurate guides to how documents relate to each other and how they are organized. The most important thing to remember is that virtually every folder on a Website contains an index document which acts as a home page for that folder. To get a good idea of how a site is organized just have a look at the index pages for the various folders.

---

www.schools.edu/shapes/circles/frisbees.html

Take the URL given in the inset. At this imaginary URL there is a document about frisbees. It is in a folder called circles. It may well be that **frisbees.html** is part of a collection of documents about circles or objects shaped like circles. To see the index page for that folder just cut off the file name, the last part of the address and go to:

www.school.edu/shapes/circles/

When a URL ends in a folder name rather than a file name your browser automatically looks for a file in the folder called **index.html**. This will usually act as a sort of home page for that folder. Some people use a different name for the index page in their folder and if you do not get any result using the folder name you can try adding some of the names commonly used like **default.html**, **home.html**, **contents.html** or **toc.html** (table of contents).

If there is no index page in the lowest level folder just go up a level and see if there is one there. In the example given here, try **www.schools.edu/**

shapes/ and if that produces nothing go back up to the domain name **www.schools.edu**.

If you do find an index page in the 'circles' folder you will have to decide if it constitutes the home page of a distinct collection of documents. If it presents itself as a home page or an index page for a site with a clearly stated title, if it provides access to an index of documents connected by a common theme, then it is a site home page, with one very important qualification. The documents on this site should belong to this site and this site alone. In general a site consists only of documents contained within and below the folder containing the site's home page. Thus the URLs of all documents on the circle site should begin with **www.schools.edu/shapes/circles/**.

This is not to say a home page will link only to pages in that site but its links outside that site are external links and it is not the home page for those documents except in rare cases. It will also link to higher levels of the site it is part of. Many new users assume that every page a site links to is somehow part of that site. It is not. When in doubt just check the URLs.

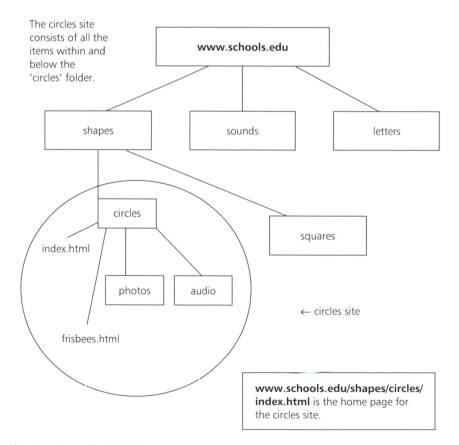

The structure of a Website

Searching by site

The most effective way to search the Web is to search by site, treating individual documents which you come across as leads to potentially useful sites rather than as sources in their own right.

Because Websites differ so much in how they are organized every new Website you come across can be fairly described as an 'unfamiliar research environment' (Basch, 1998: 182). There is a traditional research approach to such environments which can usefully be adapted and applied to Websites.

1. *Identify the starting point* When you come across a useful document the first thing to do is to identify the home page of the site it belongs to. Most of those designing Websites design them for users who enter through the home page. As a result of this it is the best starting point for exploration of a site.
2. *Identify the boundaries of the site* Scan the URLs of the links on the home page. Determine which links are internal, leading to other items on this site, and which are external, linking to documents at other sites. Follow the main internal links which seem relevant to your work until they either lead outside the service or end in substantive documents or document collections.
3. *Identify which parts of the site are relevant to you* You will have achieved much of this in the process of identifying the site boundaries.

Site-mining

Once you have become familiar with the site you should mine it thoroughly for information. Extract from it every scrap of information useful to your research. This requires you to be disciplined in rejecting the temptation to click on any of the external links on the site until you have exhausted what this site itself has to offer or have clearly identified the sections of it which you will need to return to. You do not necessarily have to mine the site in one sitting but you should not move on to any other site until you have finished with the one you are in. In exploring the site you will develop a very sophisticated understanding of its structure and of the nuances of that particular site. If you go back to the site after a long interval this information will not be as fresh in your mind and you will have a certain amount of relearning to do.

Keeping up with a site

If it is likely that new information relevant to your work will be added to a site you have mined you need to find a way to find out about it. In most cases I suggest nothing more sophisticated than returning to the site after a year or perhaps six months. This means that in perhaps the last third of your research you should go back and systematically scour the main sites which have been of use to you for new information.

There are other ways but you may well find that, unless you restrict yourself to a few major sites, they will lead to information overload. Many sites provide an email alerting service, informing you when new material has been added to the site. This is fine so long as you are prepared to visit the site every time you get an email. If not you might as well just visit the site when you are ready to. Sites will often offer some facility which allows you to distinguish newly added material from the rest. They may have a 'new additions' or 'what's new' page or alternatively may allow you to do a search of the site restricted by time. That is, their search facility will allow you to restrict your search to pages added during a particular time period. You can then just search for recently added documents. Netscape Navigator provides a facility to allow you to check if your bookmarked sites have changed. If you make sure to bookmark all the sites you want to monitor you can use this to check if anything has changed: **Bookmarks→Edit Bookmarks**, then **View→Update Bookmarks**. Sites which have changed will have an equals sign '=' beside them. Those which can't be reached will have a question mark.

The equivalent commands in Netscape 6 for this and other command sequences described in this chapter are listed in Appendix 4.

Internet Explorer 4 has a facility called 'subscriptions' (**Edit→ Preferences→Web Browser→Subscriptions**) which will inform you of changes to bookmarked sites ('favorites') which you have subscribed to. To subscribe: open favorites, highlight the favorite you want to subscribe to and then **file→get info→subscribe**.

There are also a number of services such as the Informant (**informant. dartmouth.edu**) and spyonit (**www.spyonit.com**) which will send you email informing you when new pages have been added to sites you have specified. Once again, you should only use such services if you are prepared to visit the site when you receive such a message. Otherwise it is probably just as easy to visit the site again when you are ready.

Identifying useful sites

A useful site is one which contains unique, substantive content relevant to your research. By unique I mean that it does not simply copy or distil information which is available in its original form elsewhere on the Web. Such unoriginal second-hand materials abound on the open Web. These sources are not as trustworthy as the original, as information may have been altered. Secondly, as your research involves distilling information for your own use, someone else's distillation of one or two original sources is of minimal use to you. If someone has provided an original analysis of several sources, however, this does constitute a unique contribution.

You will find such derivative documents all over the Web. Hundreds or even thousands of people thought for some reason that it would be a good idea to merge bits of information from readily available Web sources into their 'own' essay or profile of a topic or country. Thus the Web is full of articles which are composed in equal measure of thinly disguised extracts from *Encyclopaedia Britannica* (**www.eb.com**), statistics from the *CIA World Factbook* (**www.odci.gov/cia/publications/factbook**) and liberal dollops of unfounded personal opinion. Even if they are directly relevant to your subject, they are not useful sources. Better to go straight to the originals which, after all, are only a click away.

By substantive I mean the site should contain enough material to make it worth your while using it. The Web is full of small items, paragraphs on everything under the sun. It is also full of information which is very much secondary: comments on an article, for example, or a few thoughts on a political event. They are the Web equivalent of scraps of paper with interesting things written on them. There are of course exceptions but, in general, these very short items do not give you enough new information to actually make a significant contribution to your research. In practical terms it means that you should avoid very short items unless they seem particularly promising.

Monster sites

The Web may have a very short history but the weight of that history is already bearing down on its shoulders. When people started building Websites not only did they often neglect to think of the past, but also they often did not think very far into the future. Many Websites were built as though it was a one-off endeavour. The first sites were elegant, beautifully organized, sleek and trim, custom-built to provide a structure for a particular set of information. Webmasters could see that Web pages would need to be updated. Many of them, however, did not envisage that the sites would be transformed.

The result is that, four or five years on, many Websites are huge, awkward lumbering beasts. The original site structures have been stretched out of shape. Ill-fitting pieces have been welded on wherever they fit and are not easily reached from the home page. Items have been squeezed into sub-categories they do not belong to for the sake of preserving the orderliness of the overall structure. In some cases someone new has taken over the site and does not fully understand the logic which informed its organization in the first place. In the absence of an archiving policy or even a rigorous clean-out policy, collections of older documents are relegated to side-rooms, almost cut off from the main site but not from the big search engines which still return them as hits.

Websites also show the strain of relations within organizations. A site can be set up by one section of an organization. Another competing or jealous part of the organization will decide it should set up a Website too. Their sites overlap in terms of content or they even compete as the central Website for their organization. US government sites provide a classic example of overlapping authority. You can often reach the same US government document through two or three different sites, each of them providing different ways to search for the same document (Basch, 1998: 182–6). As time goes on the relationships between different sections of Websites and between original structure and subsequent additions become more, rather than less, complex. The *tabula rasa*, the clean slate which faced those early Website designers, is now dark with overlapping layers of organization. Anyone seeking to add to or further develop an existing Website is faced with the burden of a huge existing service where maintenance of existing information alone is a huge task.

The implications for the researcher are bad. Understanding Websites now requires not only an appreciation of the various ideal forms of organization which site designers try to follow, but also an understanding of the different layers of organization which have been laid down in the course of a Website's short life. This is necessary particularly in the case of many government sites where the impact of changing administrations, changing policies, shifting areas of responsibility and changing staff make Website organization a complex end-product which reflects changes within those institutions.

Masquerade sites

Because so many Web users are unaware of how the Web works there are quite a lot of 'masquerade' sites out there, pretending to be something they are not. One of the more notorious cases was the Amnesty-Tunisia site. Supporters of the Tunisian government built an entire Website devoted to illustrating how good that country's human rights record was. They called it Amnesty-Tunisia and its URL was **www.amnesty-tunisia.org** giving many people the impression that it was run by the reputable international human rights organization, Amnesty International. Amnesty International (**www.amnesty.org**) devoted Web space to publicizing this site and embarrassed the people who ran it into moving the site to a new Web address.

Particularly if you are carrying out research on controversial topics you need to be aware of the possibility that sites are not always what they claim or appear to be.

Link sites

One of the greatest sources of frustration in using the Web is that so many Web pages consist simply of links to pages on other Websites. If they provide summary information about the pages they link you to and make clear these are external links then they are providing a useful service. If not they are just contributing to the chaos and confusion out there. When you come to a page of links do a quick scan to see if they are internal or external. Run the cursor over a link. The URL will appear in the bar at the bottom of your browser. If it's on a different server you'll know it's an external link. If there are useful internal links start with them. If the page consists entirely of unannotated external links, I suggest you ignore it. You will waste a lot of time exploring promising-sounding links from here. Instead search for a good subject guide on the topic (see chapter 6).

Web browsers: advanced skills

Contents lists

Many longer Web documents begin with a contents list. This is a set of hyperlinks which point to various sub-sections of that document. URLs in the contents list will include the telltale # (the 'hash' sign) which appears before the name of the particular sub-section of the document. **Frisbees.html#red**, for example, will link you to the part of **frisbees.html** dealing with red frisbees.

There are some complications with contents lists. If you click on an item in the contents list before the whole document has downloaded you will often be brought back to the top of the page. This happens when the part of the document it links you to has not yet downloaded. The browser does not know where to bring you so it just puts you back at the top of the document.

Each time you click on a link in a contents list your browser treats it as a request for a new document even though you just want to go further down in this document. This can be a waste of time and you are often better off just scrolling through the document. One side-effect of this is that each request you make for a sub-section of a document appears as a separate item in your history list and therefore as a separate step you have to take if you use the back arrow.

Note that external links from one Web page will often link you to specific sections of another document by giving the full URL for a particular sub-section. Once again, you will know if a hyperlink does this because you will recognize the telltale # near the very end of the URL. It can actually be quite annoying to click a hyperlink and be placed somewhere half way through an entirely new document. You have no idea what the document is called and you have to scroll up to the top to find out.

Often you will come across an index page which consists solely of links, ordered alphabetically in many cases, which link you to different sections of another page. When you click on any of these links you have to download the whole document anyway, so do not bother going back to the index page if you want to look at other sections of the document. Just scroll up and down the document instead.

When 'back' doesn't work

You are looking at a Web document. You click on 'back'. The same Web document appears. If you have not been using a contents list within that document there is one other explanation of what has happened: you connected to a Web page but it was a page whose URL had been changed. Being very concerned that users should find the same page at its new location the

Webmaster has put a page at the old URL which automatically redirects you to the page's new location. It may have redirected you so quickly that you did not even notice. If you then click on 'back' you will call up the redirect page which automatically redirects you to the document you tried to go back from. Just use the history/Go list to jump back over the redirect page.

If you click on a hyperlink in a document before the document has downloaded fully your browser drops everything and retrieves the latest document you have requested even though it was only half way through downloading the first document. If you then click on 'back' to return to this first document you will find your browser will only show the part it has downloaded. To get the full document you will have to click on the reload/refresh button.

Worst Web nightmares

- Automatic spawning of new windows
- Frames
- Ticker tape displays in the status bar at the bottom of your browser
- Ticker tape news
- Java and ActiveX programs which increase download time but add little value to a site
- Parasite frames
- Fixed width pages too wide for your printer
- Home pages which consist only of an elaborate image which links you to the real home page

---

Automatic spawning of new windows

I don't know who ever thought this was a good idea but Webmasters can force your browser to open a document in a new window. Sometimes this will be obvious. The new window will overlap with your old one and you will see both of them. At other times it will completely obscure the original window and if you blink you will not notice that you are now in a new window. You can sometimes tell if a link is going to open in a new window because the URL will include 'Javascript:makeNewWindow'. Having two windows open slows down your browser a little. In addition, the 'history' of pages you visited before this new window was spawned is only available via the original window. You need to go there if you want to retrace your steps. It is a classic case of new technology allowing Webmasters to be innovative in ways which are disruptive of the use of the Web for research.

New windows

If you click on a link and hold down the right mouse button you will see a menu list. One of the options allows you to open the link in a new window.

This has certain advantages. If you have a page of links to different sections of a site you can open the various different sections in new windows while leaving the index page open in the original window. This saves you the trouble of constantly going 'back' to the index page. Be aware, however, that the more windows you open the more your browser slows down. In addition each new window has its own history list, beginning at the first document you opened in that window. It is not wise to open too many windows. The Internet is confusing enough already.

You can open a new window with your start page in it at any time (in NN, **File→New→Navigator Window**; in IE4, **File→New Window**; in IE5, **File→New→Window**).

One final thing to note: the original window you had open is no more important than the others except in having the earliest items in that session's history list. You can close it at any time without affecting the other windows.

Frame nightmares

I have already mentioned that frames caused problems for researchers when they first appeared. They still do and some users are so annoyed that they have rallied behind the slogan 'I do not want to be framed' in a 'Campaign to Recognize HTML Frames as the silly things they are'.

When you visit the home page of a site with frames you will see the URL for the site in the top bar of your browser. In the case of many sites, no matter which page you call up on the site, the home page URL will still appear there. Researchers need to know page URLs not only to tell them more about the document but for citation purposes. One way to find it is to save the page as a bookmark and check the URL of the bookmark. To bookmark an individual page within a framed site right-click on the page itself and choose 'add bookmark' (Conner-Sax and Krol, 1999: 112). Alternatively you can scan the cursor over the link to that page and make a note of the URL. When you are looking at the page itself that means clicking on 'back' and checking on the page which sent you to that document. You will also usually get the page URL by printing out the document. Since frames generally keep the home page URL up for all sections of the site your history list is of minimal use. It just shows the site name repeated over and over with no clue as to which document on the site it refers to. This is a case where you are forced to use the 'back' button rather than the history.

To stretch the Hansel and Gretel analogy a little, frames act like those pesky birds who gobble up your trail of bread so that you cannot find your way back as easily. Note that sometimes the different frames within a window can be resized. Just click on the border between the frames and drag.

Ticker tape nightmares

Ticker tape messages which run along the status bar at the bottom of your browser are another one of those great technological innovations that should have been strangled at birth. It uses up the space where URLs appear when you drag the mouse over a link so you cannot find out what URL a link is sending you to. As a result you cannot tell if it is a link to the other side of the world or to a sub-section of the site until you click on it. This one makes me despair. A site with frames and ticker tape really makes the researcher's job more difficult. You will of course always get the URL of a document on a printout and you can always check out a link's URL by clicking on it and seeing it in the top bar as it begins to download. If it is no use to you, you can click on 'stop' and 'back' to return to the page with the ticker tape. If you come across a site with this ticker tape ask yourself if you really need to use it; is there an easier way to get to the documents it links you to?

Java and ActiveX

These are two different ways of doing the same thing, running little programs within Web pages as you view them. Java came first. ActiveX is the Microsoft version of the same thing. In Java these little programs are called applets. They are responsible for innovations such as the ticker tape displays which are such a source of joy to the online researcher, slowing download time while adding virtually nothing to a site's value. One way of dealing with annoying Java and ActiveX features is to disable them on your browser. This will get rid of some annoying ticker tape displays. It will certainly speed up download time. JavaScript is another matter. It may be important for functioning, for example for login procedures at certain sites. It is probably a good idea not to disable it. To enable and disable Java: in IE4, **Edit→Preferences→Web Browser→Java→ Enable Java**; in NN, **Edit→Preferences→Advanced→Enable Java**. To enable and disable ActiveX in IE5: **Tools→Internet Options→Security→Custom Level→ActiveX controls and plugins**.

Parasite frames

This must deserve the title of worst feature of the Web. Webmasters who use frames on their site can force your browser to put their frame on every document you connect to via their site. Thus, 'idiot enterprises' could provide a page of links to a thousand other Websites. When you click on those links, whether they be to the UN, the Government of India or the Swedish Army, those sites will appear within the 'idiot enterprises' frame. It means that novice users get the impression that 'idiot enterprises' run all these sites. If you do not find a way to escape, this parasite frame will attach itself to every site you visit during the session. Parasite frames are frames in their most sinister incarnation, implicitly claiming false authority and interfering with your access to other Websites.

The way to escape is to return to the page on the parasite site where you first chose a link to another page. Click on the link you want to go to, hold down the right mouse button and choose 'open link in new window'. The link will open in a new window free of the parasite frame (Pfaffenberger, 1997: 107).

Pfaffenberger suggests you then close the original window and boycott the parasite site in future. The only thing I would add is that you might want to send an email asking the offending site to stop this practice.

Link tracking/dimmed links

If you have clicked on a hyperlink in the recent past it will appear as a dimmed link, in a lighter shade of blue than normal hyperlinks. You can change the settings on your browser to increase the length of time your browser remembers which links you have visited. Thirty days is normal. I suggest sixty days plus is more appropriate for research use. This feature can be extremely useful to a researcher. Your browser stores URLs you have requested in a history list and draws on this list when it decides which links should be dimmed.

Just say you have visited thirty sites relevant to your subject. You are looking for more relevant sites by looking at pages of links. The sites you have visited appear dimmed on these pages of links so you do not have to puzzle over them or try hard to remember whether you have visited them or not. As time goes on and the total number of sites you have visited increases you will find this incredibly useful.

It is also useful when you revisit a day or two later a site which you are systematically mining. All of the sections you have checked out appear as dimmed links and it is easy to see what is left to explore.

This can also provide a clear trail back to a document you forgot to bookmark. If you can remember the first few steps of the route you took to get to the document you will find that, on every page after that, only one or two links will be dimmed. Just follow the trail of dimmed links until you reach the lost document.

How browsers deal with URLs

Browsers try to be as helpful as they can. Sometimes they can be over-helpful. As mentioned previously most browsers will automatically add **www** at the beginning and **com** at the end if you only type one word into the bar at the top of the browser. IE4 will also try adding **.org** or **.edu** to an incomplete address, so to get most US universities or to get an organization via IE4 you generally just have to type its name or abbreviation. If your URL is very incomplete IE4 checks your 'history' to see if it can find an entry with that address. It means that just typing in the first few letters of a site you visited recently will pull it up from the history list.

Bookmarks/Favorites

Bookmarks capture two items of information, the URL of a Web page and its 'title'. The title is often not very descriptive. If this is the case alter it yourself as soon as you bookmark it. If your browser cannot detect any title for a document it will use the document's URL as the title so your bookmark then only has one piece of information for that document, the URL.

It can be tempting to use bookmarks as a method of collecting citation information. Be careful of this. The bookmark does not provide enough citation information. If you rely on bookmarks you will find yourself having to return to all the sites again to gather the rest of the citation details.

NN4 allows you to write comments about a bookmark. (To edit Netscape bookmarks: **Netscape symbol→bookmarks**. Then select the bookmark you want to add comments to and choose **edit→get info**.) You could put citation information in here. Then again you could just as easily open your word processor and paste it straight into your bibliography.

The main advantage of recording citation details in the bookmarks rather than in a word processing file is that you do not have to have the word processor open as you browse the Net. In addition, as the bookmark records the URL you do not have to copy and paste it to your typing package from the bar at the top of the browser. These are only minor conveniences, though, and eventually you will need to paste all this information into your bibliography anyway.

History/Go

The History/Go function is more advanced in IE than it is in NN4. It includes not only documents you looked at during your current session but those from previous sessions too. IE and Netscape 6 also give you the option of working offline (under the File menu). This allows you to access any of the items in your history list without having to connect to the Internet. Of course, as soon as you choose a link which is not on your history list you will have to go online again.

Error messages

'Too many connections Network connection refused by server' The site you are trying to connect to is overloaded with requests or has temporarily shut down (a lot of smaller machines are shut down for maintenance for half an hour or an hour every week or month). Try again immediately and after a few minutes. If that does not work try again later.

Error 404 This is the most common error. It means you have connected successfully to the server but the particular page you requested does not exist, at least not at the URL you have typed. Either you have made a typing mistake in the last part of the URL (after the domain name) or the page has been moved.

If you think it has been moved have a look at the index page of the folder it is in, or at the folder above it to see if you can find a link to it there. For example, if **www.schools.edu/shapes/squares.html** brings up this error look at **www.schools.edu/shapes** and **www.schools.edu** for clues as to where it has gone.

Error 400: Bad request There is usually a typing error in the URL you have typed in or in the hyperlink you clicked on.

Error 401: Unauthorized Often a password-protected page which you can only access if you have registered for the service it is part of.

Error 403: Forbidden Usually a page restricted to certain users. For example, a university server might only allow connections from computers in its own domain. No password is required. You will just be refused access if your computer does not have the right Web address.

Error 500 Internal server error. There is some problem with the server you are trying to connect to. All you can do is try again.

'Host not found' Either the domain name is wrong (try typing it again) or your computer cannot connect to your DNS server where it looks up IP addresses for servers. If the latter, it may well be there is a problem with your Internet connection.

The cache

Every Web document you look at is stored on your computer whether you save it or not. It is stored in the 'cache'. You can find the cache by just searching your file system for a file or folder which includes the word 'cache' in the title. Items are kept in the cache until it is full, that is until all the space allocated to that file or folder is taken. Older documents are constantly being deleted, 'flushed' from the cache.

The documents here are given long numbers to identify them. All of the graphics and text are stored here but it is a painful task to go and look for something in the cache. Its practical purpose is to speed up your Web browsing. The first time you click on a hyperlink during a Web browsing search your browser sends a request for the document through the Internet. If you click on it again during the same session it will go and check the cache for it and give you the copy it downloaded earlier. You can actually force it to resend the request over the Net again by clicking on 'reload/refresh' if you think the document may have changed in the meantime.

Thus, every time you click on 'back' or jump to a document in your history list your browser is just pulling up documents from the cache. The purpose is to save time. You can change the settings on your browser to force your browser to use the cache more or less often

(**Edit→Preferences→Advanced→Cache** on both IE and NN; **Tools→Internet Options→General→Temporary Internet Files→Settings** on IE5) but the default setting will do for most people.

Privacy, censorship and the researcher

Privacy and censorship are fiercely contested political issues which are at the heart of debates over the future of the Internet. (See, for example, Grossman, 1997; Ludlow, 1996; Agre and Rotenberg, 1997.) These issues have very direct implications for the future of research, for the free distribution of knowledge and information. The practice of academic research will be shaped by the outcome of these debates. In the worst-case scenario the Internet will become so restricted and controlled that its value as a research resource will be seriously eroded.

Privacy

When carrying out research on the Web you need to be aware that your movements can very easily be tracked by people in certain positions. If you are carrying out research on a controversial or contentious topic you need to be particularly aware of this.

On the Internet privacy is often eroded in a very casual way. Phil Agre (Agre and Rotenberg, 1997: 55) has argued that computers are not intrinsically hostile to privacy but the way much of the Internet has developed means that casual infringement of privacy is the norm. Many computer networks record a great deal of information about the people who have accounts on those networks. On Unix computers, for example, which host a huge proportion of the world's email accounts, a whole raft of information about users can be recorded: the time they log in and out, all of the programs they used while they were there, the commands they typed on the computer, the total amount of time the account was idle, that is the time you spent logged in without typing anything in. If you are an employee using such a network it is easy for your employer to see when you start and finish using the computer every day and what proportion of the day you actually spend working. It is used for just such a purpose in some industries.

I have already mentioned that a lot of people can read your email en route from you to the recipient. The people in charge of email at colleges or universities, unless there is an explicit policy to the contrary, can store and read anything sent by anyone using an email address at the college or university. Sometimes they do this, very casually breaching privacy.

In addition it seems that certain academic institutions carry out some monitoring of student use of the Internet, as evidenced in the case of a US student who was barred from using a university computer lab after visiting an erotic Website and a site with the title 'Hitler was a pagan' as part of her research on censorship (Marriot, 1999).

You've got a history

Your Web browser records details of all of the Websites you visit. In the case of NN it stores them in a file called 'Global history' which stays on your computer unless you delete the file. If you do delete the file NN will create it again and start over from scratch, but you can just delete the file regularly. If you do not do that, anyone who gets access to your computer can get a complete record of every Website you ever visited. If you are on a network the people who run the network are very likely to be able to get access to this file. If your research is on a sensitive topic you may not want to leave this sort of trail. In the case of IE you can view your history easily through your Web browser. You can determine how much of the history IE stores (IE4: **Edit→Preferences→Advanced→History**; IE5: **Tools→Internet Options→General→History**) and reduce this to just the last few entries so that your history never contains very much information. In IE5 you have the option to 'clear history', deleting your history completely. If you want to delete items already recorded in IE4 just open 'History.html' in a word processor and delete as required. Remember, though, that it is your history the browser relies on when deciding which links to dim. Links deleted from the history no longer appear dimmed and you will need to weigh up which is more important to you: being able to see which sites you've visited, or wiping out your tracks.

Access logs

It is not only your own computer which records your movements on the Net. Every Web server has an access log. It records details about everyone who requests pages from those servers. The people administering the Web server can read the access log. On some computers the access log can be viewed by anyone with an account on that machine and a little bit of knowledge about those kinds of computers.

If you want to avoid leaving a record of your visit in Web server access logs you can start your Web visits by going to **www.anonymizer.com**.

There is little you can do to prevent information about your site visitations being recorded on the computers you visit but you can be aware of it. Below is a sample entry from an access log showing the information recorded.

Me.anycollege.edu - - [19/Feb/1999:13:53:39] "GET/depts/pols/staff.html HTTP/1.0"200 24577

| Your computer's address | Day and time (to the last second) | Document requested | A code which tells you if the document was successfully delivered to you or not. (200 means successful.) |

If your computer has a distinctive id (say it is called **frankblack. anycollege.edu**) it can reveal a lot about your identity. If you are accessing the site from a computer that you do not own or do not have an account on, it does not leave much trace of your identity. Likewise, if you browse the Internet from home via a modem it is likely that the access log will record information about the ISP you use but will not include enough information to identify you.

Day and time is an interesting record because it measures time down to the second. If you have looked at a succession of documents it reveals exactly how long you spent on each one before requesting another.

If you are planning that your alibi for looking at a bomb-making site will be that you stumbled on it by accident and only spent a second looking at it, think again. If those investigating you get hold of the site access log there is a good chance they will know exactly how long you spent on that page, provided you went to another page on the same site afterwards.

It seems only a matter of time, if it has not already happened, before a particularly unscrupulous government or intelligence agency sets up an opposition site, watches the logs and uses them to gather information about its opponents.

Surveillance on the Net

It is a simple matter of fact that people are employed to monitor discussions in email discussion groups. One of those interviewed by Reva Basch described how he had been employed as far back as the mid 1990s to keep an eye on discussions in email groups where a lot of discussion hostile to Shell Oil company took place (1996: 77). Many public relations companies now monitor the Internet on behalf of their paying clients as they have always monitored print publications. One such company is Ewatch (**www.ewatch.com**). Ewatch not only monitors Websites, Usenet, and email discussion groups for paying customers. It also offers a service called CyberSleuth which, for a fee of about $5,000, will uncover the name of a person who is posting messages or providing a Web page anonymously. Online political activism against large companies was, at least in October 1999, one of the types of activities which Ewatch mentioned explicitly. In one sense there is nothing either sinister or surprising about such activities. For governments and large corporations concerned with monitoring hostile comment it is a logical extension of keeping an eye on press reports. The problem lies with the fact that contributors often do not realize just how public their comments are. Neither do they realize how easy it is to monitor the contributions of a particular individual.

In some cases it can be positively dangerous to send email to public lists. During the 1999 conflict over Kosovo anti-government activists in Serbia sent out information detrimental to the Serbian government's cause over the Internet. Considering how easy it is for governments to monitor this sort of activity, it was clear that some people were putting themselves in direct danger by contributing. A US company which already provided a range of services allowing people to use the Web and email anonymously, provided anonymous email and anonymous discussion facilities for such activists (**www.anonymizer.com/kosovo**) allowing them to continue spreading news with less danger of the authorities tracking them down. The same company (**www.anonymizer.com**) provides a range of services, some free, others not, which allow users to use email anonymously and to surf the Web anonymously without leaving traces in access logs. While this sounds quite worthy you may feel differently if someone uses this service to send you a threatening email.

In addition to the monitoring of email lists and public forums by a variety of interested parties, government intelligence agencies routinely monitor email traffic internationally according to several sources.

The New Zealand writer Nicky Hager has described in great detail an international surveillance system called ECHELON. ECHELON is managed by the US National Security Agency (NSA) in conjunction with intelligence agencies in the UK, Canada, Australia and New Zealand. This system routinely intercepts huge volumes of international communications, including email. Using the same keyword-searching techniques familiar to researchers using Internet search engines, it filters out messages of potential interest to the intelligence agencies concerned (Hager, 1996). Clearly, such a system could easily be adapted to monitor newsgroups, email discussion groups and the open Web. It seems highly likely that it is being used for such a purpose and one writer has recently asserted that information is fed into ECHELON from 'taps on the Internet' (Campbell, 1999), whatever that might mean exactly.

Despite all of these grounds for paranoia most researchers will not need to worry. The truth is that your research will only be of interest to those carrying out surveillance if it relates directly to an issue of current political controversy. People engaged in such research always had to deal with such issues anyway. What's most important to note on the Internet is that it is so much easier to be noted and traced than it used to be. There's one other consideration. If researchers in general are tempted to use the most easily available sources in their research there is no reason to believe that intelligence agencies do not suffer from the same malaise. They may come to focus their surveillance increasingly on the Net simply because it is such an easy place to keep an eye on. As a result the intensity of monitoring may increase.

Cookies good and bad

Yum, yum. They sound good enough to eat and certainly do not sound in the least bit sinister. Web servers automatically record information about you in their access log but many Web servers yearn for more information about you. Cookies are the means by which they collect that information. This is what happens. You visit a site that uses cookies. The first time you visit it sends a little bit of data, a cookie, to your computer, sticking it in a file or folder which your browser has set up specifically for storing cookies usually called **cookies.txt** or **MagicCookie** or **cookies**. Usually, it does not tell you it is doing this. Since you are allowing it to send you a Web page it takes the opportunity to send the cookie along with it.

The cookie will include information like the time you requested the page and which page or pages you requested. From now on, every time you go to that site it will have a look at that file and will add lines to it. In addition other sites may read and add lines to that file. Eventually the cookie will contain a lot of information about how you use that particular site. One of the main uses of cookies at the moment is for advertising purposes. If advertisers know which set of pages on a site you are looking at they can tell quite a bit about your interests and display ads targeted at those interests on all the pages you look at. Sites which are linked to one another will often write information to your cookies file which all of these sites can read. The companies which run these sites thus build up quite a complex profile of your use of a variety of sites. If you look at your cookies you'll notice that a lot of them are being sent to **doubleclick.net**, a company which uses the information to customize Website advertising to the interests of individual users.

It may seem a bit odd to you that your computer so casually allows these cookies to be placed on your machine. Most computers will allocate up to 1.2 megs of hard disk to cookies (Pfaffenberger, 1997: 131). The default on IE and NN is to accept cookies but you can change this (in IE4: **Edit→Preferences→Receiving Files→Cookies**; in NN, **Edit→Preferences→ Advanced**). You can set the browser to 'prompt before accepting cookies' or 'warn me before accepting a cookie'. This means that every time a Web server tries to send you a cookie you will be given the option to reject it. You can reject the vast majority of cookies without suffering in any way.

The great disadvantage of being warned every time a cookie is sent is that you will find that a lot of sites try to send you four or five cookies and rejecting them individually slows down your research quite dramatically. It is not a very practical option.

The Netscape option 'accept only cookies that get sent back to the originating server' has the advantage that it only sends cookies to the server you're connecting to. It rejects cookies sent at the same time by advertising companies. An alternative also allowed only in Netscape is to not accept cookies at all.

Certain sites, however, among them the New York Times on the Web, will not operate if you reject all cookies because it uses a cookie for subscriber login information.

In IE5 cookies can be altered at **Tools→Internet Options→Security** (choose the 'Internet' zone) **→Custom Level→Cookies**. It allows you to disable cookies which are already on your computer or to disable them during your Web browsing sessions.

If you change your preferences to prompt before accepting cookies you will see some scary stuff. Not only will you see more cookies than you ever expected; you will also see cookies which have been instructed to stay on your computer until the middle of the next century. Broadly speaking, if a cookie is set to expire after a short time it is less obnoxious. It is also better if a cookie is only sent back to the originating server. Increasingly cookies are sent back to 'all servers in this domain' so that any servers run by the company involved will receive the cookie and information about your browsing preferences will be distributed even further and wider. For more information about cookies see Cookie Central (**www.cookiecentral.com**).

Further measures to secure your privacy

Lehnert (1998: 483) has noted that many online services will provide somewhere on their site a form where you can withhold your consent to their selling your data to other people. She suggests you look for this and withhold consent. This is a good idea in principle but you may find it time consuming. If you do not do this you can pretty much take it for granted that data about you is being sold to commercial companies who will use it to target you for advertising. IE5 provides a facility called 'page hit counting' which essentially allows Channel Contents Providers to record what Web pages you are looking at. You can disable this by turning off the option to 'enable page hit counting' (**Tools→Internet Options→Advanced→Browsing→ Enable page hit counting**).

There are several organizations concerned with the issues surrounding the protection of privacy on the Net, among them EPIC, the Electronic Privacy Information Center (**www.epic.org**), and the Electronic Frontier Foundation (**www.eff.org**).

Censorship

Censorship is the political issue with the most direct implications for social science research on the Internet. Social scientists study aspects of human behaviour including aspects regarded by the society around them as deviant and disreputable. Censorship often cuts researchers off from evidence about these aspects of human behaviour. Definitions of what is deviant vary widely from one country or culture to another, and researchers can easily be cut off from important evidence. Much Internet censorship is ostensibly aimed at protecting children, a legitimate and laudable aim. However, this censorship tends to 'overflow' into control of adult Web use.

In all of the hubbub about the 'dangerous materials' on the Internet it has often been forgotten that many dangerous materials were always available to researchers. Take the example of documents and publications produced by the Nazi regime in Germany. It is generally agreed that the attitudes that informed such documents were and are repugnant and reprehensible. Nonetheless it was always clear that they formed a valid source of material for researchers seeking to understand and record the actions of this regime.

The effect of Internet censorship in many cases is to shut researchers off from the types of materials which they would traditionally have been able to access through archives and special collections in particular libraries. Because the contemporary versions of such materials often do not have a printed counterpart but exist only on the Net, censorship of them actually means that researchers can experience greater limitation on their sources than they did before the advent of the Net.

If censorship spreads it may well be that researchers will be retreating back into the libraries and archives to find the sort of materials which are regarded as too deviant and disreputable to be allowed on the open Web. One of the more subtle effects of censorship is that it makes material more difficult to find. In many cases censorship is not absolute. As anti-censorship activists proudly proclaim, 'the Internet treats censorship as damage and routes around it' (John Gilmore, cited in Grossman, 1997: 13). However, censored information may be forced onto such bumpy muddy backroads that it becomes much more difficult to find. Sensible Internet censors may simply redefine their job. They will not try to eliminate materials, just make them very difficult to find.

Censorship is currently being implemented on the Net at several different levels in ways which are often invisible to the user. Several organizations are working against the imposition of censorship on the Internet, among them the ACLU (American Civil Liberties Union, **www.aclu.org**) and the EFF (Electronic Frontier Foundation, **www.eff.org**).

Government

Governments all over the world have been seeking in the past few years to censor the Net at source, to stop material being made available online in the first place. In certain cases governments have succeeded in extending the effect of their laws half way across the world. When **amazon.com** removed a book on scientology from its online bookshop, because a UK court had halted its distribution in the UK, it was removed from the view of Amazon users not only in the UK, but throughout the world. In this case the book was later made available on the site again but with a feature blocking its sale to UK residents (Cooper, 1999). The nightmare scenario is that the most repressive governments in the world will succeed in removing from the Internet materials illegal in their country and thus remove them from the Internet entirely.

In certain countries the authorities have taken severe measures to restrict access to the Internet, focusing on restricting the access of individual users. China, Singapore and some of the Gulf States are among the leaders in this field (Grossman, 1997: 96–8). In some Gulf States censorship is implemented at national level, service providers being obliged to block access completely to large sections of the Net. In Singapore all Websites and discussion groups are controlled by the Singapore Broadcasting Authority (Rodriguez, 2000).

Blocking and filtering

Censorship at the level of government is one thing but censorship at lower levels has also become increasingly common. An interesting feature of censorship on the Internet is that it operates at so many different levels. Censorship can be implemented on the Web browser software itself. IE, for example, allows you to block sites according to ratings using its 'Content Advisor' (IE4: **Edit→Preferences→Web browser→Ratings**; IE5: **Tools→ Internet Options→Content→Content Advisor**). Censorship can also be implemented by other software you can buy for your computer (such as Cyber Patrol or Surf Watch). It can also be implemented at the level of the local network, or even by the search engines out on the open Web (AltaVista's Family Filter, for example). In some of these cases you will have the choice to accept or decline the censorship but in other cases censorship may be in operation which you are unaware of. One of the more disturbing features of Internet censorship is that it can be so difficult to detect.

Blocking   Blocking software works on the principle of blocking specified sites. The list of blocked sites varies from one piece of blocking software to another. In the early days software would block access to a list of specific Web addresses. Lists were updated as new unsuitable sites appeared.

Blocking software is aimed particularly at blocking pornographic sites from the eyes of children. Some libraries installed it, however, and used it to block adult access too. One of the big problems with this type of software is that it generally does not announce itself and you often do not know sites are being blocked unless you try to connect to a blocked site. You may need to ask locally to find out whether such software is installed on your local network.

Blocking software is a poor censor since it has to be updated regularly. Although it does not guarantee to block everything it will very effectively block you from large quantities of material.

Because it focuses so heavily on pornography and erotica much blocking software is not that serious a hindrance to most social science researchers. It does cause problems for those carrying out research into human sexuality. The potential of this type of software does have serious implications, however. If universities routinely use blocking software on their networks, thus almost invisibly restricting access by huge numbers of academic users, both researchers and undergraduates, it becomes a simple matter to adjust the blocking software to block sites which are deemed politically undesirable. Even in western democracies there have always been strong impulses towards the restriction of certain political views. The problem for researchers interested in studying or assessing these views is that Net censorship will be so subtle and invisible that it will be hard to tell if those views are there in the first place. Unless institutions provide lists of blocked sites it will be hard to tell what the researcher is being cut off from.

Filtering   'Filtering' relies on using keywords to block unsuitable sites. It must have seemed a good idea at the time, making it easy to identify sites to block and to keep such a list up to date. However, it is much cruder than assessing sites individually and such software packages have famously blocked not only pornographic sites but also sites concerned with sex and health and the sites of gay and lesbian political organizations (Grossman, 1997: 125–6; ACLU, 1997).

Rating

Rating, often represented as a mild and benevolent form of censorship, actually contains the seeds of a censorship far more widespread than is possible through the earlier blocking methods. It contains within it a very dangerous principle, the principle of blocking everything that is not rated while restricting access to rated materials according to their individual ratings.

Web documents are to be rated like films or video games are. It sounds a reasonable enough comparison until you realize that print literature is not rated and that the Net is at least as easily comparable with print literature as with film.

The problem with rating is that its effects will spread far and wide. At least blocking software was confined to individual computers and networks. Rating has a ripple effect.

Since it is impossible for any one body to rate pages systematically the favoured method of rating is self-rating (ACLU, 1997). People who put material on the Web will be expected to rate it themselves. If they rate it incorrectly they leave themselves open to prosecution, depending on what country they live in. If they do not rate it they risk being left so far out on the fringes of the Net that no one will ever see their sites. The ACLU has pointed out that small groups will find it hard to devote the time and money required to ensure they are rating in strict accordance with the law. Every time a page is changed or updated the possibility exists that it may have moved into a different rating. Larger, more powerful organizations will have less difficulty.

But why should unrated sites become so obscure? Surely they will be as visible as ever? For ratings to be an effective means of control unrated sites must be excluded from view. They muddy the issue. The danger is that if rating spreads far and wide enough, ultimately the big search engines and subject guides that most users rely on will limit their searches to rated sites. Rated sites will become wary of linking to unrated sites and the links from the rated to the unrated Web will decrease, making the unrated Web even less visible to most users. Even if the search engines continue to list unrated sites, they may give higher priority to rated sites, using the fact of rating as a mark of quality.

Ultimately the threat of censorship of the Internet is not that it will completely block information but that the marginal, the activist, the dissident voices which are of interest to social scientists in particular, will become so hidden away that they will be almost impossible to find. The marginal will sink so far below the surface that it will effectively be invisible to most users.

Censorship and privacy

Certain aspects of censorship have direct implications for privacy. N2H2, a company which provides a 'network-based filtering service' offered, at least in the summer of 1999, to provide the people who run the networks with reports which include lists of 'clients who most often requested blocked sites' (**www.n2h2.com/main_isps.htm**). By late 2000 it seems this was no longer explicitly mentioned on the site. There is the potential for such information to be abused, to put it mildly.

Bringing order to the chaos

In the midst of the chaos on the open Web a number of standards are emerging which suggest that, in a few years' time, there will be much more order out there.

One of the most infuriating problems for the researcher has been the fact that documents move at the whim of Webmasters. The URL, the one and only identifying mark common to all Web documents, can change. It massively disrupts the work of the search engines and subject guides dealt with in the next two chapters. One changed URL can render all links to a page useless. Sometimes hundreds or even thousands of links are affected.

In the last few years Webmasters have begun to realize the importance of keeping documents at the same URL and URL stability is increasing, more quickly in some areas than others. Stable URLs are more common in subject areas in which technical skills are more important and in which there is greater experience in use of the Web. Engineering sites, for example, are very likely to have stable URLs while classical studies sites are quite unlikely to (Parrott, 1999). As experience builds up in all disciplines good habits should spread.

In addition to this many large organizations and companies have settled on their Web addresses and in fact are 'branding' them, making sure people get to know them. They are unlikely now to move to new addresses.

XML

If stable URLs offer the hope that at least those items that are on the Web will stand still for a while, a new standard called XML (Extensible Markup Language) promises that they will be infinitely more searchable than they are now. XML offers a set of standards which will allow Web documents to be structured as clearly as items in a database.

XML allows for the creation of different types of documents with different sets of fields. Thus an academic article could be divided into the fields which the article databases use. You could restrict your Web search to documents which use this academic article template and search them just as you would search an article database.

There might be a standard template for a conference timetable, for example. You could restrict your search to conference timetables and look only for conferences that take place between certain dates or that feature particular speakers. All of this will be possible only if the people creating these documents start to use the XML standards to create standard templates for different documents. If and when this does happen it will make it possible to use the open Web to conduct the sort of searches which are now only possible on expensive databases. For further information see the XML site of W3C, the World Wide Web Consortium (**www.w3.org/xml**), and Bosak and Bray (1999).

Dublin CORE

Dublin CORE (**purl.oclc.org/dc**) is a set of standards which shares a common purpose with XML – that of making Web documents more structured and more standardized. However, Dublin CORE approaches the issue from quite a different angle. It emerges from debates among those concerned with cataloguing Web documents and Websites for libraries and archives. It consists of a list of core identifying elements which should be identifiable in all Web documents, from author to date of 'publication'. They are called the Dublin CORE because they were agreed at a meeting in Dublin, Ireland. The prime aim of Dublin CORE is to ensure that documents are fully citable. It relies on authors making an effort to ensure that all of these elements can be identified in their documents. It is a set of guidelines for good practice by Web page authors. If you want library catalogues to catalogue your Website make sure they can identify the most important of these elements. A full list of the Dublin CORE elements is provided in the inset.

Dublin CORE elements

There are fifteen Dublin CORE elements. These are the elements which professional cataloguers seek to identify when they catalogue an Internet resource, whether it be a single Web page or an entire site. You can get more detailed information about each of these elements at the Dublin CORE Metadata Initiative Website (**purl.oclc.org/dc**).

Title: The name of the resource
Creator: The author, whether an individual or an organization
Subject: Keywords or classification marks which indicate the subject the resource relates to
Description: An abstract, table of contents or short description of the resource

Publisher: The person or organization responsible for making the resource available

Contributor: A person or organization which has contributed to the content of the resource

Date: Usually date of creation or last update of the resource

Type: The general category or genre which the resource belongs to. For example, whether it is an academic article, a novel, a news service or some other type of resource

Format: For example, whether the resource is a text document, a video clip, a photo or some other type of resource

Identifier: A unique identifying number or code, such as a URL or an ISBN (International Standard Book Number)

Source: Information about any resource which the Internet resource derives from, the printed version, for example, if a printed version exists

Language: The language the resource is in

Relation: 'A reference to a related resource'

Coverage: For example, the time period or geographic area the resource deals with

Rights: Information about copyright and related rights
(Dublin CORE, 1999)

Closing doors on the open Web

A key mark distinguishing the open Web from the big article databases is that access to sites is free. This was regarded in the early days of the Net as one of its defining features. All across the open Web now, information is being gradually sealed off from non-paying users. Colleges which once allowed anyone to access their course materials and archives on the Web are increasingly treating their online materials as services which they can charge for. As academic staff are called on to provide material for online courses which attract paying students, universities may become less keen on staff distributing bibliographies or other teaching materials across the Net for free. As more and more journals put articles online they will have ever more reason to pressure academic writers not to put up freely available copies of that work on the Web. If the Web is like an ocean of information then the best beaches are being fenced off at a rapid pace.

The fencing off of useful data is not the only worrying development. In the course of 1999 a private company was given responsibility for running a search engine which would provide a comprehensive search of US government sites on the Web (Northern Light US Government Search: **www.usgovsearch.northernlight.com**, dealt with in detail in chapter 3). It charges a fee for this service. That is, although in theory the documents are freely available to use, the quickest, most comprehensive and efficient means of searching them will cost you. This puts a new twist on the concept of free information. It raises the possibility that the open Web will remain a chaotic, poorly organized realm which is difficult and time consuming to search. Those without access to pay services will waste huge amounts of time using the inefficient free search services.

Meanwhile pay search services will develop which efficiently and comprehensively search particular heavily used sections of the Web. If that is the case it will have far-reaching consequences for the way in which researchers use the Web, for the very definition of the open Web and for the contents of the Web. In conjunction with the phenomenon of rating, it raises the possibility that the large sections of the Web which remain outside the scope of these pay services and which are unrated will become ever more difficult to search. The truly open Web may become the second-rate preserve of poorer and more isolated researchers, those not connected to libraries and universities which subscribe to the pay search services. The marginal will be ever more marginal. To social science researchers interested in these voices from the edge it will be ever more important to understand how to search the open Web effectively. The following two chapters deal with searching the open Web in two broadly different ways, by subject and by keyword. Between them they provide the information necessary to do efficient and comprehensive searches of the open Web for material relevant to your research.

6

Searching by subject

Introduction

This chapter deals with services which organize and categorize Web pages according to the subject areas they deal with. The great majority of Internet users prefer to use the keyword search engines, which are the subject of the next chapter. Given that, it's worth starting this chapter by explaining the decision to deal with subject searching before dealing with keyword searching.

Keyword search engines allow you to lift items relevant to you out of a vast universe of Web documents. They are so popular because when most people go to the Web they are looking for one specific item or a few closely related items. They want to find the cure for an illness, the result of a game, information about a particular event or animal or heating-system or cloud formation, and so on.

The researcher needs to use the Web in a very different way. Certainly, there will be plenty of occasions when you will be looking for very specific items and when the keyword search engines will be the obvious tools to use in your search. But when the research process begins it is not dominated by such specific queries. Research involves an exploration of a broad area of knowledge, an exploration of what has been written and is being written in that area. The best starting point for such an exploration of the open Web is the subject guides. A good subject guide is not only more comprehensive than a keyword search engine, but also more likely to be up to date. Even where a search engine does bring up the material you are looking for a good subject guide can provide a shorter route to the same information (see Lehnert (1998: 165–7) for an illustration of this). Before you go near the keyword searchers do a good thorough search of the Web via the main subject guides in your area. You will find that by the time you come to use the keyword search engines most of the documents they retrieve will come from sites and sources familiar to you. The keyword search engines can be used for mopping-up purposes, identifying the odds and ends which the subject guides have missed or for answering very specific detailed questions which arise in the later stages of research.

Subject classification on the Web

Classification by subject is the core organizing principle for all materials stored in libraries. You can search for books by author and title but on the shelves they are grouped by subject, every book allocated a number according to its subject and surrounded by books dealing with the same subject.

Since Web documents often lack dates, titles and author details it's no surprise to find that they are not classified by subject either. In the world of print a lot of effort goes into classifying books by subject. Publishers usually provide indications of the subject areas their books relate to. Professional library cataloguers classify books according to the schemes operating in their libraries or in their country as a whole. It is a massive, ongoing and time-consuming task.

The vast majority of Web documents make no attempt to signal which subject areas they might belong to. Those concerned with classifying and cataloguing Web documents work by and large without help from those who produce the documents.

Since the earliest days of the Web people have made attempts to group or classify Web pages by subject, approaching the task from different angles, using various schemes of classification. These range in sophistication from basic 'link' pages which provide hyperlinks to almost every item on the Web which is even vaguely related to a particular topic, to the more recent efforts of professional library cataloguers to catalogue Web materials with the same precision and care which goes into the cataloguing of books.

Cataloguing the Web

Library cataloguers began a few years ago to catalogue Web resources using the established library classification schemes. Traditional cataloguing methods have been adapted for the Web, standards and rules have been laid out and this work is now well under way.

There are major problems associated with any attempt to catalogue the Web but current cataloguing efforts are showing that it's not by any means impossible. To the argument that the Web is too vast to ever fully catalogue, the cataloguers reply – that's OK, we're not even going to try to catalogue all of it (Jul *et al.*, 1998). To the argument that much of the material out there defies cataloguing they give much the same response. Cataloguers have never tried to catalogue the entire world of printed material. They do not routinely catalogue beermats, posters or handbills so why would they concern themselves with the Internet equivalent of these materials? Problems do remain, in particular the fact that Internet resources are prone to changes of address or to suddenly flickering out of existence, but these are problems which are being addressed, through a conscious decision to focus on cataloguing major stable sites.

Hundreds of US university libraries are engaged in cataloguing Internet resources, including them in their online library catalogues. Subject expertise is employed in deciding which resources should be catalogued. In the case of Harvard University, to take one example, book selectors, professionals responsible for identifying books which the library should buy in their particular subject area, are the people responsible for selecting Internet resources to be catalogued (thanks to Jeffrey Beale for this information). These libraries contribute their catalogued records of Internet resources to a 'Union Catalog' run by OCLC.

OCLC, which provides several article databases and which was discussed previously in chapter 3, provides a database of these records called NetFirst. Each record includes Library of Congress and Dewey Decimal Class numbers, the two major library classification systems (*College and Research Libraries News*, Nov. 1998, 59: 6).

Unfortunately you can only get access if your institution has subscribed. You can, however, get access to individual library catalogues such as Harvard's (see chapter 3 for information on connecting to online catalogues) and search the 'Networked Resources' in the catalogues.

As of yet NetFirst only includes a tiny proportion of academic resources on the Web. As time goes on and the number of items catalogued begins to build up it may well become one of the most comprehensive, and certainly the best organized, sources of information about Internet resources.

In the near future academic researchers may well find that their Internet searches begin not on the open Web through a subject or a keyword guide, but through a library catalogue or database which allows them to search the Net just as we currently search for books, by subject keyword and by classification numbers. When that 'glorious' day comes many of the Web subject guides will become redundant to the researcher. However, the best of them will remain useful – those which provide detailed descriptions and assessments of resources and which try to provide a comprehensive listing of all of the resources available in one small subject area. Library cataloguing will not replace these.

Understanding subject guides

A subject guide is a Web service which provides links to other Websites and documents on other Websites and which organizes these links by subject. They are also referred to variously as subject indexes, subject catalogues, directories and clearing-houses. They range widely in terms of scale. The smallest subject guides are those which deal with one very specific topic, gathering together links on a particular conflict, for example, or a current political issue. They make no further classification of these links because it is clear they all relate to one very specialized area of human knowledge. They make no pretence at fitting into any higher or broader scheme of classification. Despite this, such guides are an incredibly valuable research resource. If you find such a guide in your subject area it may well mean that half of your Web searching has been done, depending on how good that guide is.

INCORE country guides on armed conflicts

A classic example of such guides are the guides to current armed conflicts (**www.incore.ulst.ac.uk/cds/countries**) produced by INCORE (the Initiative on Conflict Resolution and Ethnicity).

One step up from these guides, in terms of scale, are the services which aim to guide you through a broader subject area. These guides are consciously engaged in attempts at classification, but only within their own particular field. Thus a service like the International Security Guide (**www.isn.ethz.ch/linkslib**) from the ISN (International Relations and Security Network), concerned with international relations, security and conflict and peace studies, is organized into sub-sections for different aspects of the subject.

Guides on this scale provide excellent introductory sources for researchers, not least because they tend to catalogue and classify sites rather than individual documents. They provide a starting point for exploration rather than providing a comprehensive listing of every relevant document out there.

At the far end of the scale are those services which aspire to being universal, which try to provide a guide to Web resources on every subject and which often describe themselves as directories. I refer to them as 'universal subject guides'. They range widely in quality, from the categories and channels provided by the keyword search engines (which by and large are of very low quality) to services such as Yahoo which, for all its flaws, makes a brave attempt at classifying huge numbers of Web pages.

In general, the more ambitious a guide is in terms of scale, the poorer it's quality. The more you try to cover the harder it is to cover it all well. That said, not all of the smaller and more focused guides are of high quality. There

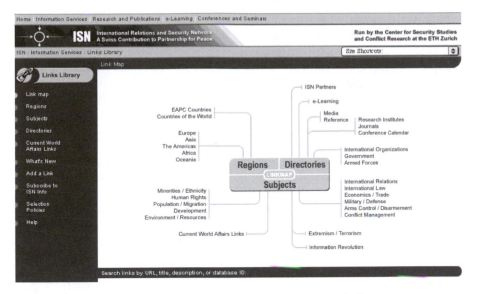

International Security Guide from the ISN: part of the Virtual Library

are many small guides out there which are worse than useless, simply providing lists of links with minimal description.

Using subject guides effectively

Before talking about how to find subject guides it's important to know how to judge how useful a guide is. As a rule, the less description of links it provides, the less useful it is. The more precise those descriptions are, the better it is. A subject guide which consists of links with no descriptions at all is usually to be avoided, unless it's a straightforward list of items such as a list of universities or of institutes or of government offices, which do not really require extra description.

If it's a large complex guide, the next step is to explore how the guide is organized with a view to identifying the categories relevant to you. You can browse down through the categories which look most promising. Many guides allow you to do a keyword search of the category headings which they use. It's worth doing this using broad search terms before you search the guide as a whole.

When you have identified and explored the main categories of interest to you, you can then do a keyword search of the entire guide to mop up any useful links or categories you might have missed. If you find a category which is directly related to your work and which is extremely useful, bookmark it. Most guides are organized so you can bookmark individual categories. You can check the category again several months later when you are checking all your major sources for new material. It's probably not worth conducting another search of the entire guide.

One of the most important marks of quality of a subject guide is how hard it tries to be both comprehensive and selective. The ideal subject guide is one which collects together everything relevant to a particular subject which is of reasonably good quality. It is about excluding as well as including. In truth only the smallest, most specialized guide can give such attention to quality and completeness. When a guide links you to materials which vary widely in quality and includes materials of minimal relevance or value, it is wasting your time. You have to question then whether the guide as a whole is useful to you.

Finding subject guides

There are a number of services which gather together lists of subject guides. These services vary in the degree of authority they exercise over the guides they list. You won't find all of the subject guides through them but you'll find a large proportion. Appendix 2 of this book provides a list of high-quality subject guides in a range of social science subjects. You can check these first to see if it lists a guide in your subject area.

The Argus Clearinghouse (**www.clearinghouse.net/searchbrowse.html**)

This is a searchable guide to subject guides. It has no authority over the guides which it lists. It exercises some quality control over the guides it chooses to list, not listing guides of very poor quality and awarding ratings to the individual guides. It provides descriptions of guides and classifies them under different subject headings. You can browse through the subject categories or search by keyword. The categories reflect Argus's focus on materials of interest to academic researchers. Note that if you search by keyword you are not searching the guides themselves, just the Argus descriptions of the guides. Use the simplest, broadest terms when searching. If looking for information relating to the Polish language do separate searches on 'Poland', 'Polish', 'language' and 'linguistic'.

Always remember: Argus has no authority over any of these guides and many of the guides Argus links you to are actually part of the Virtual Library, dealt with below.

The Virtual Library (**www.vlib.org**)

This is the original guide to subject guides. The VL appears to the user as a single organization, providing hundreds of guides on a vast array of subjects. It is in reality just an umbrella title covering guides which vary widely in quality and which are nearly all produced by different individuals and organizations. It works like this. You set up a subject guide, you contact the VL and say you'd like your guide to be part of the VL. It then provides a link to your site while you in return put its logo up on your guide, signifying that your guide is part of the VL.

The most useful thing the VL does from a researcher's point of view is to categorize guides by subject, making it easier to find guides relevant to you by browsing. As you'd expect you can also search guide titles (though not the guide contents) by keyword.

Virtual Library on Migration and Ethnic Relations, from ERCOMER

Some of the VL guides are huge complex guides in their own right, such as the Virtual Library on Migration and Ethnic Relations (**www.ercomer. org/wwwvl**) run by ERCOMER (European Research Centre on Migration and Ethnic Relations), which amounts to a collection of guides in its own right. At the other extreme some of the VL guides are of such poor quality as to be useless.

The fact that the VL makes no attempt to provide guides comprehensively for all areas of human knowledge means that the areas covered by guides are determined by those who create the guides. As a result, coverage is very uneven. You may be lucky enough to find a VL guide on your precise area of interest. It's also possible that you won't find a guide even remotely relevant to you.

About.com (**about.com**)

This service differs from Argus and the VL in two important ways. Firstly, it does have direct authority over the guides it provides, commissioning guides on particular subjects, trying to ensure all guides have the same basic format and are clearly all part of a single, coherent service. About.com at least attempts to be comprehensive to a certain degree, to provide guides in the areas of greatest public interest. In the second place it is, unlike Argus and the VL, a commercial company whose priorities are not shaped by academic research interests. As a result you are far less likely to get a guide on an obscure area of academic research in About.com than you are in the other services.

About.com provides a collection of several hundred subject guides, organized by subject category. A large number of the guides relate to areas of current political controversy, and are to be found under the 'News Issues' subject heading. Also of interest to social scientists is the 'Culture' section. Each of the guides is run by an individual who often puts quite a personal stamp on the guide. The guides are rich in descriptions of the sites they link to. They favour quality not quantity, linking to a small number of key sites in the area. Despite this the guides do vary widely in quality. More care has been taken in some of them than others. In some guides descriptions of links are sparse. In others there seems to have been quite a careless selection of materials. Links are provided, it seems, to half-a-dozen sites the guide author happens to have visited. There is no attempt to isolate the most important or useful sites in the area.

The fact that About.com, unlike VL or Argus, attempts to have a comprehensive collection of guides, to have a guide on 'everything', has its drawbacks. The fact that they want to plug the gaps means that some of the guides are written by people who are clearly not expert in the subject they are covering and whose selection of material is not particularly well informed. Such a guide can actually mislead the researcher. Because it's so professional looking it gives the impression that the sites it links to are important and worthwhile. Often they're not.

Guides to social science resources

Two major services act as guides to social science resources in general. These services do not cover any single subject in real detail but this is more than balanced by their dedication to serving the specific needs of the academic researcher in the social sciences. They are both funded by government sources and are intended to serve the research communities in their respective countries. The similarities between the two services are recognized by them and each of them provides a 'mirror' (an exact and regularly updated copy) of the other's site on their own site.

Scout Report Archives (**scout.cs.wisc.edu/archive**)

The Internet Scout Report (see inset in chapter 4) provides short descriptions of Internet resources. The Scout Report Archives provide the accumulated product of previous editions of the Scout Report, including the Scout Report on Social Sciences, in the form of a searchable database. This creates a very sophisticated guide to major online resources in the social sciences.

These archives cannot compete with the major subject guides in terms of volume. They classify thousands (rather than tens of thousands) of sites. They do not pretend to be comprehensive. What the archives lack in volume, though, they more than make up for in quality. The Scout Report Archives are no match for a good subject guide devoted to one particular subject but they are a great source of information on general social science resources.

Some of the resources they point to are individual documents dealing with very specific topics but typically the archives point to major resources of interest to people across a range of disciplines. Thus they are an excellent source of information about online data sources, like censuses, or about organizations, research projects and archives which span the disciplines.

You can start your search of the archives by using very specific terms, to check if there is anything directly relevant to your subject. After that try using simple, more general search terms relating to your broad subject area to find major sources that might be useful.

The Scout Report archives allow far more sophisticated searching than most subject guides do. You can search by title (of resources described), do a keyword search of the descriptions of resources, and search by subject keyword.

Only some of the records have been fully catalogued (see also Glassel and Wells, 1998). If you browse through the subject categories, which is well worth doing, you will only see those resources which have been fully catalogued. Subject categories are based on the Library of Congress subject headings and classification numbers which many people will be familiar with from their own library. However, they only use the broad class code so you cannot isolate records relating to a very specific area. They also classify documents according to their own system of classification, CYRUS (Classify Your Resources Using Scout).

The Scout Report Archives use a clear system of classification based on familiar academic standards. They cater specifically to social science researchers. They draw on subject expertise and devote time and care to classifying materials. For all of these reasons these archives are infinitely more valuable to the researcher than many of the guides which cover a much larger number of sources.

SOSIG (*Social Science Information Gateway,* **sosig.esrc.ac.uk**)

Pronounced 'sausage', this is in many ways the British counterpart to the Scout Report archives. It deals exclusively with the social sciences and aims to serve academic researchers. It is organized quite differently from the Scout Report archives but it also classifies records according to an established library classification scheme, in this case the 'Universal Decimal Classification Scheme' widely used in the UK and Ireland.

Unlike the Scout Report archives SOSIG does try to be comprehensive. It seems each subject category and sub-category has plenty of items in it. Each record contains a description of a resource and a set of keywords for that resource. Many categories are maintained by academic institutions or organizations which have an expertise in the subject area. You can restrict a keyword search to a particular subject category. Choose 'just this section' from within the category.

A good SOSIG sub-category on your subject can be every bit as useful as a good subject guide in your specific area. SOSIG's best features are the fact that it is targeted directly at the academic researcher and that it uses a classification system designed for such users.

Guides provided by university libraries

Many university libraries provide guides to Internet resources, arranged by subject. While usually extremely broad in their focus they have in their favour the fact that they are concerned with academia. As a result they tend to organize materials according to subject categories commonly used in universities. They tend to exercise a certain degree of quality control, including resources because they are useful and not just because they fit neatly into a certain category. These libraries can often be very selective indeed, confining their guides to resources of direct relevance to college students' studies.

If your own university or university library produces such a guide it's worth looking at it before going to other universities. Local guides are often tailored to the needs of students at that university.

Since these guides try to cover a whole world of academic knowledge, from medicine to art history, they can often be so broad as to be useless. Some guides do, however, emphasize topics in which their university has special expertise and thus certain sub-sections of these guides are quite specialized and thus quite useful. You won't know until you've had a quick look at the categories relevant to you. There is such a huge overlap in coverage between all of these various guides that you will very quickly encounter the law of diminishing returns if you use more than one such guide. Given this overlap and the related waste of human resources in compiling such guides, it seems inevitable that libraries will eventually co-operate with each other in producing them. If that happens on a large scale these guides would be much more detailed and consequently much more useful to the researcher. A few of the guides are described here.

The Librarians' Index to the Internet (**lii.org**) This is a guide, organized by subject, to Web resources which have been evaluated by librarians. It is in the process of being catalogued according to established library cataloguing procedures.

Infomine (**infomine.ucr.edu/main.html**) Infomine is the Scholarly Internet Resource Collections produced by librarians from several campuses in the University of California system. It is organized by subject, including a category for 'Social Sciences, Humanities, General Reference…'. You can also search it by keyword. It provides short descriptions of the sites it links to. Many of these sites are themselves subject guides devoted to specific topics and you will already be aware of them through the Argus Clearinghouse and the Virtual Library.

Princeton University Library (**libweb.princeton.edu/databases/web_subject_guides.html**) Princeton University Library has produced a collection of 'web subject guides'. The guides are produced by individual members of staff with expertise in the various subject areas. They vary greatly in quality and some of the weaker guides provide very little description of the sites they link to. In some cases they guide users to resources in the Princeton Library as well as to Web resources.

Other guides catering to academic researchers

The guides dealt with here are not compiled by universities but cater to academic users more directly than the major commercial guides do, focusing on subjects of academic interest.

College and Research Libraries News (**www.ala.org/acrl/resrces.html**)   This is a publication of the US Association of College and Research Libraries. Each month it includes an article on Internet resources on a particular subject. The articles are written by librarians and are generally of high quality, including short descriptions of sites. A very limited number of topics have been covered but if your topic is among them this could be a useful resource.

Explore the Internet (US Library of Congress) (**lcweb.loc.gov/global/subject. html**)   The Library of Congress provides a small collection of what it calls 'topical guides' to Internet resources. The guides vary widely in quality.

Britannica.com (**www.britannica.com**)   In addition to the full text of the *Encyclopaedia Britannica*, britannica.com provides a guide to Internet resources organized by major subject areas. It provides brief and useful descriptions of the sites it links you to (calling them 'reviews') and rates sites according to their quality. It points you to site home pages rather than to individual documents within sites. Quite a few of the sites it points you to are subject guides but, if you've checked the Virtual Library and the Argus Clearinghouse, you'll have found many of these already. The advantage of the Britannica service lies with its selectivity, trying to identify and include only sites which seem useful.

  To browse the different sub-categories choose a category from the explore menu on the site home page. Then choose 'Internet Guide' from within that category.

Academic Info (**www.academicinfo.net**)   This guide is run by an individual who provides links to resources of interest to students. The 'reference' section (**www.academicinfo.net/ref.html**) includes a list of links to the subject guides of several English-speaking universities.

Northern Light Special Editions (**special.northernlight.com**)   The Northern Light service has been dealt with previously in chapter 3. It is primarily an article database service but its 'Special Editions' are effectively subject guides which focus on major news and current events. They differ from other subject guides in that they bring together both external links to sources on the open Web and links to individual articles from Northern Light databases. A novel feature of the Special Editions is that articles which you would normally be charged for are available free if they are part of a Special Edition.

Universal subject guides

The Internet is awash now with subject guides or directories, sometimes calling themselves search engines, which partition the entire world of human knowledge into browseable subject headings. They differ from the guides already dealt with in that their ambitions are universal: to guide you to everything from cars and holidays to zoology and astrophysics.

As a rule, the more you try to cover the less well you cover it and these universal guides bear this out. Although they vary in quality the worst of them are horrendously bad.

Where the best of these guides come into their own is in providing lists of things which fall naturally into list form. If you want the Website for a particular embassy, for a sports team, for a newspaper, for a university, for a town, for anything that can be easily classified and categorized, it's worth checking a universal subject guide first to see if it has the category the item would fit into.

If you just need 'something' about a topic, 'something', for example, about the French Foreign Legion, you'll nearly always find it in one of the universal guides without the confusion of dealing with the huge number of results you would get from a keyword search engine.

The universal guides are, apart from this, of limited use to the researcher for a number of reasons. They exercise minimal quality control. They include links of very poor quality, barely relevant to the category they've been included in. They will often miss the central resources on a particular subject because they make no attempt to be comprehensive. Some of the guides seem to place higher priority on filling up categories with items than ensuring the items are useful. The universal guides generally provide no description or minimal description of the resources they link to. This almost defeats the purpose of categorizing them in the first place. They are hardly any more use than a keyword search result using an appropriate keyword (say, 'French Foreign Legion', to use the example just mentioned).

Classification and the universal guides

Subject classification   Universal subject guides generally make up their own classification schemes. Not only are the categories crude but often only minimal effort is invested in deciding which category an item belongs to. Many items end up in the wrong category. While some such services pretend to be a comprehensive categorization of the Web, no 'universal' subject guide covers anything more than a tiny fraction of Web pages. They don't come close to covering the volume of materials which the keyword search engines cover.

Most of the 'universal' subject guides are commercial operations. When 'Autos' or 'Shopping' is one of the ten main categories into which all human knowledge is divided it's a pretty good indication that commercial considerations have played a major role in shaping the classification system. As a result they are of strictly limited use for academic research.

Geographical classification   Because there are no national borders out on the open Web, because researchers anywhere in the world can use subject guides

```
Explore Excite
Autos          Health        Shopping
Business       Investing     Auctions
Careers        Lifestyle     Gift Zone
Computers      Music         Bikinis & More
Education      Real Estate   People/Chat
EntertainmentRelationships Personals
Family         Sports        Zink Teens
Games          Travel        Chat!
```

*Subject categories in Excite (**www.excite.com**)*

no matter where they are based, it is tempting to see these guides as neutral, international sources of information. In reality, the national backgrounds of these guides shape their structures in fundamental ways, most importantly in how they organize and classify the universe of human knowledge.

In addition to classifying by subject most of the universal subject guides classify geographically by country and region. In some guides the 'regional' section will include listings for every country in the world and for every region in the USA. In others 'regional' covers US regions with country categories organized separately.

If an item relates to a particular US region it will generally be placed in the appropriate regional sub-section. If it relates to a particular country other than the USA, say to Germany, or Thailand, or Kenya, there is a good chance it will be classified under the appropriate country category. So far, so good, this sounds fair enough. However, one level of geographical organization is effectively excluded from this scheme; the USA. Materials which relate to the USA as a whole tend not to be placed in any regional or country category by many US subject guides. They are placed under the appropriate subject headings, with important implications for the use of such guides as research resources. Thus an item relating to the US legal system will be classified under 'law' while an item on the German legal system is most likely to be classified under 'Germany'; an item on the US military will be under 'military' while an item on the Thai military will go under 'Thailand'. The effect is that the supposedly general subject categories are in fact very strongly tilted towards US material. The main categories such as 'Economy', 'Business', 'Government', 'automobiles' are effectively 'US Economy', 'US Business', 'US Government' and 'US automobiles', while also including material of specifically international interest (that is, related to more than one country).

If you are studying any country other than the USA you should probably head first to the relevant section in the 'country' or 'regional' categories. Afterwards you can see if the general subject categories contain relevant material.

Trying to be an expert on everything   If you're going to provide a guide to 'everything' you really need to employ someone who knows 'everything' or employ a lot of people who between them could come close to making such a claim. The latter course is the one chosen by encyclopaedias, getting contributions from a huge number of highly qualified experts. There is no evidence that any of the universal subject guides even attempt this. This seriously diminishes their reliability. People with a minimal knowledge of economics, or of psychology, or anthropology, or any other social science discipline you care to mention, are engaged in classifying sites in these areas, and often in classifying them wrongly. More serious than this is the fact that people based in one country (in most cases the USA) are classifying materials from all over the world with only the barest knowledge of the countries they're dealing with. The results can be quite disastrous. To classify newspapers from around the world, for example, requires some 'real-world' knowledge of the countries those newspapers are published in. It's important to be able to distinguish between magazines and daily newspapers and political party publications. The boundaries between them are not always obvious. When classifiers step outside their own country their reliability tends to decline, in certain instances plummeting dramatically. In short, beware of subject guides which classify material which is beyond their understanding, particularly material from countries which the classifiers clearly know little about.

The blurred boundary between subject guides and search engines

Most of the keyword search engines have their own crude subject guides or will also automatically do a search of one of the guides listed below when you search them. What makes them search engines is the fact that their main emphasis is placed on keyword searching of the open Web. As a result their subject guides are quite crude and underdeveloped. They are dealt with in full in chapter 7.

Many of the universal subject guides dealt with below also do a keyword search of the open Web, just in case you weren't confused enough already. These keyword searches are often carried out by one of the main keyword search engines. Thus, Yahoo will search its own directory first and after that will run a search on Google, one of the main keyword search engines. What marks them out as subject guides is the fact that the prime emphasis is on the guide while the keyword searches are usually performed for them by other companies. Thus, the results from Google which Yahoo presents to you are exactly the same as the results you'd get if you searched Google directly. Since subject directories respond better to simple queries and keyword search engines to complex queries you will need to search them both separately in any case, and I would suggest you ignore the keyword search engine results which come at the end of many a subject guide results page.

Yahoo! (**www.Yahoo.com**)

This is the mother and father of all universal subject guides, probably the first service with such universal ambitions. Yahoo is often mistaken for a keyword search engine, but it is actually a subject guide. When you search Yahoo by keyword you are only searching through items which Yahoo has catalogued, a smaller selection of material than you search through the key-word search engines, but a far larger selection than most subject guides provide. Yahoo employs over 150 editors to check sites for inclusion in the guide. The description of Yahoo here draws in part on an article by two Yahoo cataloguers, Callery and Tracy-Proulx (1997).

The key to making optimum use of Yahoo is understanding its classification system. Every category within Yahoo has its own Web page. Each of these category pages contains links to external Web pages which fit into that category and links to Yahoo sub-categories within that category. Only at the very bottom of the Yahoo subject tree will you find pages which only have external links. At the higher levels category pages consist primarily of links to sub-categories. In your early searches of Yahoo your prime task should be to identify useful categories, to thoroughly explore those categories and to bookmark the most useful categories so that you can check them for new additions in a few months' time. One of the great joys of Yahoo is that you can restrict a keyword search to one category or sub-category of Yahoo, searching only that category and every sub-category below it.

Understanding Yahoo categories   A look at one Yahoo sub-category will illustrate some of the main features of Yahoo. Social Science is one of the main top-level categories in Yahoo. It has over forty sub-categories of which one is Ethnic Studies. The numbers after the categories indicate how many links in total are included in that category.

This includes the total number of all links within the sub-categories which come under that category. One of the sub-categories within Ethnic Studies is Aboriginal Studies (Australia). This sub-category is several levels down the Yahoo hierarchy. The path for this sub-category, shown at the top of the page, is *Social Science > Ethnic Studies > Aboriginal Studies (Australia)*. The URL for the page also shows its place in the structure (**dir.yahoo.com/ Social_Science/Ethnic_Studies/Aboriginal_Studies_Australia./**).

To go back to a higher level category just click on its name at the top of the page. This is a convention which has been adopted by several other universal subject guides.

The higher level categories are not necessarily the best sources of good links. Cataloguers put resources in the lowest level category they can. Thus the category Ethnic Studies contains external links only to resources which cover ethnic studies in general. Anything which is more specific, targeted at a particular aspect of ethnic studies or a particular geographical region, will be in one of the sub-categories. You need to keep digging down, to the very lowest level subject categories.

- **Anthropology and Archaeology** *(1302)* NEW!
- **Area Studies** *(713)* NEW!
- **Bibliographies** *(14)*
- **Books@**
- **Chats and Forums** *(12)*
- **Communications** *(1958)* NEW!
- **Conferences** *(16)*
- **Critical Theory@**
- **Disability Studies** *(8)*
- **Economics** *(960)* NEW!
- **Education** *(28)*
- **Employment** *(5)*
- **Environmental Studies@**
- **Ethnic Studies** *(165)*
- **Futures Studies** *(24)*
- **Gender Studies** *(22)*
- **Genealogy@**
- **Geography@**
- **Gerontology** *(40)* NEW!
- **History@**
- **Humanities@**
- **Institutes** *(85)* NEW!

- **Journals** *(30)*
- **Law@**
- **Lesbian, Gay, and Bisexual Studies** *(63)*
- **Libraries** *(14)* NEW!
- **Library and Information Science@**
- **Linguistics and Human Languages** *(2855)* NEW!
- **Migration and Ethnic Relations** *(37)*
- **Organizations** *(30)*
- **Peace and Conflict Studies** *(128)*
- **Political Science** *(1187)* NEW!
- **Popular Culture Studies@**
- **Psychology** *(1440)* NEW!
- **Recreation and Leisure Studies** *(85)* NEW!
- **Rural Development** *(45)*
- **Science, Technology, and Society Studies** *(109)* NEW!
- **Sexology** *(33)*
- **Social Research** *(69)*
- **Social Work** *(171)* NEW!
- **Sociology** *(443)* NEW!
- **Urban Studies** *(329)* NEW!
- **Web Directories** *(15)*
- **Women's Studies** *(787)* NEW!

Social Science sub-categories in Yahoo!

Searching Yahoo by keyword   Yahoo is so vast that the best way to identify the sub-categories relevant to you is to do a keyword search. When you search Yahoo you are searching several layers, category and sub-category titles as well as external hyperlinks. The results page includes 'Category matches', the Yahoo category and sub-category titles which your keyword appears in, and 'site matches', external hyperlinks in which your keyword appears. Simple searching is recommended for Yahoo. It only searches titles and, in the case of external links, perhaps a few words describing the link. It does not search the text of the pages those links point you to. For details of how to search Yahoo by keyword see the inset.

Searching Yahoo

Yahoo allows very sophisticated searching, the kind which the big keyword search engines provide. Yahoo has an 'Advanced Searching' page. It provides simple drop-down menus which allow you to specify that Yahoo search for all the words in your query or search for them as an exact phase. It allows you to restrict your search to categories or to sites only. It allows you to limit your search to links which have been added recently. Thus you can limit your search to links added in the last week or month or year.

Yahoo also allows you to use a range of search commands in the main query box. Below is a list of the search commands you can use in Yahoo. All of these commands are explained in chapter 7 in the section on search options.

Boolean: AND OR NOT NEAR
Math: + − " "

Power Searching: t: (title), u: (url)

Queries should be in the order + − t: u: " "

The search results page begins with the Yahoo categories your keyword has pulled up. From their position in the Yahoo hierarchy you'll have a good idea of whether they'll be useful or not. Thus if you've searched on 'Welsh language' in pursuit of information on social aspects of the language, it will be clear to you that *Social Science > Linguistics and Human Languages > Languages > Specific Languages > Welsh* is probably relevant to you while *Business and Economy > Business to Business > Education > By Subject > Languages > Teaching and Learning Aids > Specific Languages > Welsh* is probably not.

Every external link your search retrieves is organized on the results page under the Yahoo category it's classified in. This can throw up interesting categories which did not appear as category matches. Yahoo also carries out a search on Google, a keyword search engine. These results appear after all the Yahoo results. I suggest you ignore these results and search Google separately later.

Overlapping categories   Many sub-categories can easily fit into several different higher level categories. The way Yahoo deals with this is to try to include sub-categories in all of the higher level categories they belong to. Thus the Yahoo 'Ethnic Studies' page includes a number of categories which are not actually in the *Social Sciences > Ethnic Studies* sub-category. Whiteness Studies, for example, is a sub-category in the Arts category, one of the top-level Yahoo categories. Its actual location is at *Arts > Humanities > Critical Theory > Whiteness Studies.* However, a link to it is included in Ethnic Studies for the sake of convenience and such links to related categories appear in many category pages. They are signified by an @ sign at the end of the title. As you can see in the image, Ethnic Studies includes three such convenience links.

In addition, external links are frequently listed in two different categories. As a result there is an overlap between the content of Yahoo's categories and sub-categories. Thus you may well find that certain categories in entirely different branches of the tree will be almost identical in their contents.

Criteria for inclusion   There are major problems with Yahoo's criteria for inclusion of resources. A few years ago, overwhelmed by the rapid growth

Yahoo! Category Matches (1 - 3 of 3)
Categories in the Yahoo! Directory that match your search.
Social Science > Linguistics and Human Languages > **Languages** > Specific **Languages**
  • **Welsh**

Business and Economy > Business to Business > Education > By Subject > **Languages** > Teaching and
Learning Aids > Specific **Languages**

  • **Welsh**

United Kingdom > Business and Economy > Business to Business > Education > By Subject > **Languages** > Teaching and Learning Aids >
Specific **Languages**

  • **Welsh**

Yahoo! Site Matches (1 - 17 of 18)   Grouped by category | Ranked by relevance
Sites in the Yahoo! Directory that match your search.
United Kingdom > Wales > Government > Politics > Parties and Groups

  • Welsh Language Society - political pressure group for the Welsh language.

Social Science > Linguistics and Human Languages > Languages > Specific Languages > Welsh

  • Welsh Course
  • Welsh to English Lexicon
  • Linguru - offers a free downloadable Welsh-English dictionary with content created collaboratively by users.
  • Cymdeithas Madog - Welsh Studies Institute of North America, Inc. A tax-exempt, non-profit organization dedicated to helping North Americans learn, use, and enjoy the Welsh language.

United Kingdom > Wales > Dyfed > Aberystwyth > Education > College and University > University of Wales > Departments and Courses

  • Centre for Advanced Welsh and Celtic Studies - research center promoting scholarship in the language, literature and history of Wales and the other Celtic countries.

Social Science > Area Studies > Welsh Studies > Institutes

  • University of Wales at Aberystwyth - Centre for Advanced Welsh and Celtic Studies - research center promoting scholarship in the language, literature and history of Wales and the other Celtic countries.

Results of a Keyword search on 'Welsh language' in Yahoo!

Categories

  • **Aboriginal Studies (Australia)** *(11)*
  • **African American Studies** *(48)*
  • **Area Studies@**
  • **Asian American Studies** *(12)*
  • **Directories** *(3)*
  • **First Nations Studies** *(14)*
  • **Institutes** *(16)*
  • **Latino Studies** *(10)*
  • **Mexican American Studies** *(20)*
  • **Migration and Ethnic Relations@**
  • **Native American Studies** *(24)*
  • **Organizations** *(2)*
  • **Whiteness Studies@**

Site Listings

  • Canadian Ethnic Studies Journal - subscription-based interdisciplinary journal devoted to the study of et inter-group relations, history, and cultural life.
  • UCLA Ethnic Studies Publications Catalog - interactive, searchable catalog of publications about African Asian American studies, including nearly three decades of journals.

The Ethnic Studies category page in Yahoo!

of the Web, Yahoo decided to add only sites which had been submitted to it. Obviously, commercial sites have more motivation to submit their sites to Yahoo than researchers do. In addition, Yahoo lets submitters choose which categories it will add their sites to. Yahoo has performed a certain monitoring of this, ensuring, for example, that businesses which try to sneak into other categories don't succeed and that sites under construction are not included. In pursuit of these aims Yahoo surfers do visit all sites before they are added to the directory.

This is clearly a mammoth task and it's not always possible for Yahoo to perform it effectively. Having said all that, Yahoo is probably the best of the universal subject guides. It is large enough and well organized enough to be genuinely useful. If you use only one universal subject guide this is probably the one to use.

Other universal subject guides

Galaxy (**www.galaxy.com**) Links are classified by subject and short, useful descriptions of links are provided. There seems to be some degree of quality control and there is a social sciences section which is worth a look.

Looksmart (**www.looksmart.com**) Links are organized by subject categories but, unlike Yahoo, only the lowest level sub-categories have external links. It can be a little time consuming to browse down to these levels. It's probably wiser to do a keyword search of the categories. In its favour Looksmart provides descriptions of links and exercises a good degree of quality control. On the down side, its categorization of topics is not always very clear. Looksmart's keyword search of the open Web searches the Inktomi index which is used by several other guides and search engines. For more on Inktomi see the inset box in chapter 7.

The Open Directory Project (**dmoz.org**) The argument for the Open Directory Project is well founded. Those who run the project argue that 'As the Internet grows at a staggering rate, automated search engines and directories run by small editorial staffs are unable to cope'. The diagnosis is correct but the prescription, a subject guide whose individual subject categories are run by volunteers, is questionable. It doesn't take a lot of imagination to figure out the problems with this sort of approach. One example provides a striking illustration of the problems. The Northern Ireland Politics section was, in spring 1999, jointly edited by two volunteers (at this stage the project was known as the Netscape Open Directory). One of the editors used the nickname 'Fenian Banshee', a name which to anyone familiar with Irish politics clearly identifies this editor with one particular political perspective. The validity of that perspective is beside the point. It was allowed to shape the guide to the extent that the first link in the guide pointed to the political party the editor supported. It was the only link to a political party in the guide. You can't really blame political activists for jumping at such a golden opportunity to spread their message in the form of a 'guide' but obviously such a guide is of limited use to a researcher in the area.

It might be argued that a little bit of editorial control by the Open Directory at a higher level could resolve the problem of guides which are politically biased. Certain editors could be excluded. But, in truth, it would require a lot of subject expertise on the part of US-based monitors to determine whether there were inappropriate biases in guides to German or French politics, let alone Sudanese or East Timorese or Kazakh or Finnish politics, in which there are far fewer experts available. The Open Directory uses the same kind of tree structure as Yahoo with the path of a guide given at the top of the page. As in Yahoo you can jump back to higher level categories by clicking on their name.

Netscape Search (**search.netscape.com**)   This service draws primarily on the Open Directory dealt with above, although it does also search its own 'smart browsing' database of official sites. It also does a search of the open Web using the major keyword search engine, Google (dealt with in chapter 7).

NBCi Search (**home.nbci.com**)   Choose the 'Search and Find' tab at the top of the NBCi home page to get access. This is a universal subject guide which offers very sophisticated searching options in its 'power search'. It provides pull-down menus allowing you to choose whether you want them to search for the exact phrase you've typed. It also allows you to change the number of hits shown on each page, to restrict your search by domain, date and language and even to limit the search to top-level pages which are likely in many cases to be the home pages of sites. The keyword search of the open Web which it carries out uses the Inktomi index.

Iwon (**www.iwon.com**)   This is a subject directory generated from the Inktomi index (see chapter 7). Its keyword search of the open Web also relies on Inktomi. The 'advanced search' allows you to limit your search by date and to choose AND, and 'exact phrase' options from pull-down menus.

Lycos (**www.lycos.com**)   Lycos started out as a keyword search engine but has now restyled itself as a subject guide or directory. It draws on the Open Directory for its directory results. It draws on the keyword search engine 'Fast' for its searches of the open Web and it also takes some results from Direct Hit (see chapter 7). 'Advanced search' provides drop-down menus allowing you to restrict by language and domain, to alter the display of results, to search specific fields including title and to choose AND or 'exact phrase' searches.

MSN Search (**search.msn.com**)   This draws on Looksmart (mentioned above) for directory results and Inktomi for the open Web. 'Advanced search' provides pull-down menus allowing you to limit your search by date, domain and language, to change the number of hits per page, to search in the fields 'link' and 'title', and to choose AND or 'exact phrase' searches. More detail on these options is provided in the search options section of chapter 7. It also allows you to choose the level that results are at, thus allowing you effectively to limit your search to home pages.

National versions of universal subject guides

Yahoo was the first to create national versions of its service; Yahoo UK and Ireland (**uk.yahoo.com**) and Yahoo Germany (**de.yahoo.com**) were among the first. The subject categories are generally the same as in the main Yahoo version but with additional categories and sub-categories of special relevance to the country concerned and additional links to sites relevant to the country. You can click on an option to ensure that only sites specifically related to the country are returned.

Since the country-specific Yahoos cover both the main Yahoo index and extra national-specific material a researcher concerned with a particular country might be well advised to search the Yahoo for that country rather than the central Yahoo guide.

If you are searching for material in a language other than English you should certainly search the Yahoo for the country where that language is the main language. Sites in languages other than English are generally not included in the main Yahoo directory if there is a national Yahoo where that language is the main language.

Crude catalogues: where subject guides meet keyword search engines

I was strongly tempted just to call this section 'bad subject guides' because the quality of the services I deal with here is generally so poor. Seeing how popular services like Yahoo were, a lot of the keyword search engines decided they needed to do some sort of classification of the Web by subject. They started to provide crude subject guides, calling them 'channels', 'catalogs', 'guides' or something similar. Their ambitions are 'universal' but I won't call them universal subject guides because most of them hardly merit the description 'guide'. These crude catalogues should be avoided in general. Some of them may improve with time but approach most of them warily. They can waste more of your time than they'll save. If you use them at all I suggest you leave them until the very end of your research and do a quick sweep through them then to see if they include useful material you have missed.

Some of these guides are just keyword searches dressed up to look a bit like subject categories. Thus, in the crudest of these catalogues, when you click on the Indian economy category it just does a keyword search of the Web on a few keywords related to the Indian economy. These are hardly worth the bother. You'll be able to develop a more precise keyword search on the topic yourself.

Novelty items

There are a number of technological innovations which share the common purpose of arranging Internet materials by subject, to one degree or another. They are marked out from the subject guides dealt with above by a focus on particular technologies rather than on the business of classification. The value of some of these approaches has not yet been proven and I am personally sceptical whether any of them are of value to social science researchers, at least in their present form. You will, however, come across them all over the Web. For this reason alone it's necessary to know what they involve. It may be too that some of them will in the future become useful to the researcher.

Webrings

A Webring is a collection of related sites linked to one another using Webring software. The key organizing concept for Webrings is subject. All sites in a ring deal, ideally, with the same subject or area of interest. The Webring allows you to move easily from one site to another and a list of all of the sites on the Webring are displayed no matter which site you're looking at. Webrings are co-operative efforts. People running various sites decide to set up a Webring so that people who visit each site will be made aware of other related sites. It's kind of like a club. Webrings are not comprehensive. They don't include, and generally don't even try to include, every site relevant to their subject. Individual Webrings may exercise quality control, keeping poor-quality sites out of the ring, but they don't have to. As a result there are a lot of Webrings out there which consist of several mediocre sites which have banded together out of self-interest to increase the number of visitors to their sites.

It might seem useful to have several related sites linked together but the truth is that if any of the sites in the Webring are of high quality, a good subject guide in your area should have pointed you to them already. A good guide will also provide a useful description and some assessment of the quality of the site, something you won't get from a Webring. They're good for people interested in an obscure topic for which there may only exist a few Websites.

Portals

'Portals' became a buzzword sometime around 1998 or 1999. A portal, or gateway, is a site which likes to think of itself as an entry point to the Web. You can of course enter the Web from any one of several billion points. Portal sites aimed to ensure that you entered it through them, allowing them to advertise to you and to direct your use of the Web to a certain extent. The idea was that if you became familiar with one portal site you would always use it to access the Web and that site would then be in a position to direct your attention to particular parts of the Web, to a particular bookshop or news source or search engine. The reason portals are dealt with here is that many portals were conceived as entry points for people interested in a particular subject. These subject categories tended to be very broad but promised to provide a sort of definitive entryway to Web materials on the topic. In many cases this amounted to providing subject guides on particular topics.

Subject portals are of limited use to most social science researchers because of the simple fact that they are dominated by commercial considerations and therefore there are few portals devoted to topics of academic interest.

Of course, subject guides may start describing themselves as portals, in which case we'll all become portal-users. Alternatively portals may just quietly fade away over the next few years as commercial interests realize that people have more than enough gateways to the Web.

Intelligent agents

A favourite techno-fantasy, the intelligent agent, is a bit of software which will gather information for you according to your individual needs – a search engine customized to your personal requirements. By its nature an intelligent agent is concerned with subject as this is the basis on which it will operate, collecting information on the range of subjects, however specialized, which you are interested in.

It may be that intelligent agents will become important research tools in future years, searching everything from the newsgroups through article databases to the open Web for us all at once. The ultimate intelligent agent would render this book redundant. However, if there is one thing this book illustrates it is just how much effort is required to extract information from varying types of sources. The great risk associated with intelligent agents is that they will conduct searches which are far cruder than those we could do by hand. In the first case, it is bad enough that most users think they're searching for every article ever written when they search an article database. The intelligent agent takes us back one step further from the sources we're searching and obscures the fact that these sources are not comprehensive and that we are not even efficiently extracting everything we need from them. The researcher needs to be closer to the source, to understand it better, not to have one more layer of fog obscuring it.

There is also a risk that intelligent agents will contribute to fossilizing our interests. In the course of our research our interests change, we develop new keywords and search strategies at regular intervals. To keep an intelligent agent constantly appraised of these changes probably requires more effort than it's worth. If we don't keep updating it our search fossilizes and the danger is that we become complacent, receiving information and using it and making do with it just because it's accessible to us.

Intelligent agents may yet become an important research tool in some form but for the moment the researcher can probably do without them.

Push technology

This shares with intelligent agents a concern with defining our interests, a concern inextricably linked to categorization of materials by subject. Push technology was another buzzword of the late 1990s. For a while it was all the rage. Push technology was all about sending Web pages to users, not waiting until the user decided to visit a site. Thus users were asked to define their interests and windows related to these interests would regularly pop up on their screens. You were nobody on the Web unless you were using push technology. It became so mainstream that it was built into one version of Internet Explorer. It was a classic case of one of those Internet innovations that cause confusion among users and disrupt established techniques for using the Web with little benefit.

Whenever you hear of a great new technological development on the Web, remember push technology and wait a while before you embrace it wholeheartedly.

The future of subject searching

Searching by subject has long been the academic researcher's principal method of looking for relevant research materials. This is likely to remain the case on the Internet.

Research, by its nature, is structured by subject. The researcher is looking for materials related to a particular topic, materials which are likely to fall under a few major subject headings. It seems self-evident that researchers should gravitate towards the guides and catalogues which allow them to search the Internet by subject. At the moment, however, the keyword search engines are as popular, if not more popular, with researchers than the subject guides. I don't expect that this will last. Both types of search approach are currently in their infancy. The keyword search engines right now can offer so much more in terms of sheer volume that, for that reason alone, they yield at least as much useful material as the subject guides. However, cataloguing and classification of resources, especially when it focuses on stable, authoritative and high-quality sites, is a cumulative process. While the keyword search engines expend energy in the hopeless task of indexing 'everything', the subject guides will gradually build up that proportion of the Web which is well organized and easily searchable. It is simply a matter of time before the subject guides grow to a size where they become significantly more useful than the keyword search engines.

The finest, most detailed subject guides already contain more material on their topics than the keyword search engines do. Subject guides on one topic will include all of the specialized material on that topic which is available through the search engines and the major subject guides plus more material gained through membership of email lists and newsgroups, through personal contacts and through following Web links which the search engines never bothered to follow. No keyword search engine will ever be able to compete with the quality of such hand-made guides. If their number expands, if libraries for example were to devote resources to producing such specialized online bibliographies, there is little doubt that they would become the first port of call for the student researcher venturing out onto the open Web.

Finally, the initiative to catalogue Websites with the same care and attention as is devoted to print publications will draw the researcher further away from the keyword search engines. It will provide a quick and reliable route to the online equivalent of 'major works' in the researcher's field.

As far as academic research is concerned the future lies with subject searching. In the meantime, however, the online researcher will probably find that a good half of their research work will necessarily be done through the keyword search engines which are the subject of the next chapter.

7

Searching the keyword search engines

Search engine fever

Despite all of their faults the keyword search engines are a fantastic research resource. For sheer volume no other resource can compete. They deal in the millions while most of the big subject guides deal in the tens of thousands. What they lack in organization they make up for in flexibility. They don't restrict your search to a document's title or abstract but allow you to search the full text of documents. Before the keyword search engines researchers were accustomed to using keywords to find a relevant article or book. The Web search engines opened up for the first time the possibility of searching for sentences and paragraphs rather than entire documents. They allowed researchers to pull up relevant snippets of information from documents they would never have found if they'd been searching by titles and subject categories. The freedom to search vast volumes of text using whatever words you choose in any combination you like is a truly revolutionary development. We are just beginning to feel the effects of this type of search on the way we look for relevant materials.

The search engines are the medium through which most Web users first begin to explore the Net. Most of the search engines care little about context, ignoring the site a document belongs to or the other documents it's related to. If you were in the business of allocating blame, you might reasonably place some blame on the search engines for the fact that the Web appears so chaotic and crazy and useless to so many new users.

Many of the keyword search engines have become large commercial operations spanning the globe and attracting investment and advertisers. Flawed and all as they are, they have become one of the principal means by which human beings locate information. Because the search engines have become so important they have attracted a lot of attention from journalists, academics and business people. Reams have been written about them and it seems a whole industry has grown up to analyse their effectiveness, their size and their relative merits. Among the best-known articles discussing search engines at length is Lawrence and Giles (1999).

There is also a site, Search Engine Watch (**searchenginewatch.com**), which devotes huge energy to monitoring and comparing search engines.

Some of the major search engines

In most browsers you can go to almost any major search engine just by typing its name into the bar at the top of your browser. The exceptions are listed below with their addresses in brackets. Alternatively, use a list of search engines provided locally. Don't waste time going to a list on a faraway computer which may take a lot of time to download.

   Below is a list of major keyword search engines. They are ordered alphabetically, not ranked in order of size or usefulness. Over the past few years the relative size of search engines has changed constantly. It seems as if every month a different search engine has become the largest on the Web. This rapid pace of change is likely to continue for some time.

AltaVista
AOL Search (**search.aol.com**)
Direct Hit
Excite
Fast Search (**www.alltheweb.com**)
Google
Go To
HotBot
Northern Light
Webtop

Searching the search engines

Eleven steps to effective searching

See the main text for detailed advice.

1. Use distinctive words and phrases
2. Look before you leap
3. Don't look beyond the second screen of hits
4. Use the simplified display option
5. Group hits by site
6. Don't be distracted
7. Refine your search on one search engine, then mop up on the others
8. Use a keyword search chart
9. Bookmark queries
10. Use the special search features **domain:** and **link:**
11. Ignore the 'channels' and 'guides'

Use distinctive words and phrases

Try to identify words and phrases or a combination of them which are likely to appear in a document related to your topic but which could not possibly appear in other documents. This should be the guiding principle behind your searches, the ideal that you aim for. It may sound ludicrously ambitious but it's not. By combining words and phrases you can easily create unique queries.

Take the example of a researcher looking for information on the politics of language use in California. The inset shows a right and a wrong way to search for such information

---

Good search/bad search

Searches on the politics of language use in California:

Bad searches: California language
Los Angeles Spanish
Language Politics

Good searches: +"Proposition 227" +"Los Angeles"
+"English as the official language" +California

In most search engines the '+' sign means that the word or phrase must appear in the documents retrieved. The " " means it will search for the exact phrase. Details for each search engine are given further on in this chapter.

A researcher who has already carried out some research on this topic will have gathered a lot of detailed information about it and will have built up a store of distinctive words or phrases which can be used in the search.

The 'Bad searches' given above provide a classic example of how not to search. Each of these words is incredibly common and none relates uniquely to the politics of language use in California. The 'Good searches' use specific phrases which are strongly associated with debates over language in California (proposition 227 being a proposal to end bilingual education in Californian public schools). They each add a place name to ensure that it excludes related debates in other states and countries. If these bring back an overwhelming number of hits you can narrow it further by adding other specific phrases or use other distinctive phrases instead. You can perform this exact search in AltaVista but in several search engines you will have to use the advanced search or pull-down menus to combine a phrase and a word.

Certain types of words are particularly useful in searches, not on their own of course but in combination with others. What follows is a list of these types.

Place names   If a particular place is associated with your topic it's good to add it to your query, particularly if the place is quite obscure. It does not necessarily have to be a country or city. In certain cases street names, villages, the name of a particular building even, will be linked to your topic and to virtually no other topic. This does not apply only to subjects concerned with particular places. Even the most placeless and theoretical topics will often be associated with particular places, where an experiment was carried out, for example, or where an important centre or individual was based.

Using place names has two major drawbacks. Particularly if it is a large city or town in the USA, it will appear on tens or even hundreds of thousands of Web pages. It may not act very effectively as a filter as a result. Secondly, the Internet abounds with lists of things organized geographically, lists of consulates or phone companies or shoe shops. Even the smallest country or region is included in dozens of such lists. Be very careful of using all but the most obscure place name as a query on its own. You'll bring back dozens of such lists.

People's names   You don't have to be studying a particular person to effectively use people's names in your search. For example, the name of a person associated with your topic in a peripheral way, perhaps as a minor contributor to an event or project, can be extremely effective in locating very specific information. It helps of course if the person has a reasonably distinctive name. Give the full name as an exact phrase to the search engine. If you're looking for an item written by a particular author then obviously you should use their name in your search.

Titles   The full title of a book, article, report or conference is the perfect way to search for references to that item. Just enclose it in " " in most search engines.

Other names   Brand names, the names of different categories used in your subject area (in the case of politics, for example, words like 'government', 'executive', 'legislature'), the names of organizations and institutions.

Distinctive or idiosyncratic phrases   A quote from an individual can give you a very precise search term. In addition to direct quotes there will often be distinctive phrases, a slogan or a catchphrase, a motto or a worn-out over-used cliché, which will be uniquely associated with your topic. You'll come across such phrases in the course of your research. The problem with such phrases is that they often spill over into other areas of popular culture so that searching on the phrase 'beam me up Scotty', for example, is likely to retrieve huge amounts of material which have nothing to do with Star Trek.

Look before you leap

You enter your search query, click on 'go' and get back a page of hits which match your query. If your query has brought back hundreds of hits, it will be the first of dozens of pages. At this stage the temptation for the user is to look down the first page of hits and click on the first link which looks promising. As often as not it will turn out to be a dud, useless, irrelevant; 5 to 10 minutes can have been wasted. Do this with a few more promising-looking links and you can quickly fritter away half an hour with nothing to show for it.

Visiting sites which turn out to be irrelevant is probably the biggest source of wasted time in Internet research. You can greatly reduce this waste by knowing a few simple tricks for learning more about hits without actually clicking on them. When you start using these tricks systematically you will often find that you can dismiss all of the links your search has brought back without having to visit a single one. You can then put your energy into devising a better search query, one which will actually bring back useful hits in the first screen or two.

Analyse the URL   The URL is a rich source of information about the type of document a link will lead you to. The first thing to do after looking at the title of a hit and the short text extract, is to look at the URL. URLs are dealt with in detail in chapter 5 in the section on understanding Web addresses. It's a matter of great regret that some search engines obscure the URLs of hits, among them 'Ask Jeeves' and 'Go To'. This effectively halves the amount of information available to you on the page of hits.

The first thing to look at is the domain name. Just say you're still looking for information about the politics of language in California. Clearly a hit located on a server with the domain name **www.languagepols.org** is more likely to provide substantive information than one on a server with the domain name **www.shoppingLA.com**. You can make an educated guess that any reference to language politics on **www.shoppingLA.com** is likely to be fleeting. By looking at the URL you can easily determine what country a site is based in (see appendix 1 for a full list of top-level domains) or whether it's a university or government or commercial site. This will tell you a lot about whether it's likely to be useful to you or not. The file path, the part of the URL after the domain name, can also reveal a lot. Thus **www.languagepols. org/USA/California/Englishofficial.html** suggests strongly that this is part of a larger archive on language politics in California. It would be worth cutting the URL back to **www.langaugepols.org/USA/California** where there is probably an index of all of the documents on this topic.

Check the date and size   Some search engines will provide the date on which they indexed a document and information on its size. Both of these tell you a lot about the document. A document which is only 1K, or less than a page long, is not likely to be a lengthy in-depth article. If you are research-ing an incident which occurred in September 2000 then clearly documents indexed before that date do not refer to that incident. Quickly scanning date and size can help you to avoid going to irrelevant documents.

Identify common genres   There are certain common genres of document which appear frequently when you do searches on an academic topic. They seem tantalizingly relevant to your search but in the end are of no use. If you learn to recognize them you won't have to waste your time visiting them ever again. They include:

COLLEGE COURSE DESCRIPTIONS   All over the world colleges and universities have been putting course descriptions online. They may include reading lists, times and locations of classes, a broad outline of topics to be covered, perhaps, a few paragraphs about the topic. As a result they are choc-a-bloc with keywords related to a very specific subject while at the same time providing virtually nothing of substance. Unless you are interested in looking at reading lists in your subject area or seeing how someone else has structured a course on this topic, avoid them. You can sometimes identify them because they'll have a course code in the title. If not, the URL will often reveal them as course descriptions. Look for course codes, names of faculty / staff and of departments, for example URLs like:

www.anycollege.edu/econ/Taylor/macro.html
www.anycollege.edu/psych/courses/py101.html

BIBLIOGRAPHICAL REFERENCES   Publishers, booksellers, colleges and libraries all provide documents which consist solely of lists of books. It's easy to see how a long list of books on psychology, for example, could be densely packed with very specific and obscure keywords related to the subject. You will regularly pull up such book lists in the course of your search. Once again a combination of document title and URL will often tell you this with no need for you to check out the document itself.

LISTS   The Internet is full of lists. John F. Kennedy, for example, could appear in a list of US Presidents, a list of famous visitors to Berlin, a list of people connected to Marilyn Monroe, a list of Irish-Americans, a list of prominent people from Massachusetts or any amount of other lists. These lists are almost useless to the researcher and should be avoided. Again, title and URL together should give you enough information to recognize them.

Duplication   All over the Internet pages are duplicated. Several copies of the same document can be located on different servers, at different URLs across the world. 'The life of John F. Kennedy' may well be the title of several different documents but if the short text extracts are the same for each then it's just the same document at different locations. Most of the search engines do not pick up on this and do not eliminate duplicate copies.

Link pages   Sometimes you'll get a hit which looks like it couldn't possibly be related to your search. The temptation is to have a look, to see how it is related. As a rule, don't bother. Often the reason is simply that a link has been provided to a page related to your subject.

Beware the sign of the tilde ~   This little squiggle ~ is a tilde. You'll often see it in a URL. On a Web server with a lot of users the person running the computer will often add the tilde in front of the names of all individual users. In many universities a tilde is added in front of the name of each department. It makes administration of the computer easier. If you see a tilde in a URL it often indicates the Web pages of a particular individual. Thus **www. anycollege.edu/students/~pwozniak** is probably the Website of a student called P. Wozniak. **www.anysite.com/~janeyre** is probably the Website of an individual user on *anysite*. Thus it is very often (but not always) the case that a tilde in the address means you're dealing with that unique genre of document which only exists on the Web – the 'personal home page' or as I prefer to say myself, the 'dreaded personal home page'. Obviously there are a lot of useful personal home pages. As a rule, however, this is where you will find the heaviest concentration of irrelevant, self-indulgent, unreliable nonsense on the Web. This is not to say that all such pages are useless.

Individual users are often experts in one particular field (too often, however, that's mountain-biking or surfing or stamp-collecting) or in some cases they host information for marginal organizations. In any case you should be particularly sceptical of sites bearing the sign of the tilde, if they seem to be the sites of individual users.

Don't look beyond the second screen of hits

This may sound a bit harsh but the truth is, if the item you're looking for is in the fifth or sixth screen of hits then effectively your search hasn't found it at all. It will take so long to work your way down to that screen that it is much more time-effective to change your search terms and do a fresh search.

If you don't find anything useful in the first two screens (the first twenty hits, that is) then immediately refine your search and run it again. The results of the first search will help you to do this. Look at the first screen of hits and ask yourself: 'What word or phrase is almost certain to appear in the document I'm looking for but would not appear in these dud hits?' If you find the right word it can sweep away all the dud hits and bring you straight to the document which had been buried deep down in the first search.

Use the simplified display option

Many of the search engines give you the option of displaying hits in a simpler form, with less detail from the text, for example. The option is usually available in the 'advanced search' which a lot of search engines offer. It means that you will get thirty or forty hits on a screen rather than just ten. It speeds up the process so much that, on balance, the trade-off of detail for bulk is worth it. This is especially true at the later stages of your research when you can recognize duds more quickly, without as much detailed information about them. For details of how to use this option on individual search engines see the individual profiles further on in this chapter.

Group hits by sites

One of the major search engines, Google, will group hits according to the sites they belong to. This must count as one of the best Web ideas ever. This makes it easy to use search results to identify useful sites. Rather than looking at each document on the site go straight to the site home page and thoroughly mine the site.

Where the search engine doesn't do this you can do it yourself. If several hits which look promising belong to the same site (as indicated by the URL) don't bother going to the individual documents but go straight to the site home page and mine the entire site.

Don't be distracted

Do not click on vaguely interesting-looking hits, on hits that seem to be distantly related to your subject, on hits that a friend might be interested in, or on hits which relate to a project you might tackle in the future. I know I'm being a little too harsh here. You won't be able to avoid all these temptations and if you did it would entirely remove the last shred of enjoyment involved in using the Net. But I'm sure you get my point.

Hours can be squandered before you know it on the keyword search engines because they throw up such eclectic collections of hits. They place more irrelevant temptations in front of you than the subject guides do, so you need to be that little bit more ruthless in resisting them.

Refine your search on one search engine; mop up on the others

Do not skip from one search engine to another trying random searches in no particular order. You will not extract maximum benefit from any of them. Instead do a lot of serious searching on one major search engine. Try to extract everything useful from it that you can. At the end of this you should have three or four quite complex queries that worked particularly well. That is, mining one search engine thoroughly allowed you to refine your search terms very effectively. When you go to look at the other search engines you don't need to start from scratch. You just quickly run your refined terms through them to see if they pull up anything which the first search engine didn't find. By the way, there is such a huge overlap between search engines that you will quickly experience the law of diminishing returns. It's hardly worth using more than four or five of them. In addition, many of the search engines draw off the same databases and directories, in particular the Inktomi index and the Open Directory. Details are provided in the inset on search engine families. Although they each search these indexes in slightly different ways it's probably not worth your while using more than one search engine which draws on Inktomi, for example.

If you find that one of the search engines you use for 'mop-up' is consistently bringing back more useful results than the main search engine you use, you could consider using it as your main search engine.

Bookmark queries

Most search engines will allow you to bookmark your queries. When the search engine brings back a list of hits, bookmark that page. When you go to the bookmarked page a week or a month or a year later it will automatically run your query again and bring up an up-to-date results page.

Use a keyword search chart

Draw up a chart to record search queries which have been effective. Use it to keep track of which search engines you've run the queries on and when. Recording the data gives you an indication of when it will be worth your while to run the query again, perhaps in six months or a year. If you like you can record the number of hits each search engine brings up, as an indication of its relative effectiveness.

If a new search engine appears, or you hear that a minor search engine has expanded and is now much more useful, you can just add it to the chart and run all of the queries you've developed on it.

Use the special search options **domain:** and **link:**

There are two relatively obscure search options available on several search engines which new users are usually unaware of. They are dealt with in more detail below but they are worth mentioning here because they can very effectively limit your search. **domain:** refers to the domain name of a site. Thus **+domain:edu** will ensure that you only get hits in the **.edu** domain. **+domain:gov.uk** ensures that you only get hits from UK government sites. **-domain:com** will exclude all **.com** sites. It's easy to see how useful this can be. The equivalent command in AltaVista is **host:**

link: is not quite as useful but provides an interesting back-door method of searching, akin to following academic citations. **+link:www.berlin.de/ history/JFKvisit/eyewitnesses.html** will bring back all of the Web pages which link to that (imaginary) page. If those pages are interested enough to link to this page they may well provide useful information on the topic themselves.

Ignore the 'channels' and 'guides'

That's right, ignore them completely. If you use these at all it should be at the end of a subject search to mop up items you've missed by that method of searching (see previous chapter). Although run by the search engines they are actually crude subject guides. If you use these alongside keyword searches you will only confuse your search with minimal benefit.

Search options

Some of the newer search engines don't bother with complicated search syntax. They just provide drop-down menus allowing you to specify exactly what you want. This is a great idea. Unfortunately it can be less flexible than using the search syntax. Thus my search on +"proposition 227"+ "Los Angeles" would only be possible on HotBot using the advanced search option. Although the main pull-down menus allow you to search for an 'exact phrase' they don't allow you to combine two exact phrases. Apart from this, a large proportion of the search engines don't provide such menus, so knowing your search syntax is likely to be important and useful for some time to come. An important source of information for the search options is the Search Engine Watch site (**searchenginewatch.com**) run by Danny Sullivan.

Boolean searching

It sounds technical but it's not. It's very simple and it's named after a man called George Boole, an English mathematician who devised the basic principles on which it is based. Boolean searching is a small set of simple search terms, the main ones being AND, OR, NOT. Virtually all search engines understand the Boolean search terms.

Boolean searching chart

Search term	Example	Explanation	Search engines providing this option
AND	Israel AND Palestine	Documents containing both words	Virtually all search engines
OR	Israel OR Palestine	Documents containing either word	Virtually all search engines
NOT	Israel NOT Palestine	Documents containing Israel but not containing Palestine	Virtually all search engines
AND NOT	Israel AND NOT Palestine	The same as NOT. Some search engines insist on AND NOT	AltaVista, Excite, Netscape
NEAR	Israel NEAR Palestine	Documents containing both words but only if they appear within a few words of each other	Available in AltaVista (within ten words)
*	Israel*	Documents containing words beginning with Israel, e.g. Israel, Israeli, Israelites	AOLSearch, AltaVista, HotBot, Northern Light

In addition to this, huge numbers of little databases all over the Web and the search facilities on a lot of individual Websites use Boolean terminology. So, if you learn the half-dozen Boolean terms you'll be able to use them in lots of situations. Above is a chart listing the main Boolean terms and what they do. It takes the example of a search on the words 'Israel' and 'Palestine'.

Nested queries   The OR term is often overlooked since it is the default option in most search engines. Put in two words and most search engines will automatically do an OR search for documents containing either of them. Where it does come into its own is in nested queries when you place part of a query inside brackets. Thus, **revolution AND (communist OR socialist)** is a useful query which you cannot make using the drop-down menus. The **communist OR socialist** in brackets allows you to make the strict AND search just that little bit looser.

Math searching

This is a more recent set of search terms which do much the same thing as the Boolean terms but which are shorter. They are now used by virtually all search engines.

Math searching chart

Search term	Boolean equivalent	Example	Explanation
+	AND	+Palestine +Israel	Document must include all words preceded by the + sign
–	NOT	+Palestine -Israel	Document must not include words preceded by the - sign
" "		"Palestine Israel"	Documents must include the <u>exact</u> phrase enclosed by the quotation marks
*	*	Palestin*	Documents containing words beginning with Palestin including Palestine, Palestinian

If you don't use the search terms

If you don't use any of these terms, Boolean or math, and just enter the words **Israel** and **Palestine** in a search engine search box, most of them will treat it as an OR query, and look for documents with either word, giving higher preference to documents containing the first word. Several search engines automatically treat it as an AND query or give higher preference to documents which contain both words. A few will give highest preference to documents which include it as an exact phrase. Details of which search engines take which approach are given in the individual profiles.

Capitalization

If you type in a search term in lower case most search engines will look for the word in both upper and lower case. Thus, **israel** will pull up documents including **israel** or **Israel**. If you search for **Israel** some search engines will only return documents where the word begins with a capital. You'll miss out on documents containing **israel**.

Power searching

This refers to a small set of specialized search terms which are available, in slightly differing forms, in several search engines. You can use them in combination with the math terms. These commands are quite complicated and detailed explanations of each of them are provided here.

title: (t: in Yahoo)   This searches the title field in an html document. As noted in chapter 5 this field often doesn't actually contain the title of the document. Many authors don't bother to fill it in. On large, well-organized sites, however, it usually will be filled in and a title search is most useful if the information you're looking for is likely to be located on that kind of site. For all its limitations this is the only search option which allows you to search a specific field within Web documents. As such it provides a rare chance to do a very precise search on the open Web. You should use broad simple terms related to your subject, the kind you'd use when searching for the title of a book in your library catalogue.

*domain: (**host:** in AltaVista, **site:** in Infoseek)*   This allows you to restrict your search to documents from a particular domain. The more detail you provide the more restricted your search. Thus, **domain:edu** restricts your search to US universities; **domain:harvard.edu** restricts it to Web servers at Harvard University; **domain:www.ksg.library.harvard.edu** restricts it to documents on the Kennedy School of Government server at Harvard. Note that you can only include parts of the domain address and not any part of the file path, unlike the **url** option which is outlined next.

url: (u: in Yahoo)   This retrieves documents according to their URLs. Thus, **+url:harvard.edu**, by retrieving only documents which have **harvard.edu** in the URL, effectively performs the same function as **+domain:harvard.edu**.

Because it is concerned with the entire URL and not just the domain name it can be used for a variety of other purposes. **+url:www.anycollege.edu/ courses**, for example, will retrieve a full list of all the Web documents in the **courses** folder and below (if the search engine has indexed them all). **+url:polsci**, on the other hand, will bring back documents whose URL contains 'polsci' and are therefore highly likely to be concerned with political science. **+url:polsci+domain:edu** might be a shortcut to politics departments and courses at a lot of US universities (though of course there are subject guides which will bring you there more quickly).

Power searching chart

Search term	Example	Explanation	Selected search engines and subject guides providing this option
title: (**t:** in Yahoo)	title: theory	Returns documents whose **title** includes the word 'theory'	AltaVista, HotBot, Infoseek, MSN, Nothern Light, Lycos (Advanced) Yahoo (**t:**). Some provide it via a menu
domain: (**host:** in AV **site:** in Infoseek)	domain: edu	Returns only documents where the domain name ends in **edu**	AltaVista (**host:**), HotBot, Infoseek (**site:**), MSN, Lycos (in menu)
	domain: anycollege.edu	Returns only documents where the domain name ends in **anycollege.edu**	
url: (**u:** in Yahoo)	url: psych	Returns documents whose URL contains **psych**. Subtly different from a **domain:** search	AltaVista, Infoseek, Northern Light, Lycos (in menu), Yahoo (**u:**). HotBot and other Inktomi-powered search engines let you do such a search by other means
link: (**linkdomain:** in MSN Search)	link: anycollege.edu	Returns documents which contain a hyperlink to any page whose URL includes **anycollege.edu**	AltaVista, Infoseek, Google, HotBot, MSN (**linkdomain:**)
	link: anycollege.edu/ pol/index.html	Returns documents which contain a link to this exact URL	
text:	text: Palestine	Returns documents which include 'Palestine' in the visible text only; that is, not as part of the html code. Useful if you're searching for a word such as 'text' or 'title' which could appear in the html code	
anchor:	anchor: anthropology	Returns documents containing the word 'anthropology' in the text of a link	

link: (linkdomain: in MSN Search) This returns documents containing a link to the page whose URL you specify. **link:anycollege.edu** will return all pages everywhere which link to any document on any of the *anycollege* servers. **link:library.anycollege.edu/JFKarchive/secrets.html**, on the other hand, returns every page on the Web which links to this exact document. So, if you find a really good useful page which is directly related to your topic you can use **link:** to get a list of pages which link to it. It can provide interesting leads to related items. It's like a Web version of the citation indices mentioned in chapter 3 which allow you to trace the connections between academic articles. It also provides an interesting means of studying the connections between organizations and individuals on the Web, a back door for detective work on who's connected to whom. If you've set up a Website of your own you can use this to see who has linked to it.

An advanced search using *link:* and *domain*:

+link:myserver.yesme.edu/myhomepage.html
-domain:myserver.yesme.edu

All documents which link to **myhomepage.html**, except for those located on my own (imaginary) server, **myserver.yesme.edu**

(Thanks to Arthur Kosten, then of ERCOMER, who gave us this useful search back at the FISCE conference in Derry in 1996.)

Other search options

There is a wide array of extra options offered by individual search engines, available in drop-down menus or on 'advanced searching' pages. They vary widely from one search engine to the next. The search engine profiles below provided detailed information on which options are available on which search engines.

Restricting by language   This is probably most useful if you are looking for documents which are not in English. Then you can restrict your search to documents in the language you're looking for. If you're using English words the overwhelming majority of documents you'll pull up will be in English anyway. It's not worth the effort to exclude other languages. If you're searching using terms from another language, however, you'll often find they'll pull up a confusingly large number of English-language documents which happen to contain your search term for some reason. This is simply because such a huge proportion of Web documents are in English.

Restricting by date   This is extremely useful. If you're researching a recent event you can simply restrict your search to materials which were indexed by the search engine after or around that event. If you return to a search engine to do a mop-up search six months after you first searched it this allows you to restrict your search to documents added since you last visited.

'More like this'   This is one of the less useful options available. Most search engines which offer this actually just do another crude keyword search

based on the document you've retrieved. You could more effectively get 'more like this' by continuing to refine your own search terms and avoiding this sort of distraction.

Natural language searching Several search engines now support natural language searching. The idea is that you can type in a question in plain English and receive a straight answer. I know I wasn't being fair but I couldn't resist asking Webcrawler, 'What is it all about?' It told me to 'add more words'. When I asked AltaVista, 'Why are we here?', it brought back 8.3 million hits, the first of them entitled 'Yes, Java's secure. Here's why'. One search engine, 'Ask Jeeves' (**www.askjeeves.com**), has built its entire service around this sort of searching. My own experience is that such services are so underdeveloped that they can only deal well with run-of-the-mill questions like 'What's the highest mountain in Alaska?' If you expect to be regularly hunting out answers to such questions you should buy yourself a world almanac or 'book of facts'. They're available cheaply, are easy to use and provide clearly organized lists of things like highest mountains, biggest lakes, largest cities, record sports scores. There's no need to start up the computer to find these out.

Judging documents by the sites which link to them Several search engines now use a document's 'popularity' as a principal criterion for deciding how useful it is to you. They check out how many links there are to a document from other Websites. They then check out how many people link to these other Websites and exclude those which hardly anyone bothers to link to. Thus a hit is judged on the number of popular or important Web pages which link to it. It is argued that this provides a measure of quality control, something which is utterly absent from most search engines. This approach draws in part on the citation index tradition, an approach which implies that the more people cite an article, the more important or useful it's likely to be.

Google places this at the heart of its ranking systems. There are of course major problems with this approach. Although ideally a measure of quality control, it may actually measure popularity, a different thing entirely.

The danger is that it will favour those that are dominant already. To take the example of political parties, the major political party sites will be linked to by numerous sources. Minor parties will, as a rule, be linked to by far fewer sites. As a result such a system of judging sites will bring the sites of all major parties to the top of your results page while minor parties languish on the fifth or sixth screen, the screens you never see. It may well be that both small and large parties are equally of interest to you and are equally relevant to your query. However, this popularity searching effectively means that 'biggest is best'. It's often argued that the Internet has provided a level playing field where the message of even the smallest group is just as accessible as that of the largest. If this was ever true this new method of searching ensures that it's not the case anymore.

Direct hit (**www.directhit.com**) judges the popularity of sites according to the number of people using your search term who went to the site. This may be useful for people with common popular queries but if a lot of other people have used your exact query then you probably haven't made it precise enough.

Understanding how the search engines work

What the search engines actually search

When you enter your query into a search engine it goes off and searches its own database of Web pages, stored on its own computer. It does not go out onto the open Web to do a search.

Robots and spiders   The huge databases which the search engines maintain are compiled from endless trawls of the open Web. The search engines travel through the Web just as you do, following one hyperlink after another, adding each new document to their database, recording details of its URL, title and saving some or all of the full text. The search engines employ little programs to trawl the Web for them, called 'robots' or 'spiders'. The speed at which they can work is determined by how fast they can send requests and process the documents they get back. Sometimes you find the Internet slow. Well, so do robots. After they retrieve the documents there is a further time delay before they can be searched by you, the user. The search engine database has to index these new documents. Given the vast size of the Internet and the fact that documents can change regularly you don't have to be a computer genius to realize that the databases cannot possibly stay up to date with the Web.

Out of date   When you use a search engine you're searching a database which is, unavoidably, out of date. A robot can download a page and a database can index it in a space of minutes (though at least some search engines only update their index every few hours or days). However, given the vast size of the Web, the robot will probably not have time to visit that site again for another few months. In the meantime the site may have changed beyond recognition. It may even have disappeared from the face of the earth. The out-of-date information will stay in the search engine database, and be retrieved by researchers like you, until the robot visits the site again. This is the reason why search engines often bring up hits which don't exist and why they send you to documents which don't actually contain the keyword you used.

One search engine, Google, makes clear that it does not necessarily point you to up-to-date documents. It allows you to choose between downloading the document as Google indexed it (perhaps months before) or seeing what's currently at that URL, which could be quite different.

Having emphasized how horrendously out of date the search engines are, it's important to mention that some of them do take corrective measures to deal with this problem. They give priority to sites, such as news sites, whose content changes regularly and pay more regular visits to sites which change frequently.

Still, the bald truth is that when you search a search engine, only a tiny proportion of the items it searches were collected on the open Internet on the same day as you're conducting your search. This fact reinforces the point I have made in earlier chapters that human contact, email, printed sources or subject guides will probably alert you to many new sources in your field before the search engines ever get round to indexing them.

Incomplete Not only are the search engine databases out of date, but they're also so far from being complete and comprehensive that people have begun to question their value. Through the late 1990s regular surveys of the search engines found that as the Web expanded search engines were falling behind even further. Lawrence and Giles estimated in 1997 that the largest search engine only included about a third of the Web. They estimated that this had fallen to a sixth by 1999.

Since the search engines can't even hope to cover the entire Web they have adopted a range of techniques to cope with this. In the case of large Websites they will often index just a sample of pages and not even attempt to download the whole thing. (To check how many pages from your site have been indexed by AltaVista, use **host:yourwebsiteaddress**.) If you have Web space on a free Web space provider such as Geocities, which includes thousands of pages, you are highly unlikely to be included in the search engines unless you directly submit details of your site to them (see chapter 10 for advice on how to do this). You might as well not be on the Web at all. The only people who will find your page are those you tell about it.

The search engines also clearly give priority to those sites which they regard as more important, major news sites which change regularly, or the sites of major organizations. The flip-side of this is that, once again, the minor and the marginal is pushed out of sight and neglected.

The fact that search engines often only sample sites emphasizes the importance of searching the Web by site, identifying the home pages of useful sites and mining them thoroughly. You can't rely on the search engine to have included every page on a site.

There are huge tracts of the Web which they can't index The search engines cannot reach into many online databases. They used to be able to reach into many of these until the newspapers and other database owners started shielding them behind login screens.

The search engines cannot search any site which doesn't want to be searched. When a robot visits a site the first thing it has to do is request a file called *robots.txt*. If this file says robots are refused access the robot can venture no further into the site. There are very good reasons why certain sites reject robots. If large numbers of robots are checking your site every day it can slow down the service you provide to other users. In addition you may have set up your own sophisticated search system available through your home page. This will ensure at all stages that users know they are on your site. You can let the robots in, thus letting someone else provide a crude and unreliable index of a selection of your documents, or you can keep them out allowing them only to index your home page. This ensures all users are sent to your search page. This is the path increasingly being taken by large organizations such as newspapers which can rely on users going to them on the basis of their reputation in the 'real world'. In fact, the bigger, more useful and better known a resource is the greater the incentive it has to ban robots.

This suggests that the future may be extremely bleak for the search engines if more and more large sites shut them out.

Ranking: how the search engines order your results

If you manage to refine your queries well enough your searches should only bring back short lists of documents. You needn't worry about how they've been 'ranked' because you can quickly scan all of them. If on the other hand you continue to bring back a huge volume of hits it's useful to know how the search engines rank them.

The most common and crudest form of ranking is to rank documents according to the number of times the search term appears in them. This favours documents with a lot of repetition. A lot of pornographic sites tried to achieve higher rankings for their sites by including hundreds of references to 'sex' or 'girls' or 'pics'. A major problem with this kind of ranking is that the most relevant documents will often not mention your search term frequently.

An article on a famous individual, for example, might only mention their name once, in the title. When an item is completely devoted to one subject it feels little need to regularly refer to that subject by name. It's said that until the company realized the importance of this for being listed on the search engines the word IBM didn't appear once on IBM's home page.

Most of the search engines pay attention to which part of a document a word appears in and give higher rankings if the words appear in the first few lines of a document. They also give higher ranking to documents in which the search terms appear close together. Other criteria for ranking used by the big search engines include giving higher rankings to sites which they have reviewed or which are included in their crude 'guides' or 'channels'. This seems of quite dubious value since, in many cases, very little care goes into deciding what to include in the guides.

Meta tags: a failed subject classification scheme

Any author of a Web document can add meta tags at the beginning of their Web pages. They allow the author to provide subject keywords and a short description of the page's content. It sounds fantastic, the perfect way to search the Web by subject. Some search engines used to give high rankings to documents which included search terms in the keyword meta tag. There were two problems with meta tags: the overwhelming majority of authors didn't bother to use them; and those that did were often businesses seeking to improve their ranking by including deliberately misleading keywords or descriptions. A company which sold camping equipment, for example, might choose 'Information about campsites' as a description for its home page. As a result the meta tags have become irreparably corrupted and are unreliable to the extent that some search engines ignore everything in them.

Ranking games and tricks   Some people put a lot of effort into ensuring that their pages and sites get a high ranking and are thus more likely to appear near the top of your first screen of hits. When I looked for information via AltaVista about the new censorship standard 'PICs', and which 'Search Engines' implemented it, the first screen of hits was dominated by pornographic sites. They had packed the introductory sections of their pages with the words 'pics' (as in pictures) and 'Search Engines', presumably because these are frequently used search terms.

The games played are sometimes quite hilarious. A Web page author will fill their document with popular keywords but will specify that the page should have a white background and that the keywords appear in white. When you get to the page you see none of these keywords, only the text which the author wants you to see. You'll be mystified as to why the search engine picked up this page. In some cases people create 'doorway' or 'bridge' pages packed with popular keywords in order to get a high ranking on the search engines. However, when you go to the page it automatically redirects you to another page, usually a commercial site trying to sell you something. Some search engines reject all such pages. This cat and mouse game between the search engines and businesses looking for higher rankings will interfere with your research a little but the only thing you can really do is be aware that the problem exists.

Pay ranking   This is probably one of the more sinister developments of recent years. In spring 1999 AltaVista 'sold' 500 common search terms. Those who bought the terms could be assured that their site would come out top of the list when someone searched for the term. On the plus side AltaVista made it clear that these slots had been paid for and eventually abandoned the scheme. Other search engines have taken it up, however.

If this practice spreads more widely there is a serious danger that some search engines could end up primarily as commercial directories. In a case of killing the goose that laid the golden egg this would probably drive away large numbers of users, researchers among them.

Profiling the search engines

Most of the advice given up to now applies to all or most of the search engines. However, every search engine has an individual personality, composed of a unique combination of the search features dealt with above and its own unique capabilities.

Much of the detail provided in the profiles below is drawn from Search Engine Watch (**searchenginewatch.com**). Note that alliances and relationships between the various search engines can change rapidly.

AltaVista (**www.altavista.com**)

AltaVista laid claim for a long time to the title of largest Web search engine. It has been one of the main players for a few years now. The default search is to search for the exact phrase (the equivalent of " "); NEAR will search for words within ten words of each other. The 'Ask AltaVista' option actually searches 'Ask Jeeves' while directory listings come from Looksmart. AltaVista uses the Real Names service as do several other search engines. If you enter the name of a company or organization or even of a place Real Names will look for the official site. Companies have to pay Real Names (**www.realnames.com**) to be included.

Power searching options include **link:**, **text:**, **title:**, **url:**, **host:** (equivalent to **domain:**) and **anchor:**. If you use capital letters the search will only return words which use the capitals. AltaVista performs a spell check on your search. 'Customize Settings' allows you to restrict your search by language and to adjust the number of hits per page and the level of detail included with each hit.

Advanced searching AltaVista offers three different types of advanced searching. The 'Advanced Search' itself is not particularly useful. As AltaVista used to candidly say, 'almost everything you need to search for can be found quickly and with better results using the standard search box'. Advanced searching allows you to override AltaVista's ranking.

The 'Search Assistant' provides pull-down menus for power searching options, allows you to restrict your search by date and domain and to set the number of results per page. It's more useful than the advanced search.

The 'Text-Only' search is free of the advertising and other clutter which you get on the main AltaVista search page. It is fast and lean and is highly recommended for those who can manage without pull-down menus.

AOL Search (**search.aol.com**)

If you are an AOL subscriber AOL Search will search AOL's content and the open Web together. Non-subscribers can use it to search the open Web. It uses the Inktomi index (see inset) and also searches categories in the Open Directory (see chapter 6 for more on the Open Directory). It automatically treats your query as an AND query.

Advanced searching 'Search Options' provides menus for Boolean search terms and 'exact phrase'.

Direct Hit (**www.directhit.com**)

This service is owned by 'Ask Jeeves' and it contributes results to both MSN Search and HotBot. Its special feature is the fact that it measures the popularity of sites, giving more prominence to sites which were visited by a lot of people who used the same words as you in their search.

Excite (**www.excite.com**)

Excite has subsumed two other search services, Magellan and WebCrawler, though you can still search WebCrawler individually. If you capitalize two adjacent words Excite will look for them as an exact phrase.

Advanced searching The advanced search, which is only available after you've done an initial search allows you to choose the number of hits returned per page. It provides pull-down menus for Boolean terms. You can restrict your search by language and domain.

Fast Search (**www.alltheweb.com**)

This search engine also powers some of the results in Lycos (see chapter 6 for more on Lycos).

Advanced searching   The advanced search allows you to change the display of hits, to restrict the search by domain and language, to choose Boolean options from pull-down menus and to choose 'offensive content reduction' to censor your results.

Google (**www.google.com**)

Google has some beautiful features which are unique to it. It also has a very lean and streamlined look. Rather than bringing back the first few lines of text of a document it only brings back the few words which surround your keyword or words, giving you a clearer idea of whether the document might be relevant to you. Results are grouped by site, to a certain extent. This was the first search engine to determine page rank according to the number of other pages which linked to a Web page.

Google also provides a link to the 'cache', the copy of the hit which it holds in its database. It may be different to the document currently available at the same URL. In the case of a fast-changing site the 'cached' document may actually be the one relevant to your query.

It uses the Real Names service mentioned previously.

Google automatically looks for documents containing all of your search terms. It allows the power search term **link:**.

Google also provides a search limited to US government sites (dealt with in chapter 3) and one limited to university sites (dealt with in chapter 4).

Advanced searching The advanced search allows you to limit your search by domain and language and to specify whether you want to search for the

Search in Google on Welsh language politics

exact phrase. It also allows you to choose the number of hits per page and whether to filter out sexually explicit content.

Go To (**www.goto.com**)

Go To draws on the Inktomi index. It allows math and Boolean searching.

HotBot (**www.hotbot.com**)

HotBot draws on the Inktomi index and also on Direct Hit, which rates pages by popularity. Its directory search uses the Open Directory.

It automatically matches all terms (the equivalent of AND or +). It is partially case sensitive.

Flexible pull-down menus allow you to do sophisticated searching without bothering with search syntax. They allow you to do the equivalent of **link:** and **title:** searches, to choose 'exact phrase', to restrict your search by date and language and to determine how much detail is displayed with each hit.

Advanced searching   The advanced search provides all of the options available on the main page plus the option to limit by domain or geographical region and the option to specify 'Page Depth', effectively to restrict your search to home pages.

Northern Light (**www.northernlight.com**)

Not a simple search engine, this searches the open Web and its own article databases, clustering results by topic. It was dealt with in detail in chapter 3.

It automatically matches all search terms (the equivalent of adding + or AND to your query). It allows you to restrict your search by date and to sort results by date. It provides the following power search terms: **title:**, **url:**, **text:** and **pub:**. This last option allows you to search special collection documents by journal title, restricting your search to a particular journal.

One special feature of Northern Light is that you can combine the power search terms with Boolean terms so that you can search for **url:anycollege. edu** OR **url.anycollege.edu.au**.

Advanced searching   The 'Power Search' allows you to use power search terms in pull-down menus and to limit your search by subject area and type of site, by domain and language and date.

Webtop (**www.webtop.com**)

A search engine originally established by DIALOG, one of the old online searching firms dealt with in chapter 3. When it was launched it was quite awkward to use but it has become more user-friendly in the meantime.

Search engine families

This box shows the inter-relationships between several of the major search engines and subject guides.

Search engines and subject guides which use the Looksmart directory, MSN
    Search, Excite and AltaVista.
Search engines and subject guides which use the Open Directory, AOL Search,
    HotBot, Netscape Search and Lycos.
Search engines and subject guides which use the Inktomi index, AOL Search,
    HotBot, Go To, MSN Search, Looksmart, Snap and Iwon.

You'll note that AOL Search uses the Open Directory while MSN Search uses Looksmart as their sources for subject listings. Both use the Inktomi index as their source for keyword searching. Effectively then you are searching very little that you can't find elsewhere when you use these two services. The one major exception is the fact that AOL Search also does a search of AOL material but only if you're an AOL subscriber.

Understanding Inktomi

Search engines such as Google and AltaVista build up their indexes by trawling the Web using robots and spiders as outlined in chapter 5. When you search them you search their own indexes.

Inktomi is a company which has built up an index of the Web in the same way. Instead of allowing you to search the index via an Inktomi search engine it has sold access to the index to several search engines. Inktomi just provides the index of hundreds of millions of documents. The individual search engines decide what search options to give their users and how the results from the Inktomi index will be displayed. It's hard to avoid the fact that, for all of the tweaking, you're searching the same database whenever you search using a search engine which relies on Inktomi. You probably should not bother using more than one of the Inktomi-powered keyword search engines.

Keeping up to date

When you have completely scoured the search engines for information on your topic you are left with one problem: new information is constantly being added to the Web. Clearly you need to devise some strategy for finding out about new information. The simplest strategy, and the one I recommend, is simply to run your searches again in six months' time or towards the end of your research or writing up. The keyword search chart you've kept provides a record of the queries you've used, the search engines you've used them on and when. If a new search engine has appeared on the scene in the meantime you can also run them through this.

The second option is to use a service which regularly runs searches using your queries and informs you when new pages match your query. For instance, Informant (**informant.dartmouth.edu**) will run your searches on up to four different search engines. You can choose how often Informant should run the query. It will send you email alerts letting you know if it has found anything new. One problem is that all four search engines won't have exactly the same search syntax so your query will be translated for some of them. This is likely to make the query less precise and less useful.

Some of the search engines offer updating services, informing you by email when they find new documents matching your search query. You should be very selective in using such services. It is easy to lose track of which queries you've asked the different search engines to keep track of. It's easy to find yourself inundated with email about sites which you don't have time to check out.

If you do use such services wait until you have refined and finalized your search queries, at the end of your trawl through the search engines. Only then should you go and systematically enter the same queries on all of the search engines you'd like to search. As I've said already, though, I wouldn't bother with these services at all. It's easier just to run your search again when you have time to actually look at all the new sites which have been added.

One final thing: steer clear of offers to update you every time a particular page changes. If a page changes regularly you'll be snowed under with updates. If it changes rarely you can probably leave it until your next sweep in six months to see what's new.

The meta search engines

Meta search engines are services which will run your query on several search engines at the same time. On the plus side, you don't have to waste time visiting each search engine individually. On the minus side, since all search engines have a slightly different search syntax, the meta search engines have to 'simplify', that is, crudely translate your query for search engines which don't understand it. Thus, you can't be as precise as you can when you go directly to a search engine. For this reason alone I suggest that you steer clear of them.

I have already suggested that you perfect queries on one large search engine before moving on to others. The sophisticated queries you develop will just be mangled when you put them into a meta search engine. For example, when I ran a query on AltaVista which used two + signs and a - sign, it returned eighty-seven pages. I ran the same query through a meta search engine (**www.isleuth.com**) which ran the query on six search engines. From AltaVista alone it returned 30,776 hits. That is, the meta search engine had flattened out and simplified my query so much that it defeated the purpose of developing a specific query in the first place.

The one type of query for which the meta search engines might be useful is if you have a very simple query on a very rare word. They can't do too much damage to a query consisting of one word and you can quickly run the search without having to go to the individual search engines.

Many of the meta search engines also search a wide range of databases available on the open Web. This is quite distinct from the search engine searches they do. However, few of these databases will be of interest to the researcher, ranging as they do from databases of dog breeds to databases of sports results.

Any of them which are of interest to you should already have turned up through the subject guides well before you reach the meta search engines. You can search them much more effectively and thoroughly by connecting directly to them and searching them individually rather than through a meta search engine.

So, all in all, there is little enough to recommend these services to the researcher, unless they become much more powerful and sophisticated in the type of searches they perform. A selection of meta search engines is listed below:

Beaucoup (**www.beaucoup.com**)   This is essentially a catalogue of searchable databases and Websites, organized by subject. It provides forms which allow you to search these and the search engines simultaneously.

Metacrawler (**www.metacrawler.com**)   This allows you to search the major search engines. It eliminates duplicates and you can organize results by top-level domain using the 'power search'.

All-in-one (**www.allonesearch.com**)   This meta search engine allows you to search several search engines simultaneously.

The Big Hub (**www.TheBigHub.com**)   This allows you to simultaneously search several search engines, Web directories and databases.

Dogpile (**www.dogpile.com**)   The best feature of this service is that it shows you how it has altered your query for each search engine. You can at least see exactly how it has changed your search. You can do a custom search, specifying which search engines you'd like to search, and in what order.

Internet dinosaurs? A premature announcement of the demise of the big search engines

The big search engines have universal ambitions – to index the entire Web. It became clear a few years ago just how far short of this goal they were falling. As far back as 1997 the very largest search engine at the time, AltaVista, was estimated to be indexing about a quarter of the entire Web, at the very most (Pike, 1997). The Web was still in its infancy. It only had a few years of accumulated history to be dealt with. In the meantime it has expanded rapidly and the search engines have been running just to stand still.

Even if there was a sudden halt in the creation of new Websites, existing Websites would generate huge volumes of new information every year. If the search engines can't deal with the volume of documentation which has accumulated in the few short years of the Web's infancy, how can they expect to deal with the entire Web in ten, twenty or fifty years' time?

Observing the plight of the big search engines some people have begun to develop a new kind of search engine. A domain search engine is one which limits its searching to a particular domain, a country domain like **.ru** (Russia) or an organizational domain like **.mil** (the US military). They cover one small fraction of the Web but they try to cover it well. In this sense the best of the national versions of the big search engines act as good domain search engines, services such as AltaVista France which claims to index 95% of French (**.fr**) Websites. The **usgovsearch** service, which searches US government and military sites and which aims to have a complete index to such sites, and **SearchEdu**, which only searches university sites, seem to point the way to a future where we will increasingly rely on such specialized search engines.

The domain search engines are not weighted down by the awesome and ultimately impossible ambitions of the big search engines to index the whole Web. As a result they can devote a lot of energy to indexing their chunk of the Web, coming close to covering it comprehensively. They are also likely to develop extensive expertise related to materials in that particular domain, a fact which will further improve their services.

In many ways this is a regrettable development. People have fantasized for a long time about the universal database, a single source which would contain all human knowledge. The search engines are perhaps the nearest we have ever come to such an ideal. But rather than drawing closer to the ideal it seems to be gradually receding from our reach. Soon we may all be ghettoized again in search engines covering our own specific interests. We may find ourselves abandoning the big search engines just as we were starting to get used to them.

8

Classification, evaluation and citation

Introduction

The previous three chapters dealt with finding Web documents. This chapter is about what to do with those documents once you've found them. Using Web documents as research sources is much more problematic than using print publications. It is much more difficult to judge exactly what sort of document you're dealing with and how reliable a source of information it is.

For precisely this reason you may also find a certain degree of scepticism of Web resources amongst those who are supervising or examining your work. This chapter describes procedures and standards which will help you to judge the reliability of Web documents and to reference them consistently and accurately. The very fact that you will be able to assess and cite Web documents according to rigorous academic standards is the most powerful argument you can have against the scepticism of those who are suspicious of any Internet-based source.

Reviving the lost art of scepticism

Academics are foremost among those warning us not to believe everything we read on the Web. All in all it's a good thing that mistrust of the written word is being encouraged by academics. Scepticism is a core value of scientific research. Despite this, scepticism of written materials seems to have been bred out of academic culture to a certain degree. There is a simple explanation for this. Libraries are extremely selective. The academic publications they house have passed a series of gatekeepers from publishers, editors and peer-reviewers through to librarians and the academic staff who order books. We are well shielded from non-academic materials and as a consequence it's possible for students and researchers to become accustomed to treating the written word with undue respect. The Internet has done us a favour by reminding us how important it is to take a critical and sceptical approach to all written materials. By forcing us all to develop new skills for evaluating Web documents it should help us to look more critically at printed documents. It's not only on the Internet that we should be aware of author motivation and of the ways in which authors can obscure, twist, exaggerate or even invent 'facts'.

Classification

The purpose of classification

Newspapers and magazines aside, university libraries are dominated by two types of print publication: official documents and academic publications. Both of these types of document go through a quality-control process of some kind and they both at least aspire to the ideal of objectivity. While they are of course influenced by personal and political bias this is generally muted by the requirement to at least attempt to be objective. You have to approach all research sources critically, with an eye to the subconscious biases which inevitably influence the most conscientious of researchers. Nonetheless, you can be reasonably confident that the bulk of the materials on your library shelves will not be full of deliberate lies and wild exaggerations. You don't need to worry about a classification of documents because there are only two major types and they both have high levels of reliability.

On the Web there are many other types of documents. In certain types of documents authors make no attempt to be objective and are not expected to, for example in party political publications. It would in fact be ludicrous to judge such a document by the standards of objectivity which would be applied to academic materials.

Classification of documents is not intended as a way of sorting documents according to quality but according to the genres they belong to.

Classifying means that you can put a document in a necessarily crude category and judge it by the standards appropriate to that category. Thus when you've decided a document is a news document you won't be disappointed that it's not footnoted. You won't expect an advocacy document to be even-handed and neutral. Conversely, when an academic document clearly falls short of the standards of proof and objectivity which you expect of such literature you have a right to be particularly sceptical of its conclusions. These classifications should not be treated as hard and fast categories. The boundaries between them are extremely blurred. Classification is a rough process to help you to begin to assess the reliability and usefulness of documents.

Why bother with non-academic documents?

One of the main categories dealt with below is 'academic' documents, those which meet the academic standards set for virtually all of the books and articles which make it into university libraries. Since much research has traditionally been restricted to such documents you might well ask why not just make a simple classification of the Web into the academic and non-academic and ignore the latter?

To do this would simplify matters. It would also cut us off from large volumes of high-quality research material. There are many documents which don't follow the rules of academia, such as newspaper articles, pamphlets, manifestos and reports which nonetheless bring new information to important debates. Many non-academic documents are more thoughtful, original and incisive, have a greater respect for the truth and are more useful to the researcher than some of the work which finds its way into academic journals. To draw a line between the academic and the rest would be to potentially cut yourself off from much of the high-quality writing in your subject area.

Advocacy documents

Defining advocacy   An advocacy group is a group whose prime purpose is to advocate a particular viewpoint: a political party, an NGO or a pressure group, to take a few examples. Advocacy groups are united by a particular approach to information and knowledge. Their role is to advocate certain positions. Although they will weigh up competing arguments as they develop these positions, that process of weighing up is not their prime concern. Since academics also advocate particular views and in fact are often linked directly to advocacy groups, there is often a fine line in practice between the two worlds. In theory, however, the distinction is clear. For academia the pursuit of the truth is the ideal goal. For advocacy groups the advancement of a particular point of view is the core purpose.

Certain advocacy groups systematically and deliberately distort and exaggerate facts in pursuit of this aim. For this reason you need to be particularly careful when dealing with information of any kind produced by such groups. At the other extreme are advocacy groups whose prime concern is a primarily moral issue such as human rights or minority rights. Many such groups produce work of extremely high quality which is an essential resource for academic work in their field. The work of groups such as the Minority Rights Group (**www.minorityrights.org**) and Amnesty International (**www.amnesty.org**) draws on academic standards while also seeking to make a political impact. The quality of the work of such advocacy groups is reflected in the fact that their print publications are well represented in university libraries. This emphasizes that we should be careful not to dismiss this entire class of documents. Neither should we treat all advocacy documents with unduly high levels of scepticism. Real-world knowledge of the organizations responsible for advocacy Web pages will provide the best indication of how sceptical you should be.

Recognizing advocacy documents   Generally you will recognize an advocacy document because it will be clearly marked with the name of the group which produced it. If not, the name of the group should be there on the site home page. Although the **.org** domain is used by many advocacy groups, not all such groups use the domain, so the URL does not provide a reliable guide as to whether a document is an advocacy document or not. In addition many educational organizations use the domain.

Some advocacy groups try to give their arguments more credibility by making themselves sound like academic organizations. They use titles like the 'Centre for Research on ...' or the 'Institute for the Study of ... '. This does not mean that the materials they produce are not of high quality or are not worthwhile. However, if they are driven by a clear political agenda, if they do not even attempt to follow academic standards and are clearly committed to one party to a dispute, debate or argument, then the work they produce is best classified and evaluated by the standards applicable to advocacy documents.

It can also be difficult to distinguish an advocacy document from a personal page since so many individuals put up pages advocating particular views. It is important to distinguish between the two because you need to apply particularly high standards to personal pages. In any advocacy organization, no matter how extreme, unreasonable or marginal it may be, the author of that group's materials has to take into account in some way the opinion of other members of the organization, even if there is only one other member. An individual putting up their own opinions is not answerable to even one other person in the entire world. Such an individual may well set up an organization of which they are the founder, president and sole member.

In the sense in which I use the term, such a one-person show should not be considered an advocacy group and their output on the Web should be treated as personal pages rather than advocacy documents. They should be treated with the especially high levels of scepticism appropriate for such pages.

Using advocacy documents Advocacy documents are problematic mainly because they often only give one side of a story, in many cases distorting or brushing over the main arguments of their opponents. There is one simple and obvious way to correct this imbalance: get the other side of the story. If an advocacy group is on the Web it's likely their opponents are also online. By and large, groups don't link to those who oppose them but there are many other ways of locating their opponents. To find those who oppose the 'Movement for Autonomy', for example, try searching on +"**Movement for autonomy**"+"**complete idiots**". I'm only half-joking. Regardless of the intrinsic value of the documents they provide, advocacy sites are useful to the social science researcher for two main purposes: providing information about the group and illustrating the views of the group. It used to be extremely difficult to get information about small activist groups, about their organizational structures and activities. As key social actors they are of interest in themselves to many researchers.

If you are studying a contentious issue one of the best sources of information about the principal debates on that topic are the Websites of the advocacy groups taking opposing sides in those debates.

Academic documents

Defining them Academic documents are those which follow a set of standards laid down by academia including citation and acknowledgement of sources and the aspiration to pursue 'the truth', however that may be defined and however elusive it may be. They usually undergo some sort of quality control, whether it be the examination process which a dissertation goes through, the peer-review which journal articles are subject to or the editorial process which academic books go through. Academic documents also usually carry a certain degree of authority because of the experience of authors, reflected in their academic degrees and their other publications. This isn't to say that all academic work is of high quality, merely that it has gone through a set of procedures which provide at least some sort of quality control.

On the Web it's not quite as easy to tell whether a document is an academic document or not. Academia attracts a certain amount of respect, as a source of unbiased research. Because of this certain advocacy groups, businesses and news sources try to make their documents look like academic documents. In addition there has been a growth of online 'journals' which publish articles on academic topics. Some of these do not subject articles to peer-review, one of the mechanisms for quality control in academia. While many high-quality articles undoubtedly appear in such journals (while poor-quality articles make it into peer-reviewed journals) you need to be aware that this important element of quality control is missing. In the case of such journals you are depending on the credibility of the author. If they have a record of writing and publishing in this area it adds a lot to their credibility, whether they've been peer-reviewed or not.

Recognizing them Several countries have domains which are reserved for academic institutions: **edu** in the USA, **ac.uk** in the UK, **ac.jp** in Japan, **edu.au** in Australia. In other countries the universities are easily recognized by their Web addresses. In Germany **www.uni-oldenburg.de** is Oldenburg University, **www.uni-heidelberg.de** is Heidelberg University and so on.

Not all documents on university servers are academic documents. The mountains of materials which universities provide about themselves are probably best classified as 'official' documents (see below). Many universities allow students to create Websites on the university's Web server. These are personal pages (see below), and in some cases advocacy documents, and should be treated as such. In many cases it will be clear from the URL that these are student pages. The URL may include a folder called **students/** or **personal/** or something similar, or a tilde and a name, **~jsmith** for example, indicating that this is the folder of an individual user, either staff or student.

And not all academic documents are to be found on university servers. There is nothing to stop academics and academic research projects putting their material on commercial servers.

Using them Their usefulness is clear. For all of their faults, academic documents are supposed to adhere to standards of objectivity and accuracy. As a consequence they should be more reliable sources than other types of documents.

Many academics now put draft papers or conference papers on the Web, partly to publicize their work, partly because they want to invite comments and criticism. Although these are clearly academic documents you need to be aware that you cannot treat them like published articles. In many cases authors stipulate that you should not quote from or cite these articles without direct permission from the author. It means that, although you can read them and print them, you can only use them in your research after you go to the trouble of contacting the author.

Official documents

Defining them Official documents are those produced by public institutions, and by government and international agencies. This includes documents from the smallest county council, fire department or roads authority up to national bodies such as government departments and agencies. It includes documents from the UN and all of the agencies associated with it and from all organizations which draw together the governments of several countries, from OPEC to NATO to the OSCE.

Recognizing them Many governments have their own domain (**gov** in the USA, **gov.uk** in the UK, **gov.jp** in Japan) or their government affiliation is often clear from their URL. In Germany and in Denmark, for example, government ministries have Web addresses which include abbreviations of the ministries' titles. The German environment ministry, the BMU, is **www.bmu.de**, while the URL for the Irish government is simply **www. irlgov.ie**. Many US states have their own domains. Thus **ca.gov** is the domain for the California state government. Some US states have domains which do not come under the overall **gov** domain, such as New York state whose domain is **state.ny.us**. Government domains in most cases only cover central government. Local and regional bodies often make their own arrangements and it is not as straightforward to identify them by their URLs. In the case of international organizations, although the **int** domain is reserved for their use, many of them are to be found in the **org** domain which, confusingly, is also used by many advocacy groups.

Unlike the **edu** domain which includes non-academic documents you can take it that almost every document in a government domain is an official document unless clearly marked otherwise.

Official documents have a reasonably high status in most countries and are given a lot of credibility. As a result some advocacy groups try to make themselves sound or look like official agencies. They will use official-sounding titles, 'The office of this… ', 'the bureau for that …'. This is rare enough. Just be aware that it does happen and if you have reason to doubt whether a source really is official or not just read the information that the agency provides about itself. Once again your own 'real-world' knowledge of your subject area will help you to separate the official from the advocacy document.

Using them   Governments are the main collectors and disseminators of large volumes of statistical data about their own countries, information on the economy, population and transport, for example.

Political considerations do of course influence official documents and in certain cases they shade over into clear advocacy of particular positions. While not advocacy documents, official documents which clearly argue one particular side of a case should be treated with the higher levels of scepticism which should be used when dealing with advocacy documents. That is, you should make sure to get the other side of the story and be aware that facts which undermine the argument may have been deliberately obscured.

There can be an unclear boundary between official and news sources. Many countries have official news agencies connected to government, such as Xinhua in China. Despite being government agencies their prime function is to provide news and they can be classified as news sources. Apart from this, many governments provide 'government information services' which are devoted to issuing press releases and even publications, to promote the government currently in power. These are not news services but they sometimes look like they are, particularly on the Web where it's easy to slap together a bunch of government statements and call them a news bulletin or news update.

News documents

Defining them   News documents are documents produced by organizations whose prime function is to distribute news stories, be they wire news agencies, newspapers, TV and radio news programmes or magazines. As mentioned previously, the line between government and advocacy groups and news sources can be quite unclear at times. News sources do tend to be informed by a particular political viewpoint. This is reflected in the way they cover news stories, in the stories they choose to cover, in the aspects of a story they emphasize and in the editorial positions which they take. In many cases news sources have more direct political affiliations. If you are using an unfamiliar news source you need to be aware that many news sources across the world are directly linked to political parties or governments and their approach to the news can be even more partisan than you would usually expect from a news source.

Recognizing them   The fact remains that most news sources on the Net are just the online version of an existing news service in the 'real world'. Most of these have attempted to secure domain names which include their real-world title. Thus **chicagotribune.com** is the *Chicago Tribune* online while **www.nytimes.com** is the *New York Times* online.

Most online newspapers still follow the basic layout of the printed version, a front page with short summaries of stories which appear inside, so that you recognize them as news sources immediately from their familiar layout. Likewise, the Websites of TV news services make frequent reference to the

TV version, providing still photos or transcripts of news broadcasts. The wire services, dealt with in chapter 3, provide news stories to huge numbers of other Web services but they always clearly stamp their name on the individual news stories. These are news documents no matter what kind of site they appear on.

As with academia, the news media have a reasonably high level of credibility. Some advocacy groups imitate the style and layout and terminology of news documents in an attempt to increase their credibility. Once again, it's your real-world knowledge of your subject area which will enable you to sort out one from the other.

Using them   News sources, like academia, aspire to the pursuit of the truth and to the ideal of objectivity. Unlike academia, news sources set lower formal standards of proof and referencing of sources. They are not footnoted. They can and do give the opinions of individuals as though they represent the opinions of an entire group. Standards vary from one news organization to another and those papers which attempt to be papers of record, recording all significant events with the deliberate intention of acting as a source for researchers in the future, are invaluable as research sources. Many news sources have only the barest consideration for the ideals of objectivity and truth and put considerably more weight on another core purpose of news gathering: the selling of news as a product. The desire to sell as many newspapers or attract as many viewers as possible is a powerful counterweight to the ideals of 'truth'.

Personal Web pages

Defining them   These are documents produced by a single individual on their own behalf or jointly by several individuals who are not formally organized as a group.

There is one major area of difficulty in defining personal Web pages. Many individuals use their personal Web space to host material from a particular organization. If the organization itself clearly regards this as their official site then it should be regarded as an advocacy page, not a personal page.

Recognizing them   Most personal pages belong to one of three major categories. Each of these categories has different characteristics by which they can be recognized.

1. *Student or staff pages hosted on university Web servers* They will belong to a university domain and the URL will often give an indication that you are dealing with personal pages. Thus **www.anycollege.edu/students/~jhughes** is obviously a student page while **www.anycollege.edu/depts/economics/staff/~chun** is clearly a staff page.
2. *Pages hosted on ISPs* Huge numbers of individuals who do not have access to the Web at work or at university get Web access from home through an ISP (Internet Service Provider). Most of the ISPs now offer

limited free Web space to subscribers. US-based ISPs and many outside the USA use the **.com** domain. It will often be clear from the domain and/or the file path that these are personal pages. The AOL URL, **aol.members.com**, for example, could hardly be more descriptive.

3. *Free Web space* Numerous companies now provide free Web space. One of the first and the most famous is **geocities**. You will quickly become familiar with the other main companies such as **Xoom** and **Tripod** because as part of the price for providing 'free' Web space they promote themselves on the pages of their customers.

Using them   There are of course many valuable, high-quality, personal Web pages. There are many more which are of minimal value.

There are a number of crude measures for assessing the value and reliability of a personal page. Since it is the product of a single individual its reliability will depend on this individual alone. You can look for indicators of how much trust to place in them. Consider whether they have published anything. Consider what their qualifications to write on the subject are. These qualifications can range from academic degrees to direct personal experience. Finally, evaluate them for accuracy and objectivity as outlined below.

Be careful not to dismiss personal pages too readily. It is, after all, one of the revolutionary effects of the Web that individuals can spread their ideas in this way. However, the fact that personal pages have not usually undergone any sort of editorial or quality-control process means that you do have to do some quality control of your own.

Business/marketing pages

These are pages set up by commercial companies with the core purpose of selling a product and promoting the company. While they may provide useful information about the company this information is there to promote the company and its products. When using such pages you have to be constantly aware of this fact and of the very important consequences it has for the reliability of the information provided. Be aware that businesses do sometimes try to present their materials as 'news' or 'research' to increase credibility.

The **.com** domain was created for businesses and is used by businesses world-wide. In addition many countries outside the USA have their own commercial domains, such as **.co.uk** in the UK. As mentioned previously many news and advocacy documents and personal pages use the **.com** domain. Just because a site has a **.com** address doesn't automatically make it a business/marketing site.

Entertainment sites

There is a fine line between this category and the business/marketing category since virtually all entertainment is run as a business. However, the

Web, as well as being a forum for entertainment companies to promote their products, has become a medium for entertainment. Entertainment pages usually find their home in the **.com** domain or in the commercial domain of the country they're based in.

Classification, crude but useful

Don't get too hung up on classification. The categories given above are necessarily crude and you will find many Web pages which are difficult to fit into one category or another. The effort of trying to do this is valuable in itself. In effect classification forces you to try to answer the question 'what kind of document am I looking at?' It's a question you need to have some kind of answer to before you move on to the work of evaluation.

Evaluation

One of the main purposes of evaluating Web documents is simply to identify the sort of information which is immediately obvious in print publications – information about the publisher and author and about the editing process a document has gone through. This information is essential if you are to cite Web documents accurately. A secondary purpose is to judge how trustworthy or reliable a source is. What follows is a series of checklists to help you assess authority, accuracy, objectivity, currency and quality. It draws heavily on the categories used by Alexander and Tate (1999) elaborating on and reorganizing the categories a little. One word of warning: don't apply these evaluation criteria too rigidly. Sometimes the most reliable and authoritative of Web pages do not include the basic information mentioned in these checklists. Governments, for example, often neglect to stamp their authority clearly on many documents. They often don't bother with footnoting, copyright statements or contact details. It illustrates the fact that those with most authority often feel the least need to proclaim it.

Authority

The author, the organization or institution they're associated with and the publisher of the work are the main sources of authority for print publications, in varying degree. Details for each of these is usually provided in print publications.

   On a Web page author, organization and publisher can easily be combined in the one person and they can often be quite difficult to identify. The first questions to ask are:

1. *Is it clear who is responsible for the document?* That may be an individual author, an organization or the Website owners or publishers. If you can't

find this information on the document you're looking at, check if it's available on the front page for that site.

2. *Is there any information about the person or organization responsible for the page?* That is, is there any information which would help you to make a judgement about how reliable the author is? In print publications the very fact that a book has been published by a well-established publisher with a good reputation, or has been written by someone with a higher degree in the subject they're writing on, lends it a certain credibility. If you're unsure of the quality of the page you might look to see if any information has been provided about the author or the organization.

3. *Is there a copyright statement?* In the absence of a clear statement of who the author is, this provides an alternative indication of who is responsible for the document. Don't be too upset if you don't find a copyright statement. Many people don't bother since materials are automatically copyrighted to their author regardless of whether they include a copyright statement or not.

4. *Does it have a print counterpart which reinforces its authority?* Printed documents in general are regarded as more reliable than Web documents. If a Web document also has a printed version, if it's appeared in a print publication such as a book, journal or newspaper, it reinforces its authority.

Accuracy

1. *Are sources clearly listed so they can be verified?* This is a fundamental of academic literature, in the form of footnotes and bibliographies. Although you can't expect non-academic documents to follow academic footnoting conventions you can usefully pose this question of all documents. You can use it as a measure of the quality and reliability of advocacy documents in particular.

2. *Is there an editorial input?* An editor provides an extra layer of quality control which should lead to increased accuracy. Most print publications have been through an editorial process.

3. *Is spelling and grammar correct?* You should be careful not to place too much weight on this. Minor errors creep into virtually every publication. However, poor spelling and grammar can indicate a certain carelessness which might affect the document in other ways. If an author has got their spelling wrong maybe they've got some of their facts wrong too.

Objectivity

It's unrealistic to expect anyone writing on a social science subject to be completely detached and objective. After all, if you felt completely detached from a subject why would you bother to study it? In recent years many researchers have in fact argued against the ideals of detached objectivity partly because it is a pretence which often serves to mask prejudice and bias in the research community. Even if you can never be fully objective you can at least clearly state the limits to your objectivity. The aspiration to objectivity, however impossible it may be to achieve, is a traditional value of social science research. In practical terms it means that you should not distort evidence, not make wild claims based on weak evidence and not deliberately omit evidence. You are entitled to expect academic documents to make more of an attempt at objectivity than, for example, advocacy documents. But just because a document doesn't attempt to be objective doesn't render it worthless. The questions below can usefully be applied to a wide range of documents.

1. *Are biases and affiliations clearly stated?* You can expect that an advocacy document will advocate a particular position. The problem arises when they do not make this bias clear.
2. *Is advertising clearly differentiated from information?* Advertisers often try to present ads in the form of newspaper articles or research findings to give them more credibility. This is deliberately misleading and undermines the credibility of a document.
3. *Are 'opinion' elements clearly labelled as such?* On personal pages you will often find personal opinion dressed up as an 'article' or 'report'.

Currency

Evaluating currency is important for two principal reasons. Where it's important that a document be up to date, currency means checking the date when the document was produced or last updated to see how up to date it is. If you want to know about the current state of the Nicaraguan economy, for example, it's very important that the documents you're relying on should be as up to date as possible.

In many cases it's not important to the researcher that a document be current. It's still important, though, to identify the date when a document was produced. It identifies the historical context for the document. Thus, it's important to know whether a document dealing with the Second World War was produced in the midst of the war, shortly after it or many years later. The period it was produced in will have a powerful influence on the document and knowing the date will help you to understand the document.

1. *If the document has a print counterpart is there a date of publication for that?* If there is, and the Web version is an unaltered copy of the printed version, then the date of print publication is the only significant date. It's generally irrelevant when it was put on the Web or when you viewed it.
2. *Are there dates for when the document was first produced or first put on the Web?* For a document with no print counterpart these are two different ways of determining when a Web document was first 'published'.

3. *Are there dates for when the document was last updated or revised?* For those documents which are regularly updated it's important to indicate which version you are referring to. The date when it was last updated also indicates how current and up to date the document is. Note that most Web authors don't bother to 'constantly update' the documents they put on the Web.

Evaluating email messages

It can be tricky to evaluate the reliability of email messages as research sources. Personal messages stand on their own merits. You place as much reliability on them as you would on the person who sent them. The same applies to messages sent via email distribution lists by organizations and institutions. You trust them as much as you trust the sender.

Things become more difficult when you're dealing with forwarded messages. People often forward by email news stories or other items they've gleaned from the Web. In some cases people edit or alter the stories, for legitimate reasons, highlighting the section they want to bring to your attention. In many cases, though, people edit to make news reports appear more favourable to their argument or political position. Be very very careful of quoting from an item which has been forwarded to you in the body of an email message (if it's an attachment it's a little less likely to have been altered). You really need to check the original and cite the original wherever possible.

Vonnegut, Schmich, Luhrman and the sunscreen speech: the dangers of relying on email messages

In July or August 1997 someone sent an email message which included the text of a short speech which began with the words "Wear sunscreen. If I could offer you only one tip for the future, sunscreen would be it." They described it as a speech which the science fiction author, Kurt Vonnegut, had given at a commencement ceremony at MIT in Boston. It was a clever, witty speech and a lot of people forwarded it to friends via email. People put copies of it up on Websites, attributing authorship to Vonnegut. It came to the attention of an Australian film-maker called Baz Luhrman (*Romeo and Juliet*, *Strictly Ballroom*) who decided he wanted to record a song using the text of the speech. When he started searching the Internet for contact details for Vonnegut so that he could buy the rights to the words he came across Web pages which discussed the speech. It turned out that Kurt Vonnegut had never made such a speech, had never in fact spoken at an MIT commencement ceremony. The original piece had been written as a column in the *Chicago Tribune* by columnist Mary Schmich in June 1997. Why the person who first included it in an email message described it as a speech by Vonnegut is a mystery but as a result thousands of people believed it was. There are still Web pages out there which attribute it to Vonnegut and even two years after the controversy I heard the song described on a TV music show as being based on a Vonnegut speech.

This story has one simple moral. Be very careful of anything which has been forwarded to you by email. Do your best to find the original source for the information.

Citation

The purpose of citation

Before discussing Internet citation in detail it's worth taking a quick look at the basic principles behind the citation of printed materials. One of the purposes of citation is to acknowledge your sources, to give credit where credit is due. A second purpose is to provide information about the source, such as date, publisher and author, which help us to understand the context in which the source was produced. At its heart, however, citation has a single core purpose: to make it possible for the reader to track down and consult the original sources the writer has used. This allows the reader to check whether you have correctly quoted or represented the views of people you cite. It also allows them to see whether you have copied from the original source and points them to further reading on particular points you dealt with. It also allows them to assess themselves the value of the sources on which you're relying.

When you're citing a Web document you need to bear in mind this core purpose. A URL alone is not enough to guide a reader back to a document. URLs change. Web documents also raise new issues for citation as a practice, issues which can only be dealt with by adding new elements to citations.

The particular need for good Internet citation

Many people are already sceptical of the value of Web-based materials. If you can't properly cite the materials you use, if you can't mark out a path which will allow the reader to find the original source you're referring to, they'll be even more sceptical. People might legitimately argue that it's unacceptable to use a source which a reader can't check up on.

Complete and accurate citation is even more important for Web documents than for print publications. Catalogues of print publications are so comprehensive and well organized that even with an incomplete citation it's easy enough to find a particular item. Author and title would be sufficient in most cases.

On the Web it's much harder to locate an item if you have just a few scraps of information. Even with full citation details it may be impossible to find it again, if the person responsible for the document has removed it from the Web or altered it. For this reason you can never be certain that the reader will be able to find the document you cited. Although it is an imperfect strategy, you should save copies of all of the Web documents you cite. Make sure to save them as 'html' or 'source' so that you preserve the format of the original. This doesn't provide proof positive of the original document; you could easily alter it on your own word processor. However, in the doomsday scenario where the document disappears from the Web for ever and the reader is absolutely insistent on looking at the original source, you can print out a copy yourself and give it to them. This is particularly advisable if the reader is an examiner.

Emerging citation standards

Shortly after the Web came into existence the first schemes for citing Web documents were devised. In recent years some of the main authorities responsible for setting standards for the citation of printed documents have laid down guidelines for Internet citation. The American Psychological Association (**www.apa.org/journals/webref.html**) and the Modern Languages Association (**www.mla.org/style/sources.htm**) have both made citation guidelines available online. Neither of these are widely used by social scientists, however, and they are useful for illustrating general guidelines rather than providing exact citation formats. *The Chicago Manual of Style* provides one of the principal set of citation guidelines used by social scientists but at the time of writing it had not yet produced official guidelines for Internet citation.

The examples of citation given below use the basic format of the Harvard style which is widely used in the social sciences and which is used in this book. I use this style so that I have a consistent style with which to illustrate the difficulties around Web citation. My principal concern is not to lay down hard and fast rules. Rather it is to provide intelligent guidelines which will help you to cite Web documents whichever citation style you choose.

Internet citation: the main elements

The principal elements in a book citation are author, title, date, publisher, place of publication. Page number is included when referring to a specific page. For a journal article or book chapter you need to add, respectively, the name of the journal or book which it appeared in in order to show the wider context in which the article or chapter is located. You can omit publisher and place of publication in the case of a journal. In Web citation you need to use most of the elements of a book citation, adapted to suit the Web. You also need to identify the wider context in which a Web document is located, as you have to do with a journal article. On the Web that wider context is the 'site' which a document belongs to. The other extra element in a Web citation is the URL.

Web citation can be complicated. It is to be hoped that it will get easier as authors learn to include citation information on their documents. For the moment, however, the researcher needs to cite Web documents as fully as possible, to do their best to ensure that their reader can locate the original sources.

What follows is a detailed discussion of each of the elements of a Web citation and of the various problems you'll encounter in each case.

Elements of a Web citation

Author
Title
Site
Date
Page or section
URL

Author   If the author of a Web document is clearly identified on the document you're in luck. If not, there are a number of ways to determine the author. If the document is produced by an organization of any kind, whether that be a government, an advocacy group or a business firm, it may well be that the organization itself is the author. You can assume this if no author is specified. In the case of news items, journalists are often not given a 'byline'; that is, their name does not appear with the article. In that case you do not need to give an author name. The news agency or publication is effectively the author and it will appear in the citation in any case.

If all else fails **view→pagesource** (Netscape Navigator) **view→source** (Internet Explorer 4 and 5) to see if the author has included their name in the html document. For reasons best known to themselves some Web authors put author details and dates in their html documents which are only visible if you view the source.

In certain cases the author of a site will put their name on the site home page but will neglect to put it on every document on the site. In such a case just locate the site home page and check for an author name there.

Title   There are two different places where the title of a Web document usually appears: in the bar at the top of your browser or at the top of the Web page itself. My rule of thumb is, if it looks like the title it probably is the title. All Web documents have a 'title' field the author can fill in. This is what appears in the bar at the very top of your browser. Many authors don't fill it in and many who do put a different title here to the one visible on the page itself. If the two are different I advise you to use the title which is visible on the page.

Site   When you cite a published journal article you always include the name of the journal it was published in. It is equally important in Web citation that you cite the Website a document belongs to. It is an essential citation element which explains the wider context in which the document is located. Refer back to chapter 5 for a detailed explanation of what constitutes a site.

Date   There are three different dates related to a Web document which are important in citation. For many documents only one date is needed for a citation – the date when the document was first written or the closest equivalent, such as the date it was first put on the Web. A huge proportion of documents are not changed or updated after they go onto a Website. Many Web documents are simply online versions of an existing printed document. The date of publication of the printed version is generally the only date necessary for your citation in this case and you can cite it as an ordinary printed document adding the URL at the end to make it easier for people to locate it on the Web. The second important date, for documents which have been changed or are subject to change, is the date on which it was last updated. This indicates the version of the document which you saw. You are not guaranteeing that the document will look the same after the next update.

The third type of date is only relevant to documents which are undated or to documents which change but do not provide a 'last updated' date. In this case and in this case only you should put down the 'date viewed'. This indicates that you are citing the document as it appeared on the day you viewed it. You are not guaranteeing that it will look the same if it is updated after that date.

Below are four different ways to cite the same document depending on the information it provides about dates and on whether it is updated. It's an imaginary document called 'Small victories in the kitchen' by an imaginary author, Anna Lee. It is one of several documents by the same author on a site called *Rat Wars*.

No information about dates is provided
Lee, Anna (2001) 'Small victories in the kitchen', *Rat Wars*. Viewed on 12 March
    2001 <www.anysite.com/members/~annalee/ratwars/kitchen.html>.

A date when it was first written or first put on the Web is provided. It is clear that
the document has not been updated since and is unlikely to be updated
Lee, Anna (1999) 'Small victories in the kitchen', *Rat Wars* <www.anysite.com/
    members/~annalee/ratwars/kitchen.html>.

A date when it was first written or first put on the Web is provided. It has been
updated since and the date of last updating is provided
Lee, Anna (2000) 'Small victories in the kitchen', *Rat Wars*, 1999, last updated
    on 10 September 2000 <www.anysite.com/members/~annalee/ratwars/
    kitchen.html>.

A date when it was first written or first put on the Web is provided. It has been
updated since but the date of last updating is not provided
Lee, Anna (1999) 'Small victories in the kitchen', Rat Wars. Viewed on 12 March
    2001 <www.anysite.com/members/~annalee/ratwars/kitchen.html>.

Page or section   When you refer to a particular sentence or paragraph in a printed document you give the page number so the reader can find it easily. Giving page numbers for Web documents presents some difficulties. If the document is in PDF form, where all of the pages are clearly numbered, there's no problem. Most Web documents are not clearly numbered. When you print out a document your printer will number each page. However, your printer will be set up quite differently from a lot of other printers. A Web document which is seven pages long on your printer could easily be five or nine pages long when printed out on another printer. Thus you can't rely on this for page numbers. One way around this problem is to give the total number of pages in the document, citing it as '2 of 7', for example. This gives a clear indication of which part of the document the quote appears in, even to someone whose printer is set up differently or who is viewing it through their browser. Alternatively if a document is divided into named sub-sections you could give the name of the relevant sub-section rather than a page number.

In some types of printed documents, such as parliamentary debates or legal documents, it is established practice for paragraphs to be numbered. You cite the paragraph rather than the page number. Although it would be quite ugly looking, it would make a lot of sense to number and cite Web documents by paragraph. Where a Web document is numbered by paragraph you can cite these rather than page number.

Finally, bearing in mind that the core purpose of citation is to be able to locate the original, one of the most effective ways for a reader to locate a quote in a Web document is to view the document on their browser and use 'Find' to locate the quote.

URL   Many people citing Web documents assume that providing the URL is sufficient. It fulfils the core purpose of citation after all: to allow people to find the document again. Unfortunately it doesn't always do this. Some Webmasters do rename files and move them around, thus changing the URL. Apart from this it means that very little information is provided on context such as date and author.

It is very common for newspapers, to take one example, to move documents to different URLs. Many newspapers use the same URL for their main news story each day. Thus a URL like **www.anynewspaper.com/ mainstory.html** might be reserved for the main story of the day. As a result its contents will change completely every day. The URL in this case provides very little assistance to those looking for the document originally cited.

In addition Webmasters sometimes remove documents from the Web entirely. Thus a URL alone does not guarantee you'll be able to retrieve a document. If you have the other details you have a better chance of locating it again. Even if you don't, full citation details give you a lot of information about these documents.

There are a few complications around citing URLs. Many URLs end in *#whatever*, indicating the sub-section of the document referred to. In general there is no need to include this part of the URL in your citation.

Many services create pages 'on-the-fly'. That is, the page is created for you in response to your request. For example, a news service with a huge archive of news stories may offer you the option of clicking on stories on crime. However, the page it retrieves is not a pre-existing Web page which would have its own URL. Rather it is the result of a search query. The URL will reflect this, being very long, full of numbers and making no sense. In this case it's often impractical and of little use to cite the full URL and it's more important to get details of author, title and site.

Frames can also cause major problems for Web citation by obscuring the URLs of pages you are looking at. If you keep seeing the same URL in the bar at the top of the browser as you move to different pages then this is the URL of the frame itself, not the pages you're looking at. To see the URL you can print out the document or use 'back' to return to the previous page and scan over the link to see the URL. You can also bookmark an individual page on a framed site and check the URL of the bookmark. Click on the page with the right mouse button and choose 'add bookmark'.

Citing email messages

These are a lot simpler to cite than Web documents, requiring minimal detective work. The author is usually the person who sent the message. If their email address is publicly associated with the message, if for example it was sent out on a public mailing list or if it is available on a Website or in a public archive, you can give the email address in the citation. If not, if it is a private message or one intended for a strictly limited audience, you should probably ask permission to include the address. If it's a personal message you should ask permission before you quote it or cite it at all. The date is usually the date it was sent first and the title is the subject heading or an obvious title at the beginning of the message. For email messages, the equivalent of 'site' is the discussion list or mailing list which the message came from, if it came from a list. If it is unclear from the name of the list that it is an email list put the mailing address for the list after its name, just to make this clear. If it came directly to you from an individual then 'site' is irrelevant. In the case of such private messages you should include the name of the person the message was sent to. If an email is archived on the Web you can also give the URL to allow people to locate the original easily.

Below are two different ways to cite the same imaginary email message depending on whether it was a private message or one sent to a discussion list.

Message sent to the Quitsmoking-L discussion list
Mulcahy, Dara (1999) <dara@mulcahynet.ie> 'Giving up cigarettes in Belfast', *Quitsmoking-L* 28 December 1999 <http://www.quitsmoking.ie/list/message432.html>.

Private email message
Mulcahy, Dara (1999) <dara@mulcahynet.ie> 'Giving up cigarettes in
    Belfast', private email message to Niamh Quinn 28 December 1999.

Citing newsgroup/Web forum postings

You cite these in much the same way that you cite email messages. Author,
date and title are all straightforward enough while the newsgroup the
message is posted to is the equivalent of the site. In the case of a Web forum
you should provide the URL for the forum.

   Below is a sample newsgroup citation using the same imaginary message
which was used to illustrate email citation.

Mulcahy, Dara (1999) <dara@mulcahynet.ie> 'Giving up cigarettes in
    Belfast' 28 December 1999 <soc.ireland.smoking>.

Citing articles located through online databases

I've mentioned already that where a printed version of a Web document
exists you should give the citation for the printed document. I'd just like to
make one qualification to this. When you locate a document through an
online article database, whether it be OCLC FirstSearch or Northern Light or
any of the others, give the print citation but also give the name and URL of
the database you located it in. You don't need to bother with the exact URL
of the document or about how exactly you located it. Simply naming the
database makes it much easier for the reader to locate the original.

Citation of an imaginary article located through a search of OCLC FirstSearch
Lee, Anna (1999) 'Small victories in the kitchen' *Journal of domestic conflict
    studies* 3: (2) OCLC FirstSearch<www.oclc.org>.

The Internet: calling into question the basic principles of citation

Web documents can flicker out of existence in the second that it takes a
Webmaster to delete a file. Documents which share the same title, author
and URL can have totally different contents depending on the date they're
viewed. Among the difficulties which the Internet presents for citation are
problems which go to the core of the practice of citation. No matter how diligent you are in citing, the reader may never be able to view the document
you cite, simply because it has been taken off the Web.

   While you can take the imperfect step of printing out or saving documents
so that you have at least some proof of the source you're citing, this problem
does raise serious questions about the practice of citation itself. In the long

run we can expect that those who wish to be cited will take the necessary steps, through the consistent archiving of Web documents, to ensure that they can be cited. In the short term, however, we will have to accept that some of the documents we cite will flicker out of existence shortly after we've viewed them.

9

Archives and statistics

Patricia Sleeman

Archives

> Books are easy. Ninety-five percent of them exist in multiple copies and are now easily accessible through international databases...it is the scholarly resources hidden in archives that we need to make more visible. David Stam, Syracuse University Librarian emeritus (cited in Research Libraries Group, 1999)

In the long term it may well be that the greatest contribution which the Internet makes to research is to provide easier access to archives. Because of the difficulties in gaining access to them, archives have been an under-utilized research resource and many researchers are barely aware that they exist at all.

Archives are an underused resource for the study of history, society and people. They consist of materials created or received and accumulated by a person or organization in the course of the conduct of their affairs and preserved because of their continuing value. The term has usually been used to refer to non-current records deposited in an archival institution (Ellis, 1993: 2). Governments in particular keep them to enable informed planning and decision making, to support accountability, continuity, consistency and effectiveness of human action.

Archives exist in a wide variety of formats and can consist of paper files, photographs, maps, architectural drawings, films, sound recordings and electronic records.

Archives differ from books and other published materials because as organic products of activity they result in a unique record. While libraries hold multiple copies of published materials, archives usually hold the unique unpublished record. However, in today's increasingly electronic environment concepts such as 'unique' and 'multiple' or 'published' and 'unpublished' which were previously useful in distinguishing archival sources from library materials are becoming significantly less meaningful. An electronic document can contain links and pointers to many other files or documents challenging the concept of a document as an integral and independent record.

The traditional image of the world of archives and the archivist is that of 'a rarefied, arcane world that is of little relevance to contemporary life…surrounded by dusty parchments' (Hoon, 1998: 5). Despite the fact that many archivists still view their role as being agents of *Überlieferungsbildung* (Gilliland-Swetland, 1998) – the handing down of culture and civilization from generation to generation – technology and telecommunications, particularly the developing Internet, have caused the focus to shift.

Archives were once the most inaccessible type of research resource, despite the fact that many of them have a public service mandate. Just finding out which collections were held by the different archives involved quite a lot of research. The Internet provides the potential for archives to provide easy access to information about their collections and thus to make their collections much more widely accessible. Ultimately, if archivists put the actual materials online, the Internet will be the medium for releasing into the public sphere a vast number of unique research resources. At the very least the Internet, by allowing easy access to archive catalogues and guides, has already made it much easier to search archives without actually visiting the archives themselves. At present the inaccessibility of archives and the element of mystery which surrounds them mean that many researchers never use any archive in their research work.

Understanding archives: organization and context

What distinguishes archives from published sources are the methods of organizing archival collections, the most widely used being the principles of provenance and original order. To preserve their original intellectual integrity 'records groups' are formed on the principle of preserving together records generated by the same office, department or other bureaucratic cell or person. The principle of original order involves keeping records in the order in which they were accumulated as they were created, maintained or used and not rearranging them according to some latterly imposed subject, numerical, chronological or other order (Ellis, 1993: 11). These principles strive to safeguard the authenticity and preserve the context of records and it is on these basic principles that their strength and value as sources for research depend. The Internet has transformed patterns of research practice as researchers are now able to search many databases of various media at one time and move rapidly from one to another at various levels. However, simple physical access or its virtual equivalent is not enough; additional information and explanations are needed in order for researchers to understand and make use of collections and materials (Walworth, 1996). The archive profession has years of experience in presenting not only information but a context within which to understand this information.

Archivists see it as vitally important to use the Internet as a means of making their knowledge of the context and the content of the records available to avoid researchers drowning in a sea of information.

Archivists must transcend 'mere' information and 'mere' information management if they wish to search for and lead others to seek knowledge and meaning among the records in their care, as Cook puts it (1984–5: 49).

It has been said that the existence of the Internet is an indication of a fundamental change in society, representing a move from searching for knowledge to searching for data and information (Cox, 1997). Clifford Stoll comments that 'what the information highway *promises* is a lot of knowledge.…In fact, it delivers mostly just data. And data is just bits and bytes; and words and paragraphs, without context or content' (1995b).

In a sense the whole profession of archiving revolves around the theme of context. Out on the Net, where context is so often difficult to identify, archives stand out for their dedication to making context clear.

Archivists provide contextual information about their holdings in various resources known traditionally as 'finding aids'. These allow the researcher to understand fully how a record was created. In recent years the advent of the Web has offered the archives profession a means of representing information about archival holdings in many possible relationships to other series or fonds (Cox, 1998: 109). In this way the integrity of the complex structure of arrangement of archives can be not only maintained but considerably enhanced in an electronic environment such as the Internet.

Hypertext mark-up language is of great benefit to archives as it provides the ability to link documents of different types together in various ways and thereby provides a context or an environment in which many disparate files can be inter-related in meaningful ways. This allows for the contextualization of documents and the further contextualization of already contextualized archival documents when these are linked together imaginatively on an archival Website (Cox, 1998: 108).

Using online archives

An increasing number of archives are establishing an Internet presence. Many archival Websites function simply as online brochures and offer contact details, and general information on holdings. For research purposes archivists also construct Websites that provide information about the repository through the posting of traditional finding aids, information about the contents, context and structure of archives in conjunction with the means of retrieving this information. This includes, but is not limited to, guides, catalogues and indexes. At the other extreme are complex sites providing archival documentation, exhibitions, access to records and advanced searching facilities.

Some archives make some of their holdings available online. Many do not, owing to the sheer cost as well as the physical and technical problems inherent in scanning thousands of records as well as complicated issues such as copyright.

One of the main disadvantages of accessing information about an archive via the Internet is the lack of professional help compared with that usually available in a real-life reading room. However, many archives provide information online for researchers, some giving a step-by-step guide on how to conduct research, sometimes covering topical areas of potential interest and highlighting the collections of records which the researcher may want to see according to their area of research. If an archive does provide a large amount of its finding aids / catalogues online, it will often allow the researcher to search its catalogues by keyword or by subject. Some archives provide online help, allowing researchers to contact a specialist in a particular area by email.

Major online archives

Listed below are a number of the major archives based in English-speaking countries

National Archives and Records Administration of the United States (NARA) (**www.nara.gov**) NARA provides an online research room informing the researcher of opening hours and locations as well as the regulations for using its records and includes a section on how to do research at NARA. It provides the researcher with a useful list of research tools including its Guide to Federal Records in the National Archives of the US, NARA Archival Information Locator (NAIL), and Presidential Libraries' finding aids. Its holdings are listed by Federal Government Organization, by media, and by selected topic. The most comprehensive tool for searching NARA's holdings is NAIL, a searchable database containing information about NARA's holdings across the USA. NAIL can be used to search descriptions of collections, to search by keyword or by topic, and to retrieve digital copies of selected records. Although NAIL contains more than 124,000 digital copies, it represents only a limited portion of NARA's holdings. There is also a 'What's new' section where additions to NAIL are noted.

Public Records Office, England (PRO) (**www.pro.gov.uk**) The PRO has committed itself to providing its users with electronic access to its services and to its records in the twenty-first century. One of the main services for researchers is an online catalogue of its holdings consisting of a database of over 8 million document references with descriptions of the documents and descriptions of the classes in which they are categorized. This will be replaced in 2001 by PROCAT, the PRO's online catalogue. The catalogue will not contain digitized images of the records themselves by 2001, as this would be a vast project in its own right, but it does lay the foundations for this. From the catalogue, users will be able to order documents online so that they are awaiting them on arrival when they visit the archives in person. PROCAT will also become the main finding aid in the reading rooms at Kew.

Other finding aids available online are The Public Record Office's Research Information Leaflets covering many areas of research, developed by individual researchers and by the PRO. They cover a wide range of topics from sources for the study of Anglo-Jewish history to treaties. They isolate the records which cover these specific areas, often including a bibliography.

The National Archives of Australia (**www.aa.gov.au**)   The National Archives of Australia provide 'fact sheets' describing their holdings in different subject areas. Various guides to their holdings are advertised including 'Federation', the guide to holdings on Australia's states. It contains lists of materials from other national and state archives, libraries, museums and art galleries, as well as parliamentary, city council and university archives in Australia. The National Archives of Australia provide two searchable databases. The items database (also known as ANGAM) describes approximately 2 million individual items held by the National Archives and the Australian War Memorial. The agency / series database (also known as RINSE) describes the entire archives collection, but at a broader level than ANGAM, describing record series (groups of related items) and the government agencies and individuals who created them.

VIRGO (University of Virginia) (**www.lib.virginia.edu/speccol/ead/**)   This 'Special Collections' Website contains online guides to manuscripts and archival materials at the University of Virginia. About 40% of its manuscript holdings are represented in its online catalogue, VIRGO.

Guides to online archives

Ready, net, go! (**www.tulane.edu/~1miller/ArchivesResources.html**)   Leon C. Miller's excellent guide includes 'Masters Lists of Archives'. This is an index of indexes, lists and databases of archival resources around the world.

Repositories of primary sources (**www.uidaho.edu/special-collections/Other-repositories.html**)   A simple but useful collection of links to the Websites of over 4,000 archives and manuscript repositories around the world, organized geographically.

American Heritage Project (**sunsite.berkeley.edu/amher**)   This is a collaboration between the University of California, Berkeley, Stanford University, Duke University and the University of Virginia funded in part by the National Endowment for the Humanities in the USA. The project is creating a shared database of finding aids describing and providing access to collections documenting US history and culture.

EAN (European Archival Network) (**www.european-archival.net**)   Intended as the main site for searching for information about European archives, this is maintained by the Swiss Federal Archives. It provides a list of European archives organized alphabetically and geographically. It gives contact details and Website addresses where they exist.

ARCHON, Archives On-Line (**www.hmc.gov.uk/archon/archon.htm**)   Hosted and maintained by the UK's Royal Commission on Historical Manuscripts,

ARCHON is the principal information gateway for British archivists and users of manuscript sources for British history. From here you can access information on all repositories in the UK and all those repositories throughout the world which have collections of manuscripts which are noted on the British National Register of Archives.

Opening up the archives

No longer is access to information about archival holdings necessarily restricted to the lucky few who have the time and the money to travel to distant repositories. There is a lot of unjustifiable hype about the Internet. Archives are one important area in which the hype is quite justified. Vast hidden resources are being made accessible and searchable to researchers in a way which is genuinely new.

Statistics

One of the first uses which social scientists made of computers was to use them for storage and analysis of statistics.

Entering the data into a computer database has long been an intrinsic part of the process of collecting statistics. Statistical data is a type of social science research resource which is almost always available in computerized form. Even in the earliest days of the Internet it was clear that one of its greatest potentials was to give easy access to statistical data. That data was already sitting on computers all over the world. Now it just had to be opened up to outside researchers.

Of course not everyone who has a collection of statistics has made them freely available online. In many cases you will still have to make the physical journey to a particular institution if you want to analyse its data. However, many of the largest collectors and disseminators of statistics about human society are making a proportion of their information available online. Chief among these are government statistics offices and universities.

These bodies provide statistics in three different forms. In the first place they put statistical tables up on the Web. These are the sorts of tables which you would have found in a government census publication, listing numbers according to age or birthplace or nationality or whatever. You can print them out and look at them. They're useful in their own right but they're static. You can't manipulate the data. You can't play around with it and ask for different results.

The second form in which such agencies provide statistics is in the form of datafiles. These are files containing the raw statistical data which you can download to your own computer. You can then open them up on a piece of statistical software on your own computer, such as SPSS, and perform very sophisticated analysis of the statistics. Agencies are less likely to provide this service. In many cases you can only get access to datafiles if you are a registered user or if you pay for them.

There is also a third way which lies half way between the two options listed above. Increasingly statistics providers allow you to manipulate and analyse their data on their Websites. That is, you can't download the data yourself but you can use pull-down menus and query boxes on the Websites to crunch the numbers yourself and produce tables customized to your own research needs. This is less flexible than having the data yourself but it means you have an easy-to-use interface and you don't need to buy, or learn how to use, a complex piece of statistical software. For many researchers who are not particularly comfortable with using statistics but wish to use them to supplement their research, this is perhaps the most attractive option, where it's available.

I have categorized statistical resources on the Web into two major groups. The first is statistics Websites, the Websites of agencies which collect statistics and make them available online, chief among them government census agencies. The second is data archives, electronic archives of datasets, usually based at universities. On the statistics Websites you can usually view tables and can sometimes manipulate data online. The data archives provide indexes to datasets gathered by a wide variety of organizations and research projects. In many cases they allow users to download the full datasets to analyse them on their own computers.

Statistics Websites

Statistical resources on the Web (**www.lib.umich.edu/libhome/documents. center/stats.html**)   This service from the University of Michigan Documents Center is the largest and most elaborate guide to statistics Websites that I have come across. It organizes links by broad subject categories, including several social science categories such as sociology, economics and politics.

Statistics Canada (**www.statcan.ca**)   This provides census tables and statistical tables on a wide range of topics related to Canada.

Statistics Sweden (**www.scb.se/indexeng.htm**)   This contains simple statistical tables on a range of topics.

Swiss Statistics (**www.statistik.admin.ch/eiindex.htm**)   This is an excellent large collection of tables on everything from migration to forestry.

National Statistics: the Official UK statistics site (**www.statistics.gov.uk**)   This contains UK government statistics, organized by subject areas such as migration, education, economy. The site provides information about newly released datasets.

US Census Bureau (**www.census.gov**)   This is a huge elaborate site providing tables of data from US censuses.

FedStats (**www.fedstats.gov**)   This provides access to the statistical data produced by a huge number of US federal government agencies. It aims eventually to include all federal statistics. You can search individual agencies or search them all together. The search is not, however, limited to statistics and can bring back official documents which contain no statistics.

Data archives

Data archives hold and preserve data deposited by researchers or other bodies such as governments or any other institution, public or private. Datafiles may exist in a definitive version and be generated by a project or business function with a finite timespan; or a datafile may be dynamic, constantly evolving, generated by a project or business function with no finite timescale (Feeney, 1999: 10). Owing to rapidly changing computer technology and the fact that information encoded in digital form is entirely dependent on technology to allow access, preservation of data which might otherwise become inaccessible to the researcher is a major concern of the data archives.

ICPSR (The Inter-university Consortium for Political and Social Research) (**www. icpsr.umich.edu**) Located within the Institute for Social Research at the University of Michigan, the ICPSR is a membership-based, not-for-profit organization serving member colleges and universities in the USA and abroad. ICPSR provides access to the world's largest archive of computerized social science data. Access to the datasets is restricted to those affiliated with member colleges and universities. Everybody can get access to abstracts and other documentation related to many of the datasets. You can search for datasets by subject, title and keyword.

CESSDA (Council for European Social Science Data Archives) (**www.nsd.uib.no/ cessda/**) CESSDA allows you to simultaneously search the catalogues of data archives in several countries, mostly in Europe but also including the ICPSR in the USA. It also provides links to these catalogues.

The Data Archive (University of Essex, UK) (**dawww.essex.ac.uk**) The Data Archive has an extensive collection of datasets and related documentation in the social sciences and humanities. The collection consists mainly of datasets which were gathered in the course of publicly funded research projects in the UK. Many of these are surveys carried out by government agencies or public bodies. You can search by subject and keyword.

It also provides access for academic researchers in the UK to some of the ICPSR datasets and to European-based data archives.

National Digital Archive of Datasets (NDAD) (**ndad.ulcc.ac.uk**) NDAD preserves and provides access to computer datasets from UK government departments and agencies. The service is aimed at all those with an interest in records of twentieth-century government decision making and planning, including researchers, social historians and historians of computing. NDAD provides open access to the catalogues of all its holdings, and free access to open datasets following a simple online registration process.

Social Sciences Data Archives, The Australian National University (**ssda.anu.edu.au**) This is a searchable guide to datasets held by the SSDA including datasets on Australian opinion polls, the Australian census and research studies in Australia and New Zealand.

10

Publishing on the Internet

Internet publication versus print publication

If you have written a substantial article you should definitely try to get it published in a print publication. There are a small number of peer-reviewed online journals in the social sciences which have no printed version. Some of them are recognized widely in the discipline but these are few and far between. If you try to publish in a purely online journal make sure it is one of these. It's hard to recommend choosing the Web <u>instead</u> of print. If you only put your article on the Web people will ask, however unfairly, 'was it not good enough to make it into print?' You can, however, do your best to ensure that you can also place your print publications, or portions of them, on the Web. This may involve some negotiation with the publisher. One way around publisher permission is to put a draft of the article online. This allows you to spread your work on the Web while the publishers can be satisfied that readers will still have to consult the final printed version if they wish to cite it in a piece of academic research. Some people involved in publishing have found that putting a printed publication on the Internet actually increases sales of the printed version. The Internet version publicizes it to many more people and a lot of them find it more convenient to buy the published version than to print out an unwieldy copy from their printer.

There are a few good reasons why you may not want to devote too much energy to Web publication. If you want your results to reach people interested in your subject, publishing them in a major journal may well allow you to reach more relevant people than the open Internet does. Major journals are included in the online databases dealt with in chapter 3. In many cases the full text of articles is included. These databases are so much more clearly structured than the open Web that it is far easier to find material in them. Those who have access to these databases are much more likely to locate an article published by you in a major journal than they are to find an article you've placed on the open Web. The same applies to any thesis or dissertation which you complete. If you make sure it is registered with UMI or another company which provides dissertation abstracts online you will probably reach more people working in your area than you will by placing it on the open Web.

What to publish

Documents which belong on the Internet

In the two paragraphs above my focus has been on putting documents online which would traditionally have been print publications. The Internet has, however, given rise to different genres of documents which take full advantage of the Internet's capabilities, which are truly Internet documents and which do not fully make sense in printed form because they were designed to be read online. These range from documents which make innovative use of hypertext to allow readers to take any number of routes through the material, to documents which are concerned above all to reach people quickly, to documents which act as guides to other documents on the Internet.

Putting such documents on the Web makes a lot more sense than putting existing printed documents online. Rather than just using the Internet as a distribution network, and one which is severely flawed, you are using it as a medium, creating the kind of materials which could not exist in printed format, or which would be very expensive to produce in that format. What follows are some suggestions for the type of documents a researcher might focus their Internet publishing efforts on.

Online bibliographies

In the course of your research you build up a bibliography, a list of the sources you have consulted. Your bibliography is a valuable resource in its own right to other people carrying out research in your area, bringing together a concentrated collection of materials on a very specific topic.

You could of course make your entire bibliography available online but it makes particular sense to put up on the Web a bibliography of the Internet sources you've used, providing links to the URLs. Even if your work is published this document is still uniquely valuable because it allows people to quickly view your sources, clicking on links rather than laboriously typing in the URLs. It would be particularly valuable to refer an examiner of your work to it.

This provides a genuinely useful resource to specialists in your field, complementing rather than competing with the related print publication. A bibliography of online sources is particularly useful because the Web is so less well charted than the world of print publications. You are charting out territory which, unlike the relevant print publications, is new and confusing to many researchers in your field.

Subject guides

With a little bit of work you can turn your online bibliography into an Internet guide, a very high-quality and focused subject guide. If you expand the bibliography to ensure that you include all of the central resources on your specific topic and add precise informative comments about each source you will have created such a guide. You needn't provide full citation details for all documents, as you do in an online bibliography, but it's a good idea to include author and, of course, title. Those comments should make some assessment of the quality of the source, provide information which helps the reader to understand the context for the source and describes the substantive content available at that source.

Do not cast your net too widely. The more exclusive, the more focused it is on your specific topic, the more useful it is to people working in the same area.

Don't be deterred by the fact that there are large numbers of subject guides in your general area or by the fact that so many people are busily classifying the Web. Print cataloguing has not yet made printed bibliographies redundant. Online guides, provided that they focus on a very specific topic, are a type of resource, produced by an individual expert, which no amount of Internet cataloguing will replace.

While your online bibliography will be of interest to academic researchers in your area, a subject guide which provides a little more information about sources and which makes sure to include central sources is a resource of use to undergraduate students and to anyone carrying out a short research project on the topic.

You should try to make your guide comprehensive, to include all of the useful resources in this specific subject area. One way to ensure this, while simultaneously publicizing the guide, is to create a first version and then ask people to point out omissions while reserving to yourself the final decision on what resources to include.

If you teach a course on the subject you can refer students to the guide as an online reading list for the course, to supplement their reading list of print publications.

Guidelines for creating a subject guide

What will mark your specialist guide out from so many other guides is that it will point to individual documents rather than vaguely directing users to sites. It will also be marked out by the quality of the description of the items you point people to. Another of your main contributions is to identify clearly the context for documents. To this end you should be careful always to link to the main site which each document in your subject guide belongs to as well as to the individual documents. Some people have taken to asking permission to link to pages from the person who is responsible for the page they're linking to. My view is that this should not be necessary so long as you make clear that you are not the author or provider of that document. Asking permission for links in this case is like writing to ask permission from authors to include their books in your bibliography. It's too time consuming and it seems a real infringement of intellectual freedom. It should be enough that you make clear that these documents belong to other sites for which you are not responsible.

Photographs

It might be the case that you take photographs in the course of your research which illustrate and illuminate your work. Even if you do get your research published the publisher may not publish all or even any of these photographs owing to the expense involved. If you want to make them available to a wider audience the Web provides a relatively cheap way to do this. You can add text and create a sort of photo gallery of your own. If it relates to work you've published you might provide the URL for the photo gallery in the published work. Remember, though, that once you put these images up it's an easy matter for someone else to copy them.

Updating

Constant updating is an impossible dream if you are maintaining a Web page on a part-time voluntary basis. It requires too much effort and after a while you will become bored with this topic and resent the fact that it takes time away from new projects you're working on. You need to be much less ambitious if your site is to have a useful long-term existence. One option, which is appropriate for an online bibliography, is not to update at all – ever. You simply accept that your work will become less useful as time passes and as some of the documents you point people to change their Web addresses. Since the bibliography provides full citation information, those who are particularly keen have all the information they need to try and track the source to its new location.

A second option, appropriate for a specialist subject guide, is to update at regular but infrequent intervals. Updating once a year or once every six months should ensure that your guide remains reasonably up to date. If you use the guide to support teaching you could update it just before the teaching semester or term begins.

It is a much more efficient use of your time to make a lot of changes to the document in one sweep than to have to turn your attention to the document every few weeks.

One principal reason to update a document is to update the content. You might put an article up on the Web and then decide to update it because of new material which has come to light. There is a precedent for this in the print world; new and revised editions of books. If you update a Web document in this way you should make it clear that this is a new version, giving a date of revision or updating. If you intend this as a serious contribution to research you should also ensure that you continue to make earlier versions of the document available and that readers can easily reach older versions from the current version of the document, and vice versa. If you don't do this you could cause a lot of confusion for people citing different versions of your article in their own research.

A second major reason for updating is to fix broken links, links to other Web documents which have since changed their URLs. This is particularly important for online bibliographies and subject guides whose main purpose is to provide links. Thankfully more and more people are trying to ensure that their documents stay at the same URLs over time. Many documents don't, however.

Publicity

On the Internet publicity is distribution

Publishers don't just print materials. They also distribute and publicize them. The two traditional publishing functions of distribution and publicity can be boiled down to one function in Internet publishing: publicity. On the Internet publicity is distribution. If someone with Internet access is aware of your document and its URL then they can access it.

By publicity I do not mean an elaborate campaign to ensure that the whole world knows about your work. I mean a careful strategy to ensure that your target audience is made aware of it. If your work has taken hours, days or weeks to prepare then it is worth devoting at least an hour or two to letting people know that it exists.

Thinking about the user

Before you begin your publicity ask yourself who you're trying to reach. If the answer is 'everyone' or 'as many people as possible' then forget the Web. If you really want to try to reach everyone on the planet try making a big film, getting involved in a popular TV show or writing for a major newspaper. These media all have much greater reach than an individual Internet site. When you think about it for a while you'll probably realize that you don't actually want to reach 'everyone'. Trying to do so can waste a lot of energy. If the answer is 'anyone' think hard about whether you really mean that. Would you be happy if thirty or so people with no interest in your topic stumbled on your Web page by accident and immediately clicked on the 'back' button? It would be slightly more expensive but you could achieve this effect equally well by leaving thirty copies of your article in any local bar or café near your house. The truth is that most researchers would like to see people who are actually interested in the topic they deal with reading their material. It is by no means guaranteed that any such people will find your Web page unless you direct your publicity very carefully. Do some serious thinking about your target audience. That target audience could be as narrow as a single class at a particular university or as broad as anyone interested in your subject, from other researchers to students to commentators and people whose daily lives are affected by the phenomenon you're studying.

A publicity strategy

Careful publicity Indiscriminate mass emailing for publicity purposes comes under the heading of spam (see chapter 4). If you send spam you will annoy a lot of people, possibly invite retaliation and will probably reach very few of those you would like to reach. So many people see the Internet as the perfect medium for cheap publicity that Internet publicity itself has a bad name. Your publicity strategy has to be a sensitive one, otherwise its principal effect will be to drag your name through the mud.

Starting in the real world It's no surprise that so many Internet companies pay for billboard, TV and newspaper advertisements. These real-world media provide very effective means of publicizing Web-based services. In your case, real-world publicity can be as basic as telling people you meet about your materials on the Web. It's surprising how many people don't bother to do this. You should also put your Web address on any printed materials that you produce such as business cards.

Placing The very fact of placing your work on a site which is heavily used, has a high degree of credibility and/or is focused on your broad subject area, makes it more visible. Good placing is an act of publicity in its own right and has very important knock-on effects for the keyword search engines, increasing the likelihood that your pages will be quickly included in them. While it is a perfectly good approach to put your materials up on a Website of your own you might consider trying to place them more prominently. If there is a service devoted to putting up materials in your subject area you might place it there, while retaining copyright. Such a service called CAIN (**cain.ulst.ac.uk**) exists for research on the conflict in Northern Ireland. The service is heavily used by students of the conflict. Researchers into the conflict who place materials on this site greatly increase their visibility.

If there is no such site in your field the next best option is to put materials on your college or university's Web server if you are a student or member of staff. Some universities allow students, as a matter of course, to put up their own Web pages. If not you might ask if you can put your work on your department's site. Placing your pages on a university site will give them a reasonably high profile as such sites are heavily used by students and staff. It will also give them some academic credibility simply by locating them in an academic context.

Placing your pages on a commercial server is a poor second best. It is very tempting because many companies now offer free Web space. Be extremely careful of putting research work on such services. The **www.anysite.com/members/~1076** type of address erodes the credibility of the work a little but there are other, more serious problems. The free Web space providers usually make their money by selling advertising space on pages like yours. If you have put a lot of work into ensuring that your research is as accurate and as objective as possible you may want to consider the damage that might be done to it if it appears to readers to be associated, by advertising, with commercial companies or even political groups which you or they find objectionable. It might well diminish the impact of the work. If this seems like an abstract issue not worth bothering about then worry about advertising for another reason: the pages on some free Websites are so covered in ads, including pop-up ads which can appear every minute or so, that it is extremely hard to read the material. The last time I viewed a document on one of these sites I read only a few paragraphs before giving up in frustration. The ads were coming so fast and furiously that it was an ordeal to read the document. If you are registered with an Internet Service Provider which provides Web space without advertising on it this is far preferable. In the end I think it's well worth paying in order to have Web space which is not wrecked by advertising.

One final word of warning about the free Web space providers. In 1999 there was a public controversy after Yahoo Geocities introduced new conditions for its free Web space. The agreement which users were asked to sign up to granted Yahoo 'royalty-free, perpetual, irrevocable, non-exclusive… license to use, reproduce, modify, adapt, publish, translate, create derivative works from, distribute, perform and display…' the content of users' 'free' Web pages. Yahoo later altered this provision under immense public pressure. The new provisions still granted Yahoo 'the World-wide, royalty-free and non-exclusive licence to reproduce, modify adapt and publish the content, …for so long as you continue to be a Yahoo Geocities homesteader' (*The Irish Times*, 12 July 1999). You need to be aware that when you use free Web space you may be losing full ownership of your work. No matter where on the Web you place your work you should be certain that you're not casually handing over rights to it to someone else.

The subject guides   There are likely to be at least a handful of subject guides devoted to your subject area. Send a short note, giving the title, URL and a brief and useful description of your site to the people running these sites and suggest or request that they provide a link to your pages. You should be able to find their email addresses from the guides themselves.

Where a guide has an existing procedure for people to submit such information use that procedure. Do not mass-mail Web guide maintainers. They may take you less seriously. Inclusion in high-quality guides not only raises the profile of your pages, but also increases your chances of inclusion in the major keyword search engines.

The universal subject guides   Of the universal subject guides Yahoo is still the most heavily used and you should make a special effort to be included in this. Yahoo allows you to choose one or two sub-categories in which to place your Web pages. You have to go to the Web page for the sub-category and choose the 'suggest a site' link at the bottom of that page. You then get a lengthy form to fill out. If Yahoo doesn't think your pages belong in the sub-category you've chosen it won't include them there, so choose carefully.

Other Web authors   In the course of your research you will have come across Websites directly relevant to your topic. If you have produced a subject guide or online bibliography you will provide hyperlinks to many such sites. You should inform the people running these sites of your Web page and of the fact that you have linked to them (if you have). By doing this you reach people directly concerned with your topic who are active in using the Web in connection with this topic, a very specialized group likely to have a real interest in your work.

Email lists   Do not bother with the low-quality lists in your field. These are so clogged up with spam that users are likely to regard any publicity notices with cynicism or annoyance. They are so discredited that notices posted here are unlikely to reach those people who are seriously interested in your topic. Rather you should direct your efforts, very carefully, at one or two high-quality lists devoted to your subject area. If these lists regularly publicize useful Web resources in your field then you can send a straightforward email notifying them of what you provide. If they do not you can still request that they pass on the URL and a short description on the basis that it will be of real interest to many people on the list. In the last resort you might mention the resource in a discussion which it's relevant to. Needless to say, it's a good idea if you're an established subscriber and contributor to any list which you wish to publicize your work through.

The keyword search engines   For many people the search engines are the beginning and end of their publicity strategies. Many commercial companies go to extraordinary lengths and devote huge energy to trying to achieve a high ranking for their sites. There is an entire industry devoted to advising you how to achieve a high ranking in the search engines. I suggest you ignore this industry.

Commercial companies put so much effort into this because they have so much competition from other firms trying to sell similar goods or services. They want to ensure that people doing searches on common terms such as 'CD' or 'car' or 'cuddly toy' will be brought to their sites.

The academic researcher will generally not face such intense competition. People interested in your specific topic will be using keywords which are relatively rare. You shouldn't worry too much about using elaborate tricks to increase your ranking.

You should, however, ensure that all of the major search engines know that your pages exist. It's a curious feature of the Internet that if nobody at all links to your pages (not even your own university or department or employer) you are, in a way, not on the Internet at all.

The search engines search the Web by following links. If no one links to your pages they won't ever find them unless you submit the details directly to them. This emphasizes the importance of asking guides and other Web authors to link to you. The more links there are to you from other sites the more likely it is that the search engines will find out about you. In addition, some of them will give you a higher ranking according to the number of high-quality sites which link to you.

All of the big search engines allow you to submit details of your Web pages to them. They may take weeks or, in some cases, months to include you in their index, though. Some of them won't guarantee inclusion at all. Once again this emphasizes the importance of making sure that people can reach you through the subject guides. Some of the search engines will also ask you or allow you to choose a category from their crude guides in which your Web pages should be included.

You can submit your page details directly to individual search engines. On virtually all search engines there is a link on the main page to a page called 'submit your site', 'add URL' or 'suggest site'. Many of them differ slightly in how they treat submissions and going directly to them allows you to tailor your submission to suit each search engine, choosing appropriate categories where that's an option. I suggest you submit to five or six of the largest search engines in one sitting, copying and pasting the details to each from a text file you should have open on the screen. If you have a lot of Web pages you might be well advised to submit just your home page.

There are a number of services such as Submit It! (**www.submitit.com**) which will submit your Web page details to lots of search engines at the same time. The advantage of this is that it saves you time. It is a little crude, though, and I suggest that the extra twenty minutes or so which it will take you to submit directly to five or six of the largest search engines are well worth it. Submitting to more than five or six is of limited value in any case since the vast majority of users will run their search through at least one of the big search engines.

Understanding usage of your Web pages

All Web servers have an access log where details are recorded of every request for a page on that server. A request is more popularly known as a 'hit'. The people running the server on which you place your Web pages should, as a matter of course, provide you with information about usage of your pages, just to let you know whether anyone is using them. They can also break down results by domain, letting you know which countries your users are in or what universities they are at. Thus you can make a crude assessment of who your users are and plan for the future on this basis. If, for example, very few people in your own university or town are using your pages, you could consider directing a little more of your efforts towards local publicity.

You need to be very careful in analysing figures from access logs. The number of hits does not represent the number of people visiting your pages. There is really no limit to the extent to which hits can exaggerate usage and they are often deliberately manipulated for these purposes. A much more accurate measure of how your pages are being used is unique visitors or unique users, effectively the number of different individuals who have viewed your pages. It is not unusual for this figure to be only 10% or 5% of the number of hits. For an explanation of why see the inset.

No matter how detailed, access logs can only give you limited information about your users. If you are really interested in how and by whom your pages are being used you should make sure your email address and an invitation to contact you are prominently displayed on your pages. Alternatively you might put a short user questionnaire online (if your computer support people will help you to do this). One way to get people to use this would be to offer a token prize which would be awarded randomly to one of those who completed the questionnaire within a set period of time.

Five ways in which hits exaggerate usage of a site

1. Images: every image on a Web page counts as a hit. If you have ten images on your page then eleven hits are registered in the access log every time that page is requested.
2. Cancelled requests: if a user gets tired of downloading your page and cancels without viewing it this is still registered as a hit.
3. Stop and reload: if someone reloads a page it counts as another hit.
4. Mistaken visits: the average user visits a number of sites before finding the information they're looking for. This suggests that the majority of visits to any given site are made by mistake – as part of a quest for information. These users will register as hits but won't read your pages.
5. Robots: search engine robots visit and regularly revisit your pages to update their indexes, not just the big search engines you're familiar with but also a brace of search engines devoted to specific subjects or to specific geographical areas. They can account for a significant proportion of your hits if yours is a lightly used site.

Writing Web documents

It's easy

There is a certain mystique around the writing of Web documents, much of it generated deliberately by people who run Websites and don't want other people to know how easy it is and by companies which charge a lot of money to design Websites. Anyone who knows how to use a computer can learn the skills necessary to write a very basic Web page in an hour or less. Here's two ways to do it.

Using a text editor

1. Open a text editor (see chapter 2 if you don't know how to find your text editor).
2. Type or paste in the text you'd like to put on the Internet.
3. Save it, giving it an **.html** extension (or **.htm** if your computer only accepts three-letter extensions).
4. That's it, you've created a Web document.

In a word processor

1. Open a new file in your word processor.
2. Type or paste in the text you'd like to put on the Internet.

3.   Save it as 'plain text' or 'text only' giving it an **.html** or **.htm** extension. If you're using a recent version of Microsoft Word be sure that you <u>don't</u> save it as **html**.
4.   That's it, you've created a Web document.

The point I'm trying to emphasize is that, when it comes right down to it, a Web document is just a simple plain text document. Note that if you're using Microsoft Word 98 you can't edit this document. It insists on adding html code without your permission. It's better just to use a plain text editor.

You can make the document look pretty using html code but even without a line of html you can create a 'Web document'. You can have a look at how it will appear on the open Web by viewing it in your Web browser (NN: **File→Open→Page in Navigator**; IE4: **File→Open File**; IE5: **File→Open→ Browse**).

Note that you save the document as 'text only' in your word processor. 'Text only' is what your text editor always uses. It means text without any of the embellishments which a word processor adds like bold, underline, headings or different fonts. Plain text is limited to the characters on your keyboard that you can see on a document. It doesn't even recognize tabs. To add any of this sort of formatting to your Web document you have to add html code to it.

There are a lot of html editors available which will add the html for you. Two of the most widely used are Frontpage Express (part of Internet Explorer) and Netscape Composer (part of Netscape Communicator). Many people use these editors and never learn about the html code. I will deal with them in a little more detail further on. Even if you do use these editors you will find it very useful to know some basic html.

Understanding html

Hypertext mark-up language is a 'mark-up' which you add to your document. It provides instructions on how your text should be displayed. Anything between angle brackets, like these < >, is html. Web browsers treat the text inside the angle brackets as instructions on how text should be displayed. There are two types of mark-up tags. The first are single tags which give an instruction. <P>, for example, means start a new paragraph, <HR> means place a horizontal line in the document. There are also pairs of tags which enclose items of text and give instructions on how these pieces of text should be displayed: <B>**this text will be displayed as bold**</B>. <B> stands for bold and the </B> at the end marks the end of the bold text. Html is not case sensitive. It doesn't matter if the tags are in upper or lower case or a mixture of both.

Basic html

In this section I want to describe some of the simplest and most commonly used pieces of html code. I'll do this by analysing one simple html document. The screen shot shows how the document looks on a Web browser.

The inset is the html document itself, viewed in a plain text editor.

```
<html>
<head>
<title>Oh my God !</title>
</head>
<body>
<h1>Well, of all the things . . .</h1>
<p>
<i>at first it was difficult to make out the shape in the darkness</i>
<p>
<b>as the sun rose the shape became fully visible</b>
<br>
<hr>
<p>
<a href = 'http://www.anycollege.edu'>A link to Any College</a>
<p>
<ul>
<li>a dog
<li>a cat
<li>a group of sheep
<li>two rats
```

```
<li>lice
</ul>
</body>
</html>
```

Below is a step-by-step explanation of what each piece of code means.

\<html\> \</html\> This tag, placed at the beginning and end of the document, tells the Web browsers that this is an html document.

\<head\> \</head\> This marks off the header of the document. In this document the only thing in the header is the title but you can also place other information about the document in here, such as keywords.

\<title\> \</title\> The text you put here appears in the title bar at the very top of the browser. It is the title which the search engines use when listing your document. Make sure it's the same as the main title visible on the page (unlike the author of this document).

\<body\> \</body\> Like the header tags this is really for the benefit of browsers, to indicate that this is the document itself. If you were creating a more elaborate document this is where you would put information about how the whole document should look, what the background colour should be, for example.

\<h1\> \</h1\> Header 1, the main heading on the page. You can use headings from \<h1\> all the way down to \<h6\>, each one smaller than the other. A good rule of thumb is to use \<h1\> for the title of the document and \<h2\> for the main sub-headings. Different browsers display the headers in different ways. One browser may display \<h1\> as 22 point and another as 24 point text, but all of them will display \<h1\> as bigger than \<h2\>, \<h2\> as bigger than \<h3\> and so on. Text following the header is automatically put into a new paragraph.

Text appearance

\<i\>\</i\> italic
\<b\>\</b\> bold
\<ul\>\</ul\> underline

Use italic text sparingly, it can be very difficult to read on many Web browsers.

Spaces and breaks

\<p\> paragraph; starts a new paragraph leaving a line of blank space between it and the previous text.

\<br\> break; starts a new line without leaving any blank space.

\<hr\> horizontal rule; creates a line which runs the width of the screen, no matter how wide or narrow the screen is. Useful for dividing a document into different sections.

If you put many <p> one after the other in order to create more blank lines it won't work. To create extra blank space enclose the <p> in the code for preformatted text; <pre><p><p><p><p></pre>, for example. This insists that the browser treat every <p> as a blank line.

Lists   In an unnumbered list, each <li> is a bullet point while <ul> marks the beginning and </ul> the end of the list:

<ul>
<li>
<li>
<li>
</ul>

Links   Linking to other Web documents is simple. To provide a link to **www.anycollege.edu** just insert:

<a href = "http://www.anycollege.edu">A link to Any College</a>

The text "A link to Any College" appears in the Web browser as blue-underlined text. When someone clicks on it they'll be brought to **www.anycollege.edu**. It's as simple as that. The <a> stands for 'anchor' by the way, the official name for a link.

Internal links   If you're linking to one of your own documents located on the same server you don't need to give the full address. If it's in the same folder just give its name:

<a href = "surfing.html"> a file about surfing</a>

for example. If it's in a sub-folder you have to give the folder name, **/watersports/surfing.html**, for example. If you're linking back up to the main document from a sub-folder the easiest thing to do is to give the full URL.

Html which is a little more advanced

Images   For information on the practicalities of putting photographs and other images onto your computer refer back to chapter 2. To put an image in your Web document you provide a link to it. If the image is in the same folder as your Web document you just need to put in the name of the image file <img src = "myphoto.gif">, for example. The **img src** stands for 'image source'. It's a good idea to keep your images together in a single 'images' folder.

You can point to an image in this folder from any file by putting in the full URL, <img src = "http://www.anycollege.edu/yourfiles/images/myphoto.gif">, for example.

You can align the image on the page in several different positions, on the left or right of the page, for example, using the align tag. <img src = 'myphoto.gif' align = right> puts it against the right margin. Just replace 'right' with 'left' to put it against the left margin. Other options are top, bottom, middle, which align it in relation to the text around it. (See Lehnert (1998: 382–91) for detailed advice on html code related to images.)

To separate the image clearly from the text on either side of it just put <br> before and after the <img src> tag.

Colour Colour on a Web page is produced by using codes based on the RGB (Red Green Blue) scale. A colour is signified by six characters signifying the proportions of red, green and blue and the hue, saturation and lightness of the colour. Thus 000000 is black, a complete absence of colour. ffffff is white. The best way to find out the code for the colour you want is to use an html editor. Choose a colour from its palette and look at the html code to see what the code for that colour is. Once you have the code for the three or four colours you use regularly you won't have to worry about this again.

One of the best uses of colour is to change the dull grey background colour. I suggest you change it to white. You put this in the body tag near the start of the document, <body bgcolour = '#ffffff'>.

Changing the colour of the main text is generally not recommended but one good way to use colour is to make your headers stand out. <font color='#990000'></font> around the text you want to change will make it a dark red.

Tables These are the key to creating an attractive layout for your document. Create a table with two columns and only one row. This effectively divides your page into two halves, allowing you to create a more attractive looking document. The simplest way to create a table is to create it in an html editor and then copy the code into your own document. The inset lists the html code for a simple table with four rows and two columns. <table></table> is the mark-up for a table. <tr></tr> is the code for a row. <td></td> is the code for an individual cell.

```
<table border+0>
<tr>
<td>Wake up:</td>
<td>10 am</td>
</tr>
<tr>
<td>Go to the beach:</td>
<td>11 am</td>
```

```
</tr>
<tr>
<td>Lunch:</td>
<td>1 pm</td>
</tr>
<tr>
<td>Siesta:</td>
<td>3 pm</td>
</tr>
</table>
```

The screen shot shows what the table looks like on a Web browser.

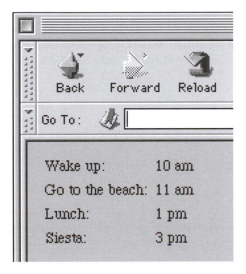

The border is '0' so it's invisible. Use higher numbers to create borders of different thicknesses. You can put as much text or as many images as you like or a combination of both in a single cell.

More about html

If you want to learn more about html there are a host of Websites devoted to providing tutorials on writing html documents. Among them are 'A Beginner's Guide to HTML' (**http://www.ncsa.uiuc.edu/General/Internet/ WWW/HTMLPrimer.html**) from the NCSA, perhaps the most famous such guide. Many of the Internet search engines have entire sections on 'Web authoring' or 'Web publishing' in their crude subject catalogues, providing links to numerous resources on writing html documents. In addition, try searching for 'beginner's guide to html' in any keyword search engine to pull up a variety of guides using this title or a variation on it.

Online bibliography: a template

This is a very simple template for an online bibliography with two sub-sections. You'll have to tinker with each of your bibliography entries, making some of the text italic and adding links to the documents, but that shouldn't be too difficult. Instructions are in capital letters.

```
<head>
<title>THE TITLE OF THE BIBLIOGRAPHY</title>
</head>
<body bycolor= '#ffffff'>
<h1><font color= '#990000'> THE TITLE OF THE BIBLIOGRAPHY
</font></h1>
Author: YOUR NAME AND AFFILIATION HERE AND A LINK TO YOUR
    DEPARTMENT OR ORGANIZATION'S HOME PAGE OR TO YOUR OWN HOME
    PAGE.
<br>
<hr>

<h2>THE TITLE OF THE FIRST SUB-SECTION</h2>
<ul>
<li>AN INDIVIDUAL BIBLIOGRAPHY ENTRY
<li>AN INDIVIDUAL BIBLIOGRPAHY ENTRY
<li>AN INDIVIDUAL BIBLIOGRAPHY ENTRY
</ul>
COPY AND PASTE THESE SIX LINES OF CODE TO CREATE AS MANY
    SUB-SECTIONS AS YOU NEED.

<hr>
Document information<br>
Author: YOUR NAME AND AFFILIATION<br>
This document was first created on ADD DATE. It was last updated on ADD
    DATE.
```

Putting your documents on the Net

The way in which you actually place your documents on the Net once you've finished them varies dramatically according to where you're putting them. If you're on a university server the person running the server may just ask you to give the documents to them to put up. If you use free Web space the individual company will provide you with instructions and software. Either way it's worth knowing how it's done and just how simple it is.

On most Web servers there will be Web documents from several different users. The person running the server will create folders for each different person and they will turn over ownership of that folder to the person concerned. Owning the folder means not only that you can put documents in the folder, you can also create sub-folders within that folder to organize your Web documents.

The simple fact of putting a document on a Web server puts it 'on the Internet'.

The big question is how do you put the documents on? You do it through FTP, File Transfer Protocol, which is very simple to use. Get a free FTP software package (such as Fetch for the Mac or WS-FTP for the PC – see chapter 2 for details). Connect to the Web server by typing in its address. You'll need to give your username and password. Go to the folder you've been allocated. On most servers you'll automatically be connected to this folder. If not, you'll need to get this information from the person running the server. Then just 'upload' your files to the server with the click of a button. When you want to change a file just change it on your own computer then FTP it up to the server to replace the older version.

Html editors

Html editors allow you to add html code using drop-down menus. Instead of typing <b></b> around text you highlight a piece of text, go up to the menu and select 'bold', just as you would in a word processor. 'Why don't I just use one of these editors?' is the reaction of most people when confronted with html code. The thing is, these editors are still at quite an early stage of development. There are a lot of problems with them and it probably takes as much effort to learn to use one as it does to learn simple html. Even if you do use them, knowing html will help you to repair your documents when the editors cause problems with them.

Among the major problems with the two main editors, Microsoft Front Page Express and Netscape Composer, are:

1. Both editors use some non-standard html which can only be viewed by those using the related browser (IE and NN respectively).
2. If you open a plain html file or a file created in another html editor in one of these there's a chance they'll mangle the original document.
3. They add huge amounts of extra and unnecessary html code, increasing the size of your files and adding in things that you didn't really want to add. It makes it more difficult to make simple changes by hand.
4. It's easy to create a page in these editors but complications can arise when you try to alter an existing page.

Even if you're writing html code yourself the editors can be extremely useful. If you want to put a table in your document, for example, create it in an editor and then just paste the code into your html document (FPE: **Table→Insert Table**; NSC: **Insert→Table**).

FPE: **View→HTML** and NSC: **View→Page Source** let you view and copy the code of documents which you've created in these editors.

If you intend to create ambitious Web pages, heavy in graphics, or including other special features, then you would be well advised to learn how to use an editor. If, however, you're just providing plain text, simple html is all you need and these editors may just complicate matters.

Good design practice

An entire industry has grown up which is devoted to discussing Website design (see, for example, Nielsen, 2000; Spool *et al.*, 1999). Many Web page authors make some very basic design mistakes which alienate users, make their pages difficult to use and ultimately decrease their impact and usage. What follows are a set of simple basic guidelines to bear in mind when publishing on the Web.

Site structure

Design doesn't just refer to pretty pictures and layouts. It begins at the most basic level of site structure. If you put more than one or two Web pages up you need to be careful about how these pages are inter-related. Many of your users will reach your pages through a search engine which provides little information on the context in which the pages exist. For this reason you have to ensure that people can easily understand the context from the information provided on the page itself. Thus, every page should have a link to the home page of the site it belongs to. The heading at the top of each page should also indicate what site it belongs to or the larger organization or structure it is affiliated to.

Folders and files   Use folders to organize the different files on your Website. Each folder should correspond to a distinct section of the site. Thus, if your site consisted of two distinct sets of documents, one related to coffee and one related to tea, you might put them in two folders called 'coffee' and 'tea'. In this way the URL helps users to understand the structure of the site. You should also give distinctive meaningful names to documents, not only for the benefit of the user but to remind you of their contents. A URL like **mysite.edu/coffee/java.html** tells the user a lot more about the document than one like **mysite.edu/webdocs/one.html**. Do not mix upper and lower case letters or use special characters in file and folder names. It makes it more likely that people will make mistakes when typing in the URL. Call your home page **index.html** (or **index.htm**), the standard name for the main page in a folder. If a user types in **www.yoursite.edu** they are automatically brought to **www.yoursite.edu/index.html**.

URL stability   Do not rename pages or move them into different folders once you have put them up. Doing so breaks every link to those pages from anywhere on the Web.

Thinking about the long term   If you think you may expand your site in the future make sure the structure allows for expansion – that you don't set up an elaborate structure which will be disrupted if you add new sections to your site.

Information about documents   Users should not need to go to your home page to find basic information such as the name of the author. You should ensure your name is on every document on your site as well as the title of the document, date produced and updated and any other citation details you wish to add.

Template building   Decide what features you want to include on all of your Web documents and create a template including all of this information. Whenever you create a new Web document you just open the template and start from there.

Page design

Keep it simple   Large images make for slow download times. Fancy features such as animated graphics or scrolling text do the same thing. Research also indicates that they frustrate many users (Spool *et al.*, 1999: 89–91). Unless you're a skilled or talented graphic designer don't use fancy backgrounds or lots of different coloured text. It's too easy to get it wrong and make your Web pages confusing or even illegible. If you are making maps, photos, diagrams or other images available provide them on separate and distinct Web pages and provide an index to them which consists solely of text. It is possible to make clever use of small graphics to make a page of text look attractive but it needs to be done very carefully.

Don't break up documents   If you split a long document into lots of different Web pages you create one major problem for most users: printing. If they want to print the entire document they'll have to visit and print all the separate sections individually. This wastes time.

Give descriptive names to links   Don't provide hyperlinks with titles like 'more information here' or 'click on this'. It makes life much easier for the user if the hyperlink clearly describes the document it links to (Spool *et al.*, 1999: 33). Usually the hyperlink text should be the full title of the document it links to.

Keep internal and external links separate   You should ensure that users can easily distinguish between internal links, to other documents provided by you or your organization, and external links to other Web services.

Be careful of where you place links   Web users downloading a page seem irresistibly drawn to clicking on the first link on that page. If you prominently display a link near the top of your Web page make sure it's a page you really want people to go to. If it's a link to another site you may find that many users simply click through and out of your site without even noticing it.

Check how your pages look on other browsers NN, IE and other major browsers each display Web pages differently as do the different versions of each browser. You should check how your pages look to people using the various browsers. If your pages are unreadable to users of one of the big browsers you'll want to make changes. There are a number of services which allow you to check the compatibility of your pages with the various browsers, including Bobby (**www.cast.org/bobby**) and Tom (**lunch.nasa.uiuc.edu/tom**) (sites mentioned in Conner-Sax and Krol, 1999: 308).

Be careful of copyright

Almost everything on the Web is copyrighted by someone, unless it is explicitly stated that it's not. You don't need to put a copyright notice on something for it to be copyrighted. That means you have to be careful of using other people's work in your Web pages.

Don't copy large chunks of other people's work from the Web and put it on your site without asking them. You can copy and paste a limited amount under 'fair use' guidelines.

Fair use generally allows you to quote up to 300 words from a book or 150 words from a newspaper or magazine article where the excerpt is less than 20% of the original work. You have to give full credit to author and publisher, citing the original document fully. There are a few other minor restrictions (Lehnert, 1998: 468). These are only rough guidelines, however, and exact definitions of fair use will vary in individual cases.

Don't copy images from other sites and use them on your own site without asking the person providing them first or unless they clearly give permission to people to do this. You cannot scan a published photo from a magazine and put it on the Web. People have been successfully sued for doing this.

Linking has become a tricky issue in recent years as some people deliberately create the impression that they are the authors of the information they link to. In a famous case in Scotland an online newspaper, *The Shetland News*, linked to the stories of its better known competitor, *Shetland Times*, in a way which gave people the impression that they were providing the stories. A Scottish court granted an interim injunction in 1996 banning *The Shetland News* from providing links to its competitor's stories. If you are linking to individual documents on someone else's site you should also link to their home page, as a matter of courtesy. If a site asks you to link only to their home page you should respect this request or ask permission for an exception to be made in your case.

Copy and paste: Internet plagiarism

Plagiarism is copying other people's work or portions of their work and presenting it as though it was your own. People often reword things slightly when they're plagiarizing. At its most extreme plagiarism involves presenting as your own work an entire essay or piece of research which has been written by someone else.

Plagiarism has always been an issue for researchers. It's not only student essays which are sometimes plagiarized. Some people plagiarize in their PhD dissertations or even in published work.

The Internet has changed the nature of plagiarism for ever, bringing both benefits and disadvantages for those who wish to plagiarize. The Internet makes it easier to plagiarize than ever before. To copy and paste from a few different Websites on your subject takes virtually no effort. The old-time plagiarizer had to laboriously copy out passages from books. This mindless and boring labour is now a thing of the past.

Keyword searching allows the plagiarizer to find material related to their essay or research topic quickly and relatively easily, without the work of physically searching the library shelves.

There are disadvantages, however, to plagiarizing from the open Web, apart altogether from the fact that it's unethical and bad practice. Low-quality sources mean you could produce very poor work, getting a fail mark despite plagiarizing. It's also very easy to get caught. An examiner can just pick a few distinctive phrases, search for them on a couple of major search engines and very quickly find the plagiarized material.

A second source for plagiarism is the databases of journal articles online. It's possible to copy and paste directly from high-quality academic articles. Once again, plagiarism can often be detected by a keyword search of a few of the major article databases.

A third source is the banks of essays and research projects, known as Internet paper mills, which are now available on the Web. Services exist to sell essays on common topics, to write new essays on specific topics and even to sell PhD dissertations, services such as **cheater.com**, **schoolsucks. com** and **cheathouse.com**. Some universities are responding to this by buying essays in bulk from certain services in order to check for plagiarism, or by blocking access to such sites from university computer labs. Once again, while the Internet makes it easier to plagiarize, it also allows examiners to easily find out about these services and even get copies of plagiarized essays.

In response to the growth of Internet plagiarism a number of pay services have grown up offering to detect plagiarism. **Plagiarism.org**, for example, searches the open Web, the Internet paper mills and their own database of essays in search of plagiarism.

A last positive word on Internet publishing

For all of the harsh things I've said about Internet publishing, I've been happily doing it myself for several years now. It has brought a lot of benefits. It brings your work to the attention of the most unexpected of people. It is cheap and it is quick and easy once you've put in the initial work to learn a bit of html code or how to use an html editor. Perhaps the best aspect of it is the freedom it allows you. You don't have to negotiate with an editor or publisher over what's worthwhile or valuable, over what should go in and what shouldn't. You can put up the sort of bits and pieces which might never find a home in any print publication anyway, not because they're not valuable, but because they don't fit neatly into a particular genre of documents.

Appendix 1:
Top-level domain names

The last part of an Internet address is called the top-level domain. It tells you which country the computer is based in or, in the case of the USA, what sort of organization runs the computer. This appendix provides a list of all top-level domains. New organizational domains may be created in the future.

Organizational domains

COM	Commercial
EDU	Educational
GOV	Government
INT	International
MIL	US military
NET	Network
ORG	Non-profit organization

Country domains

AD	Andorra	BA	Bosnia-Herzegovina
AE	United Arab Emirates	BB	Barbados
AF	Afghanistan	BD	Bangladesh
AG	Antigua and Barbuda	BE	Belgium
AI	Anguilla	BF	Burkina Faso
AL	Albania	BG	Bulgaria
AM	Armenia	BH	Bahrain
AN	Netherland Antilles	BI	Burundi
AO	Angola	BJ	Benin
AQ	Antarctica	BM	Bermuda
AR	Argentina	BN	Brunei Darussalam
AS	American Samoa	BO	Bolivia
AT	Austria	BR	Brazil
AU	Australia	BS	Bahamas
AW	Aruba	BT	Buthan
AZ	Azerbaidjan	BV	Bouvet Island

BW	Botswana	GI	Gibraltar
BY	Belarus	GL	Greenland
BZ	Belize	GM	Gambia
CA	Canada	GN	Guinea
CC	Cocos (Keeling) Islands	GP	Guadeloupe (French)
CF	Central African Republic	GQ	Equatorial Guinea
CG	Congo	GR	Greece
CH	Switzerland	GT	Guatemala
CI	Ivory Coast	GU	Guam (US)
CK	Cook Islands	GW	Guinea Bissau
CL	Chile	GY	Guyana
CM	Cameroon	HK	Hong Kong
CN	China	HM	Heard and McDonald
CO	Colombia		Islands
CR	Costa Rica	HN	Honduras
CS	Czechoslovakia	HR	Croatia
CU	Cuba	HT	Haiti
CV	Cape Verde	HU	Hungary
CX	Christmas Island	ID	Indonesia
CY	Cyprus	IE	Ireland
CZ	Czech Republic	IL	Israel
DE	Germany	IN	India
DJ	Djibouti	IO	British Indian Ocean
DK	Denmark		Territory
DM	Dominica	IQ	Iraq
DO	Dominican Republic	IR	Iran
DZ	Algeria	IS	Iceland
EC	Ecuador	IT	Italy
EE	Estonia	JM	Jamaica
EG	Egypt	JO	Jordan
EH	Western Sahara	JP	Japan
ES	Spain	KE	Kenya
ET	Ethiopia	KG	Kirgistan
FI	Finland	KH	Cambodia
FJ	Fiji	KI	Kiribati
FK	Falkland Islands (Malvinas)	KM	Comoros
FM	Micronesia	KN	Saint Kitts Nevis Anguilla
FO	Faroe Islands	KP	North Korea
FR	France	KR	South Korea
FX	France (European Territory)	KW	Kuwait
GA	Gabon	KY	Cayman Islands
GB	Great Britain (UK)	KZ	Kazachstan
GD	Grenada	LA	Laos
GE	Georgia	LB	Lebanon
GF	Guyana (French)	LC	Saint Lucia
GH	Ghana	LI	Liechtenstein

LK	Sri Lanka	PK	Pakistan
LR	Liberia	PL	Poland
LS	Lesotho	PM	Saint Pierre and Miquelon
LT	Lithuania	PN	Pitcairn
LU	Luxembourg	PT	Portugal
LV	Latvia	PR	Puerto Rico (US)
LY	Libya	PW	Palau
MA	Morocco	PY	Paraguay
MC	Monaco	QA	Qatar
MD	Moldavia	RE	Réunion (French)
MG	Madagascar	RO	Romania
MH	Marshall Islands	RU	Russian Federation
ML	Mali	RW	Rwanda
MM	Myanmar	SA	Saudi Arabia
MN	Mongolia	SB	Solomon Islands
MO	Macau	SC	Seychelles
MP	Northern Mariana Islands	SD	Sudan
MQ	Martinique (French)	SE	Sweden
MR	Mauritania	SG	Singapore
MS	Montserrat	SH	Saint Helena
MT	Malta	SI	Slovenia
MU	Mauritius	SJ	Svalbard and Jan Mayen Islands
MV	Maldives		
MW	Malawi	SK	Slovak Republic
MX	Mexico	SL	Sierra Leone
MY	Malaysia	SM	San Marino
MZ	Mozambique	SN	Senegal
NA	Namibia	SO	Somalia
NC	New Caledonia (French)	SR	Surinam
NE	Niger	ST	Saint Tome and Principe
NF	Norfolk Island	SU	Soviet Union
NG	Nigeria	SV	El Salvador
NI	Nicaragua	SY	Syria
NL	Netherlands	SZ	Swaziland
NO	Norway	TC	Turks and Caicos Islands
NP	Nepal	TD	Chad
NR	Nauru	TF	French Southern Territory
NT	Neutral Zone	TG	Togo
NU	Niue	TH	Thailand
NZ	New Zealand	TJ	Tadjikistan
OM	Oman	TK	Tokelau
PA	Panama	TM	Turkmenistan
PE	Peru	TN	Tunisia
PF	Polynesia (French)	TO	Tonga
PG	Papua New Guinea	TP	East Timor
PH	Philippines	TR	Turkey

TT	Trinidad and Tobago	VE	Venezuela
TV	Tuvalu	VG	Virgin Islands (British)
TW	Taiwan	VI	Virgin Islands (US)
TZ	Tanzania	VN	Vietnam
UA	Ukraine	VU	Vanuatu
UG	Uganda	WF	Wallis and Futuna Islands
UK	United Kingdom	WS	Samoa
UM	US Minor Outlying	YE	Yemen
	Islands	YU	Yugoslavia
US	United States	ZA	South Africa
UY	Uruguay	ZM	Zambia
UZ	Uzbekistan	ZR	Zaire
VA	Vatican City State	ZW	Zimbabwe
VC	Saint Vincent and		
	Grenadines		

Appendix 2:
Subject guides

I argued strongly in chapter 6 that one of the best places to begin your Internet research is with a good subject guide in your area of interest. This appendix provides a list of high-quality subject guides in a range of social science disciplines. I have chosen one or two guides in each subject area. These are not the only high-quality guides but they are all of good-enough quality to provide a useful starting point in their own subject area. It is easy enough to locate these and other subject guides through the methods outlined in chapter 6 and you should not restrict yourself to the guides listed below. Don't forget the services dealt with in chapter 6, particularly the Argus Clearinghouse (**www.clearinghouse.net**), the Virtual Library (**www.vlib.org**), SOSIG (**sosig.esrc.bris.ac.uk**) and About.com. Each of the guides below will also provide links to other guides.

Anthropology

WWW Virtual Library: Anthropology (**vlib.anthrotech.com**), sponsored by Anthro TECH, LLC.

Archaeology

ArchNet (**archnet.uconn.edu**), WWW Virtual Library: Archaeology, Dept. of Anthropology, University of Connecticut.

Conflict studies

WWW Virtual Library: International Security Resources (**www.isn.ethz.ch**), International Relations and Security Network (ISN).

Economics

RFE, Resources for Economists on the Internet (**rfe.wustl.edu/EconFAQ.html**), WWW Virtual Library: Economics, Bill Goffe, SUNY Oswego, USA.

Environment

Environment Web Resources (**www.herts.ac.uk/lis/subjects/natsci/env/envweb**), Learning and Information Services section at the University of Hertfordshire, UK.

Ethnic studies

WWW Virtual Library: Migration and Ethnic Relations (**www.ercomer.org/ wwwvl**), ERCOMER – the European Research Centre on Migration and Ethnic Relations.

Geography

About.com: Geography (**geography.about.com**).

Governments

Government Resources on the Web (**www.lib.umich.edu/libhome/ Documents.center/govweb.html**), University of Michigan Documents Center.

History

History Guide (**www.sub.uni-goettingen.de/ssgfi/aac-hist**), State and University Library of Göttingen.

Languages

Yamada Language Guides (**babel.uoregon.edu/yamada/guides.html**), Yamada Language Center, University of Oregon.

Human Languages Page (**www.june29.com/HLP**), WWW Virtual Library: Languages, Tyler Chambers.

Law

World Law (**www.austlii.edu.au/links/world**) from AustLII, the Australasian Legal Information Institute.

Maps

Perry-Castaneda Library Map Collection (**www.lib.utexas.edu/Libs/PCL/ Map_collection/Map_collection.html**), University of Texas at Austin.

Philosophy

Guide to Philosophy on the Internet (**www.earlham.edu/~peters/ philinks.htm**), Peter Suber, Earlham College, Indiana, USA.

Philosophy in Cyberspace, A Guide to Philosophy-Related Resources on the Internet (**www-personal.monash.edu.au/~dey/phil**), Dey Alexander, Monash University, Australia.

Politics

Political Science Resources on the Web (**www.lib.umich.edu/libhome/ Documents.center/polisci.html**), University of Michigan Documents Center.

Poly-Cy: Internet Resources for Political Science (**www.polsci.wvu.edu/ PolyCy**), Robert Duval, West Virginia University.

Political Science Resources (**www.psr.keele.ac.uk**), Richard Kimber of Keele University, UK.

Psychology

Psychological Science on the Net (**www.psychologicalscience.net**).

PsychREF (**www.psychref.com**), Vincent Hevern, LeMoyne College, USA.

Research methods

SOSIG: Social Science Methodology (**www.sosig.ac.uk/social_science_ general/social_science_methodology/**), with sub-sections on Qualitative Methods and Quantitative Methods.

Social Policy

World-Wide Web Virtual Library: Social Policy (**www.bath.ac.uk/~hsstp/ world3.htm**), Theodoros N. Papadopoulos, University of Bath, UK.

Sociology

WWW Virtual Library: Sociology (**www.mcmaster.ca/socscidocs/ w3virtsoclib**), Dept. of Sociology, McMaster University, Canada.

Statistics

Statistical Resources on the Web (**www.lib.umich.edu/libhome/ Documents.center/stats.html**), the Documents Center at the University of Michigan.

Women's studies

WSSLINKS (Women's Studies Section Links) (**libraries.mit.edu/humanities/ WomensStudies/wscd.html**), the Women's Studies Section Collection Development Committee of the US-based Association of College and Research Libraries.

Women's Studies/Women's Issues Resource Sites (**umbc7.umbc. edu/~korenman/wmst/links.html**), Joan Korenman, Center for Women and Information Technology, University of Maryland, Baltimore.

Appendix 3:
A brief history of the Internet

Beginnings

Roughly speaking, the first connecting of computers to one another across long distances was carried out between US universities in the late 1960s and the early 1970s. Research agencies developed these connections through the 1970s and in 1982 a new technical standard which forms the basis of the 'Internet' connections we know today emerged. For what it is worth, it was called TCP/IP. (See inset.)

TCP/IP

TCP – Transmission Control Protocol
IP – Internet Protocol

The word protocol, borrowed from the language of diplomacy, refers to an agreed set of terms for communication between two sides who may not have much in common. TCP/IP is a set of terms for communication between computers which operate very differently and normally would not understand each other. When you send a request from your PC for a file on the Internet that request could easily go to a Macintosh server or a Unix computer. The fact that you have TCP/IP software on your machine means that your request is sent in terms which any computer, Mac, Unix or PC, will understand, so long as it also has TCP/IP software. To be on the Internet essentially means to have a computer with TCP/IP software. There is no need for the user to worry about this. If you have access to the Net then, by definition, you have TCP/IP.

TCP, the Transmission Control Protocol, prepares data for transmission and assembles incoming data. That is, it prepares your request for transmission while also dealing with the file which comes to you in response to that request.

IP, the Internet Protocol, sends and receives the requests and files, dealing directly with the other computers.

If IP is the delivery service, TCP is the mail sorting office, kind of (see also Lehnert, 1998: 25–6).

Any computer with TCP/IP could now connect to any other computer with TCP/IP. Nonetheless, very few people were connected to the 'Internet' and most of them were computer scientists. In 1984 only a thousand computers were linked by TCP/IP. Then in 1986 the US National Science Foundation (NSF) set up the NSFNET which was primarily aimed at linking US university computers with one another. There was an explosion of connections from universities. By 1987 there were 10,000 computers linked using this new standard. By 1989 there were 100,000, the vast majority of them at US universities (see Zakon, 1994; Kitchin, 1998: 26–45). But still this 'Internet' looked nothing like the Internet we are using today. In the late 1980s the connections between computers allowed you to do three things;

- Email, which allowed you to send messages to other people's computers.
- Telnet, which allowed you to connect from one computer to another and use programs on the faraway machine that you might not have on your own machine.
- FTP, File Transfer Protocol, which allowed you to transfer files of any kind from a faraway machine back on to your own machine where you could print them out or make further changes to them.

Using each of these functions involved learning a lot of old-fashioned computer commands and understanding the way files and folders were organized on a computer. There was no 'windows' system, there was no 'mouse'. If you wanted the computer to send an email or connect by telnet to another computer you had to type in a long list of commands. It took a lot of learning. Telnet, for example, was initially most important for the small number of people who used it to get access to the 'super-computers', extra-powerful computers running complex programs for analysing numbers.

Gopher

In 1992 Gopher appeared. It was the first tool which made it possible for the novice user to quickly learn how to connect to other machines on the 'Internet' and look through them for information. The appearance of Gopher in 1992 marks the birth of the Internet which we, the general users, find useful. Gopher provided a tree structure in which people could arrange the files they wanted to make available to the outside world, arranging them in a logical hierarchy. Then, people using the Gopher searcher could move down through this tree structure just by selecting one item from a number of menu items. At the bottom of the 'tree' was the actual content, documents or images usually.

As a windows version of Gopher was developed it became simple to use. Universities began to set up Gopherservers which were used to provide information about the universities. By late 1993 there were several hundred Gopherservers, most of them at US universities. But by then, a year after it appeared, Gopher was already being overtaken by a new tool which made Gopher look like it belonged to a previous century – the World-Wide-Web. For more on the history of the Web see 'Understanding the Internet' in chapter 1.

Appendix 4:
Netscape 6 commands

Netscape 6 is the most recent version of the Netscape Web browser. It succeeds Netscape Navigator 4. Netscape leapfrogged the number 5 in an apparent attempt to appear to be more modern and up-to-date than Internet Explorer 5. A large number of command sequences for NN4 and IE4 and IE5 are given in chapters 2 and 5 of this book. This appendix provides the equivalent commands in Netscape 6 for Macintosh.

Changing the start-up page
Edit→Preferences→Navigator
In the 'location' box type the address of the Web page you would like to have as your start-up page.

Adding a bookmark
Bookmarks→Add Current Page

Connecting to a Web address
File→Open Web Location

Browsing without images
Edit→Preferences→Advanced→Images

Opening a local file in your Web browser
File→Open File

Updating bookmarks
Bookmarks→Manage Bookmarks (select the bookmark you want to update) **Edit→Properties→Schedule**

Opening a new window showing your start-up page
File→New Navigator Window

Enabling and disabling Java
Edit→Preferences→Advanced→Enable Java

Editing bookmarks
Bookmarks→Manage Bookmarks (select the bookmark you want to edit) **Edit→Properties→General Information**

Altering the cache
Edit→Preferences→Advanced→Cache

Rejecting and controlling cookies
Edit→Preferences→Advanced→Cookies

Bibliography

Acker, Stephen R. (1995) 'Space, collaboration, and the credible city: academic work in the virtual university', *Journal of Computer-Mediated Communication*, 1 (1). <http://www.ascusc.org/jcmc/vol1/issue1/acker/ACKTEXT.HTM>.

ACLU (American Civil Liberties Union) (1997) 'Fahrenheit 451.2: Is cyberspace burning? How rating and blocking proposals may torch free speech on the Internet', *Cyber-Liberties, ACLU Freedom Network*. <http://www.aclu.org/issues/cyber/burning.html>.

Adams, Douglas (1979) *The Hitch Hiker's Guide to the Galaxy*. London: Pan Books.

Agre, Philip E. (1996a) 'Some thoughts about political activity on the Internet', *Red Rock Eater News*. <rre@weber.ucsd.edu>. 11 August.

Agre, Philip E. (1996b) 'The art of getting help', *Red Rock Eater News* <rre@weber.ucsd.edu>. 8 October.

Agre, Philip E. (1998) 'Stanton McCandlish on action alerts', *Red Rock Eater News* <rre@weber.ucsd.edu>. 18 March. <http://www.tao.ca/wind/rre/0380.html>.

Agre, Philip E. (1999) 'Rethinking networks and communities in a wired society', paper presented to the American Society for Information Science, Pasadena, May. <http://dlis.gseis.ucla.edu/people/pagre/asis.html>.

Agre, Philip E. (2000a) 'Networking on the network', 1993–2000 (version of 3 July 2000). <http://dlis.gseis.ucla.edu/people/pagre/network.html>.

Agre, Philip E. (2000b) 'Infrastructure and institutional change in the networked university', *Information, Communication, and Society* 3, (4): 494–507. Draft version at <http://dlis.gseis.ucla.edu/people/pagre/cenic.html>.

Agre, Philip E. (2001) 'Information and institutional change: the case of digital libraries', in Ann P. Bishop, Barbara P. Buttenfield and Nancy Van House (eds), *Digital Library Use: Social Practice in Design and Evaluation*. Cambridge, MA: MIT Press. Draft version at <http://dlis.gseis.ucla.edu/people/pagre/dl.html>.

Agre, Philip and Rotenberg, Marc (eds) (1997) *Technology and Privacy: the New Landscape*. Cambridge, MA/London: MIT Press.

Ahrens, Frank (1999) 'The cyber-saga of the "Sunscreen" song', *The Washington Post*, 18 March. <http://www.washingtonpost.com/wp-srv/style/features/daily/march99/sunscreen0318.htm>.

Alexander, Janet E. and Tate, Marsha Ann (1999) *Web Wisdom: How to Evaluate and Create Information Quality on the Web*. Mahwah, NJ/London: Lawrence Erlbaum Associates.

Barrett, Daniel J. (1997) *Netresearch: Finding Information Online*. Sebastopol, CA: O'Reilly.

Basch, Reva (1996) *Secrets of the Super Net Searchers: The Reflections, Revelations, and Hard-Won Wisdom of 35 of the World's Top Internet Researchers*. Wilton, CT: Pemberton Press.

Basch, Reva (1998) *Researching Online for Dummies*. Foster City, CA: IDG Books Worldwide.

Bell, Judith (1993) *Doing your Research Project: A Guide for First-Time Researchers in Education and Social Science*, 2nd edn. Buckingham, Philadelphia: Open University Press.

Bertot, J.C. and McClure, C.R. (1996) 'Electronic surveys: methodological implications for using the World Wide Web to collect survey data', in S. Hardin (ed.), *Global Complexity: Information, chaos and control*. Medford, MA: Information Today.

Bosak, Jon and Bray, Tim (1999) 'XML and the Second-Generation Web', *Scientific American*, May. <http://www.sciam.com/1999/0599issue/0599bosak.html>.

Callery, Anne and Tracy-Proulx, Deb (1997) 'Yahoo! Cataloging the Web', *Journal of Internet Cataloging*, 1 (1): 57–64.

Campbell, Duncan (1999) 'Careful, they might hear you', *The Age*, 23 May. <http://www.theage.com.au/daily/990523/news/news3.html>.

Ciolek, T. Matthew (ed.) (1998) 'The Internet: opportunities and disadvantages to scholarly work. Results of an online brainstorming session', *Research School of Pacific and Asian Studies, Australian National University*, 10 March. Last updated on 13 March 1998. <coombs.anu.edu.au/Depts/RSPAS/DIR/PAPERS/Brainstorm-98.html>.

Cline McKay, Sharon (1999) 'Accessing electronic journals', *Database*, 22 (2): 17–23. <http://www.onlineinc.com/database/DB1999/mckay4.html>.

Conner-Sax, Kiersten and Krol, Ed (1999) *The Whole Internet: the Next Generation*. Beijing/Cambridge, MA : O'Reilly.

Cook, Terry (1984–5) 'From information to knowledge. An intellectual paradigm for archives', *Archivaria*, 19: 28–49.

Cooper, Charles (1999) 'Amazon reverses decision on book ban', *ZDNet News*, 20 May. <http://www.zdnet.com/zdnn/stories/news/0,4586,2263095,00.html>.

Cox, Richard (1997) 'US National Inventory of Archives and the Internet', paper presented to *Access Unlocked*? Society of Archivists Annual Conference, University College, London.

Cox, Richard (1998) 'Access in the digital information age and the archival mission: the United States', *Journal of the Society of Archivists*, 19 (1): 25–40.

Da Silva, Stephanie and Da Silva, Peter (1999) 'Getting off a mailing list', *Publicly Accessible Mailing Lists*, 13 April. <www.neosoft.com/internet/paml/gettingoff.html>.

Dervin, Brenda and Nilan, Michael (1986) 'Information needs and uses', *Annual Review of Information Science and Technology*, 21: 3–33.

Drew, C.J. (1980) *Introduction to Designing and Conducting Research*, 2nd edn. St Louis, MO: C.B. Mosby.

Dublin CORE Metadata Initiative (1999) 'Dublin CORE Metadata Element Set, Version 1.1: Reference Description', Dublin CORE. <http://purl.oclc.org/dc/documents/rec-dces-19990702.htm>.

Duffy, K.P. (1998) 'Everybody's free to wear sunscreen'. <http://www1.tpgi.com.au/users/kpduffy/sunscreen4.htm>.

Ellis, Judith (1993) *Keeping Archives*, 2nd edn. Port Melbourne: Thorpe in association with the Australian Society of Archivists.

Feeney, Mary (ed.), National Preservation Office (1999) *Digital culture: maximising the nation's investment*. London: British Library.

Gilliland-Swetland, Ann J. (1998) 'An exploration of K-12 user needs for digital primary source material', *American Archivist*, 61 (1): 136–57.

Glassel, Aimée D. and Wells, Amy Tracy (1998) 'Scout Report Signpost: design and development for access to cataloged Internet resources', *Journal of Internet Cataloging*, 1 (3): 15–45.

Grossman, Wendy (1997) *Net.wars*. New York: New York University Press.

Hager, Nicky (1996) *Secret Power: New Zealand's Role in the International Spy Network*. Nelson, New Zealand: Craig Potton.

Harnack, Andrew and Kleppinger, Eugene (1998) *Online! A reference guide to using internet sources*. New York: St Martins Press.

Hewins, Elizabeth T. (1990) 'Information need and use studies', *Annual Review of Information Science and Technology*, 25: 145–72.

Hine, Christine (2000) *Virtual Ethnography*. London: Sage.

Hoff, Jens, Horrocks, Ivan and Tops, Pieter (eds) (2000) *Democratic Governance and New Technology: Technologically mediated innovations in political practice in Western Europe*. Routledge/ECPR Studies in European Political Science, London/New York: Routledge.

Hoon, G. (1998) *Proceedings of 'Electronic access: archives in the new millennium'*. London: Public Records Office.

ICRA (Internet Content Rating Association) (1999) 'Internet Content Rating Association formed to provide global system for protecting children and free speech on the Internet', *RSAC (Recreational Software Advisory Council)*. 12 May. <http://www.rsac.org/fra_content.asp?onIndex=86>.

Issacs, Margaret and TERENA (Trans-European Research and Education Networking Association) (1998) *Internet Users Guide to Network Resource Tools*. Harlow: Addison-Wesley.

Johns, Cecily (1997) 'Cataloging Internet resources: an administrative view', *Journal of Internet Cataloging*, 1 (1): 17–23.

Jones, Steve (ed.) (1998) *Doing Internet Research: Critical Issues and Methods for Examining the Net*. London: Sage.

Jul, Erik, with deep thought from Eric Childress and Eric Miller (1998) 'Now that we know the answer, What Are the Questions?', *Journal of Internet Cataloging*, 1 (3): 9–14.

Kaye, Barbara K. and Johnson, Thomas J. (1999) 'Research methodology: taming the cyber frontier: techniques for improving online surveys', *Social Science Computer Review*, 17 (3): 323–37.

Kelly, Richard (2000) 'Click click, you're caught', *The Irish Times*. 4 March.

Kennedy, Angus J. (1998) *The Internet: The Rough Guide*, 4th edn. London/New York: Rough Guides.

Kitchin, Rob (1998) *Cyberspace: The World in the Wires*. Chichester: John Wiley.

Kollock, Peter and Smith, Marc (eds) (1999) *Communities in Cyberspace*. London/New York: Routledge.

Lawrence, Steve and Giles, C. Lee (1999) 'Searching the World Wide Web', *Science*, 280: 98–100.

Lehnert, Wendy (1998) *Internet 101: A Beginner's Guide to the Internet and the World Wide Web*. Reading, MA: Addison-Wesley.

Ludlow, Peter (ed.) (1996) *High Noon on the Electronic Frontier: Conceptual Issues in Cyberspace*. Cambridge, MA and London: MIT Press.

Mann, Chris and Stewart, Fiona (2000) *Internet Communication and Qualitative Research: A Handbook for Researching Online*. London: Sage.

Manning, Kate (1997) 'Archivists and the Internet', *Journal of the Irish Society for Archives*, 4 (2): 20–3.

Marriott, Sarah (1999) 'Fighting the cybercensors', *The Irish Times*, 24 May.

McKim, Geoffrey W. (1996) *Internet Research Companion*. Indianapolis, IN: Que Education & Training.

Members of the Clever Project (1999) 'Hypersearching the Web', *Scientific American*, June. <http://www.sciam.com/1999/0699issue/0699raghaven.html>.

Neely, Mark (1998) *Find what you want on the Internet*. Harrogate: Net.Works.

Negroponte, Nicholas (1996) *Being digital*. New York: Vintage Books.

Nesbary, Dale K. (2000) *Survey Research and the World Wide Web*. Boston, MA: Allyn and Bacon.

Neuman, William Lawrence (1997) *Social Research Methods: Qualitative and Quantitative Approaches*, 3rd edn. Boston, MA/London: Allyn and Bacon.

Neumeister, Susan M. (1997) 'Cataloging Internet resources: a practitioner's viewpoint', *Journal of Internet Cataloging*, 1 (1): 25–45.

Nielsen, Jakob (2000) *Designing Web Usability*. Indianapolis, IN: New Riders Publishing.

Page, Melvin E. (1996) 'A brief citation guide for Internet sources in history and the humanities' (Version 2.1), *H_Africa*. February 20. <http://h-net.msu.edu/~africa/citation.html>.

Parrott, Jim (1999) 'URL-stability index for the Scholarly Societies Project', *University of Waterloo Scholarly Societies Project*. Last updated on 3 May 1999. <http://www.lib.uwaterloo.ca/society/URL_stability_index.html>.

Pfaffenberger, Bryan (1996) *Web Search Strategies*. New York: MIS Press.

Pfaffenberger, Bryan (1997) *Official Microsoft Internet Explorer 4 book*. Redmond, WA: Microsoft Press.

Pike, John (1997) 'Flawed AltaVista search engine', email message to Phil Agre forwarded on *Red Rock Eater News*. <rre@weber.ucsd.edu>. 26 March.

Quercia, Valerie (1997) *Internet in a Nutshell*. Sebastopol, CA: O'Reilly.

Research Libraries Group (1999) 'RLG's archival resources', *Research Libraries Group*. Last updated on 29 June 1999. www.rlg.org/arr.

Rheingold, Howard (1995) *Virtual community: finding connection in a computerized world*. London: Minerva.

Rodriguez, Joseph (2000) 'A comparative study of internet content regulations in the United States and Singapore: the invincibility of cyberporn', Asian-Pacific Law & Policy Journal, 1 (1). <http://www.hawaii.edu/aplpj/>.

Schmich, Mary (1997) 'Advice, like youth, probably just wasted on the young', *Chicago Tribune*, 1 June. <http://chicagotribune.com/news/columnists/schmich/0,1122,SAV-9706010178,00.html>.

Spool, J.M., Scanlon, T., Snyder, C., Schroeder, W. and DeAngelo, T. (1999) *Web site usability: a designer's guide*. San Francisco: Morgan Kaufmann.

Staunton, Denis (1999) 'Electronic spies torture German firms', *The Irish Times*, 16 April.

Stein, Stuart (1999) *Learning, Teaching and Researching on the Internet: A Practical Guide for Social Scientists*. Harlow: Longman.

Stoll, Clifford (1995a) *Silicon Snake Oil: second thoughts on the information highway*. New York/London : Anchor Books, Doubleday.

Stoll, Clifford (1995b) 'Highlights of interview with Clifford Stoll', in interview with Russell D. Hoffman, *High Tech Today*, 25 May. <www.animatedsoftware.com/hightech/cliffsto.htm>.

Van Alstyne, Marshall and Brynjolfsson, Erik (1997) *Electronic Communities: Global Village or Cyberbalkans*? March. <http://web.mit.edu/marshall/www/papers/CyberBalkans.pdf>.

Walker, Janice R. and Taylor, Todd (1998) *The Columbia Guide to Online Style*. New York: Columbia University Press.

Walworth, Julia (1996) 'Insular institutions: problems and possibilities', *Enhancing Access to Primary Sources Internationally*, paper presented to a Joint RLG-CURL Symposium, University College London, September. <http://lyra.rlg.org/pswal.html>.

Zakon, Robert 'H'obbes' (1994) <hobbes@hobbes.mitre.org>, 'Hobbes' Internet Timeline v1.1'.

Index